London, Londoners and the Great Fire of 1666

CW00523379

The Great Fire of 1666 was one of the greatest catastrophes to befall London in its long history. While its impact on London and its built environment has been studied and documented, its impact on Londoners has been overlooked. This book makes full and systematic use of the wealth of manuscript sources that illustrate social, economic and cultural change in seventeenth-century London to examine the impact of the Fire in terms of how individuals and communities reacted and responded to it, and to put the response to the Fire in the context of existing trends in early modern England. The book also explores the broader effects of the Fire in the rest of the country, as well as how the Great Fire continued to be an important polemical tool into the eighteenth century.

Jacob F. Field has taught history at Massey University and the University of Waikato, New Zealand. He is currently a research associate at the University of Cambridge.

Routledge Research in Early Modern History

For a full list of titles in this series, please visit www.routledge.com

The Business of the Roman Inquisition in the Early Modern Era
Germano Maifreda

Cities and Solidarities
Urban Communities in Pre-Modern Europe
Edited by Justin Colson and Arie van Steensel

James VI and Noble Power in Scotland 1578–1603
Edited by Miles Kerr-Peterson and Steven J. Reid

Conversion and Islam in the Early Modern Mediterranean
The Lure of the Other
Edited by Claire Norton

Plural Pasts
Power, Identity and the Ottoman Sieges of Nagykanizsa Castle
Claire Norton

Witchcraft, the Devil, and Emotions in Early Modern England
Charlotte-Rose Millar

Early Professional Women in Northern Europe, c. 1650–1850
*Edited by Johanna Ilmakunnas, Marjatta Rahikainen,
and Kirsi Vainio-Korhonen*

**The Solemn League and Covenant of the Three Kingdoms and
the Cromwellian Union, 1643–1663**
Kirsteen M. MacKenzie

London, Londoners and the Great Fire of 1666
Disaster and Recovery
Jacob F. Field

London, Londoners and the Great Fire of 1666

Disaster and Recovery

Jacob F. Field

Taylor & Francis Group

LONDON AND NEW YORK

First published 2018 by Routledge

2 Park Square, Milton Park, Abingdon, Oxfordshire OX14 4RN

52 Vanderbilt Avenue, New York, NY 10017

Routledge is an imprint of the Taylor & Francis Group, an informa business

First issued in paperback 2019

British Library Cataloguing-in-Publication Data
A catalogue record for this book is available from the British Library

Library of Congress Cataloging-in-Publication Data
Names: Field, Jacob, author.
Title: London, Londoners and the Great Fire of 1666 : disaster and recovery / by Jacob F. Field.
Description: New York : Routledge, 2018. | Series: Routledge research in early modern history | Includes bibliographical references and index.
Identifiers: LCCN 2017028242 (print) | LCCN 2017028721 (ebook) | ISBN 9781315099323 (ebook) | ISBN 9781138207141 (hardback : alkaline paper)
Subjects: LCSH: Great Fire, London, England, 1666. | Fires—Social aspects—England—London—History—17th century. | Disasters—Social aspects—England—London—History—17th century. | Disaster relief—England—London—History—17th century. | Urban renewal—England—London—History—17th century. | London (England)—History—17th century. | London (England)—Social conditions—17th century. | London (England)—Economic conditions—17th century.
Classification: LCC DA681 (ebook) | LCC DA681 .F54 2018 (print) | DDC 942.1/2066—dc23
LC record available at https://lccn.loc.gov/2017028242

ISBN: 978-1-138-20714-1 (hbk)
ISBN: 978-0-367-88972-2 (pbk)

Typeset in Sabon
by Apex CoVantage, LLC

For my parents, and in memory of my sister

Contents

List of figures   viii
List of maps   ix
List of tables   x
Acknowledgments   xi
List of abbreviations   xiii
Key to maps of parishes   xv

Introduction: a new history of the Great Fire of London   1

PART ONE   5

1   A brief account of the Great Fire   7

2   Rebuilding London   30

PART TWO   57

3   Household movement after the Great Fire   59

4   London's economic topography after the Great Fire   99

5   Cultural reactions to the Great Fire   131

Conclusion: the impact of the Great Fire   160

Index   165

Figures

1.1   Panoramic view of London by Nicolaes Visscher (c. 1666)   8

1.2   View of the Great Fire seen from across the River
Thames (1666)   13

1.3   Plan of the City of London and surrounding area after
the Great Fire of London by Wenceslaus Hollar (1666)   19

2.1   Designs for rebuilding London after the Fire by
Christopher Wren and John Evelyn (1748)   32

2.2   View of Monument's west side and adjacent buildings
by William Lodge (1676)   46

3.1   Number of hearths per household in London
before the Fire (%)   67

3.2   Number of hearths per household in London
after the Fire (%)   67

3.3   Number of hearths per household in twenty-four parishes,
1666 and 1675 (%)   69

3.4   Number of households in twenty-four parishes,
1666 and 1675   70

3.5   Change in number of hearths per household, c. 1666 and
1675 (%)   81

5.1   Frontispiece of *Pyrotechnica Loyolana* (1667)   135

Maps

1   The City of London and surrounding parishes   xiii
2   London parishes, 1666   xiv
3   Ward map of the City of London   xix

Tables

3.1 Number of Households in London before and after the Fire, by City ward, c. 1666 and 1675   65

3.2 Non-movement of Londoners linked in the Hearth Tax, c. 1666 and 1675   74

3.3 Movement of nominally linked Londoners from the Hearth Tax, c. 1666 and 1675 (%)   78

3.4 Distance of residential movement of nominally linked Londoners from the Hearth Tax, c. 1666 and 1675   79

3.5 Changing locality of nominally linked Londoners from the Hearth Tax, c. 1666 and 1675 (%)   84

4.1 Place of business, Merchant Taylors, 1652–66, 1666–80 (%)   106

4.2 Geographical distribution of London booksellers, 1663–5, 1667–9 and 1676–8 (%)   107

4.3 Movement of Merchant Taylors, 1652–66 and 1666–80 (%)   110

4.4 Occupational groups of Merchant Taylors, 1652–66 (%)   113

4.5 London's male occupational structure, 1641–1700 and 1710–12 (%)   115

Acknowledgments

Without the support of my family, friends and colleagues, the researching and writing of this book would have been impossible. Firstly I would like to thank my parents, Ellen and Paul, who have unconditionally supported and inspired me. I owe them more than I can express. To my late sister, Eowyn Jane, I miss you every day. I would also like to thank my parents' partners, Ian and Pam, as well as the rest of my family from across the world, especially my grandparents – Grandma Billie and the late Albert Cretella, Aussie Granddad and Nana. Finally I must thank my wife Emily, who makes me feel lucky every day and never stopped believing in me; I will always be thankful for this and for her. I would also like to thank my in-laws, the Bell family, for welcoming me so warmly into their midst.

My friends have kept me from getting too lost in the seventeenth century through their good company and encouragement in the twenty-first. I would like to thank my 'second families': the Tomiczeks (Caroline, Isaac and Safiya) and the Blitzes (Biggi, Barry, Jonas and David), as well as the Greenwalds (Ava Seave, Bruce and Diana), who have provided generous support throughout my academic life, and Mark Ravenhill. I would also like to thank: James, Samir, Ali and Al; the Greens (especially my goddaughter Isabel); Niheer, Dan, Rich, Tina, Neil, Jillian, Chris, Laura, Josh and the Heortons; and Elly, Corin, Toby, Pete, Alli and Ellie.

This book could not have been undertaken without the help of the people who care for the records it depends upon. I have relied heavily on the help and advice of those who work at the Guildhall Library, the London Metropolitan Archives and the National Archives. I have also used the resources of the Robinson Library at Newcastle, the British Library, the London Library and the Wellcome Library.

My greatest academic debt is to my doctoral supervisor at Newcastle University, Jeremy Boulton, who has been a constant source of knowledge and constructive criticism, and whose expertise and assiduousness has been invaluable. I would also like to thank my second supervisor Helen Berry. This book has benefited greatly from the input of the two examiners of the doctoral thesis upon which it was based: Ian Archer and Rachel Hammersley. My colleagues during my postdoctoral work at the University of Cambridge have also been incredibly helpful and stimulating – in particular Amy Erickson, Gill Newton, Max Satchell, Leigh Shaw-Taylor and Tony Wrigley. I have also been blessed with wonderful support from my colleagues at Massey and Waikato universities, especially Michael Belgrave, James Beattie, Peter Lineham and Rowland Weston. I am also grateful for conversations, correspondence and advice with many other historians over the years, including Sylvia Brown, Ian Doolittle, Vanessa Harding, Philippa Hubbard, John Landers, David Marsh, Joseph Monteyne, Osamu Saito, Chiaki Yamamoto and Matthew Yeo. I would also like to thank the two anonymous peer reviewers of this book for their perceptive and constructive comments, as well as the editorial team at Routledge.

I have been privileged to have received generous financial support from the Arts and Humanities Research Council in the form of a three-year doctoral award at Newcastle University, without which I could not have undertaken the doctoral research upon which this book is based. I would also like to thank the Leverhulme Trust for their generous funding of 'The occupational structure of England and Wales c.1379 to c.1729' (F/09/774/G), held by Dr Leigh Shaw-Taylor and Professor Sir E.A. Wrigley, which financed my collection of the data for the Fleet Registers used in this book. Finally, I also received kind bursaries to attend conferences – one from the organisers of the 'London in Text and History, 1400–1700' conference, and one from the School of Historical Studies at Newcastle University.

Abbreviations

BL: British Library
GL: Guildhall Library
LMA: London Metropolitan Archives
LPL: Lambeth Palace Library
PA: Parliamentary Archives, United Kingdom
TNA: The National Archives, United Kingdom

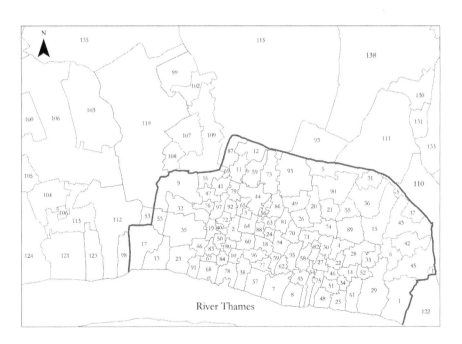

Map 1 The City of London and surrounding parishes. Created by Dr Max Satchell.

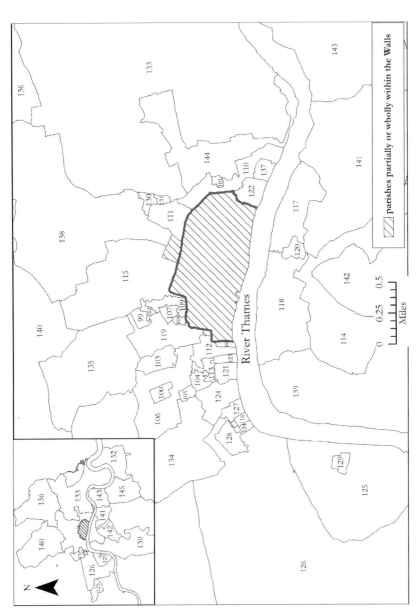

Map 2 London parishes, 1666. Created by Dr Max Satchell.

parishes partially or wholly within the **Walls**

Key to maps of parishes

Within the Walls

1. All Hallows Barking
2. All Hallows Bread Street*
3. All Hallows Honey Lane*
4. All Hallows Lombard Street*
5. All Hallows London Wall
6. All Hallows Staining
7. All Hallows the Great*
8. All Hallows the Less*
9. Christchurch Greyfriars*
10. Holy Trinity the Less*
11. St Alban Wood Street*
12. St Alphage London Wall
13. St Andrew by the Wardrobe
14. St Andrew Hubbard*
15. St Andrew Undershaft
16. St Anne and St Agnes*
17. St Anne Blackfriars*
18. St Antholin Budge Row*
19. St Augustine Watling Street*
20. St Bartholomew by the Royal Exchange*
21. St Benet Fink*
22. St Benet Gracechurch Street*
23. St Benet Paul's Wharf*
24. St Benet Sherehog*
25. St Botolph Billingsgate*
26. St Christopher-le-Stock*
27. St Clement East Cheap*
28. St Dionis Backchurch*
29. St Dunstan-in-the-East**
30. St Edmund the King and Martyr*
31. St Ethelburga Bishopsgate

32. St Faith under St Paul's*
33. St Gabriel Fenchurch Street*
34. St George Botolph Lane*
35. St Gregory by St Paul's*
36. St Helen Bishopsgate
37. St James Duke's Place
38. St James Garlickhithe*
39. St John the Baptist Walbrook*
40. St John the Evangelist Friday Street*
41. St John Zachary*
42. St Katherine Coleman
43. St Katherine Cree
44. St Lawrence Jewry*
45. St Lawrence Pountney*
46. St Leonard East Cheap*
47. St Leonard Foster Lane*
48. St Magnus the Martyr*
49. St Margaret Lothbury*
50. St Margaret Moses*
51. St Margaret New Fish Street*
52. St Margaret Pattens*
53. St Martin Ludgate*
54. St Martin Orgars*
55. St Martin Outwich
56. St Martin Pomroy*
57. St Martin Vintry*
58. St Mary Abchurch*
59. St Mary Aldermanbury*
60. St Mary Aldermary*
61. St Mary-at-Hill*
62. St Mary Bothaw*
63. St Mary Colechurch*
64. St Mary-le-Bow*
65. St Mary Magdalen Milk Street*
66. St Mary Magdalen Old Fish Street*
67. St Mary Mounthaw*
68. St Mary Somerset*
69. St Mary Staining*
70. St Mary Woolchurch Haw*
71. St Mary Woolnoth**
72. St Matthew Friday Street*
73. St Michael Bassishaw*
74. St Michael Cornhill*
75. St Michael Crooked Lane*
76. St Michael-le-Querne*

77. St Michael Paternoster Royal*
78. St Michael Queenhithe*
79. St Michael Wood Street*
80. St Mildred Bread Street*
81. St Mildred Poultry*
82. St Nicholas Acons*
83. St Nicholas Cole Abbey*
84. St Nicholas Olave*
85. St Olave Hart Street
86. St Olave Jewry*
87. St Olave Silver Street*
88. St Pancras Soper Lane*
89. St Peter Cornhill*
90. St Peter-le-Poer**
91. St Peter Paul's Wharf*
92. St Peter Westcheap*
93. St Stephen Coleman Street*
94. St Stephen Walbrook*
95. St Swithin London Stone*
96. St Thomas the Apostle*
97. St Vedast-alias-Foster*

Without the Walls

 98. Bridewell Precinct
 99. Charter House
100. Gray's Inn
101. Holy Trinity Minories
102. Liberty of Glasshouse Yard
103. Liberty of Saffron Hill
104. Liberty of the Rolls
105. Lincoln's Inn
106. St Andrew Holborn
107. St Bartholomew the Great
108. St Bartholomew the Less
109. St Botolph without Aldersgate
110. St Botolph without Aldgate
111. St Botolph without Bishopsgate
112. St Bride Fleet Street*
113. St Dunstan-in-the-West
114. St George the Martyr Southwark
115. St Giles without Cripplegate
116. St John the Baptist Savoy
117. St Olave Southwark
118. St Saviour Southwark

119. St Sepulchre Holborn**
120. St Thomas Southwark
121. Temple***
122. Tower of London
123. Whitefriars Precinct***

*   Parish where church was destroyed in the Fire
**   Parish where church was seriously damaged in the Fire
*** Extra-parochial areas that the Fire also spread to

Westminster city and liberties

124. St Clement Danes
125. St Margaret Westminster
126. St Martin-in-the-Fields
127. St Mary-le-Strand
128. St Paul Covent Garden
129. Westminster Abbey

Out parishes and beyond

130. Liberty of Norton Folgate
131. Old Artillery Ground
132. St Alfege Greenwich
133. St Dunstan Stepney
134. St Giles-in-the-Fields
135. St James Clerkenwell
136. St John Hackney
137. St Katherine by the Tower
138. St Leonard Shoreditch
139. St Mary Lambeth
140. St Mary Islington
141. St Mary Magdalen Bermondsey
142. St Mary Newington
143. St Mary Rotherhithe
144. St Mary Whitechapel
145. St Nicholas Deptford

Map 3 Ward map of the City of London. Created by the author.

F: Farringdon Within (detached)
T: Tower (detached)

Introduction

A new history of the Great Fire of London

The Great Fire started on 2 September 1666 in a baker's shop on Pudding Lane. Over the next four days it spread across the City of London and beyond, destroying most of the historic core of the metropolis. Thousands of houses were destroyed and tens of thousands of people were made homeless. Dozens of parish churches and livery company halls were left in ruins and St Paul's Cathedral was gutted. The disaster took place at a vital moment in England's history, in the aftermath of the Civil Wars and the Restoration. By the time of the Fire the lustre of the restored monarchy was beginning to dim. In 1666 England was recovering from a serious outbreak of plague and was at war with both the Dutch Republic and France. Over time, the Great Fire would become an iconic moment in both the history of London and England. London's destruction by flame and resurrection through the industry of her citizens has proved an enduring idiom, buoyed during the twentieth century by the experience of the Blitz. The Fire is a 'transcendent event' in London history, retaining its relevance to the present day.[1]

The destruction of much of London had the potential to seriously destabilise the rest of England. London was by far the largest city in the nation. Yet it was not just significant because of its population – it was the political, economic and social centre of England.[2] London was vital to the English demographic system. It attracted migrants from across the nation and its high mortality levels prevented excess population growth.[3] By the end of the seventeenth century one in six adults in England either were living, or had lived, in London.[4] Given London's importance and centrality, the Fire had the potential to seriously disrupt not only local, but national, demographic and economic patterns.

The Fire clearly was, and remains, a moment of national importance. This is reflected in the length of writing on the Fire in the past century. For the most part, this encompasses narratives of the Fire and accounts of the rebuilding. Most of these accounts view the Fire and subsequent events almost wholly through a metropolitan prism, and devote little to the impact of the Fire outside London. The demographic and economic context of the Fire, and what degree of continuity there was after the Fire, has not been systematically analysed. The Fire also occurred at a key moment in London's topographic development. Vanessa Harding has argued that it created a more open and clear City, forcing poorer residents into overcrowded suburbs. Therefore the Fire widened the contrast between London's disorderly periphery and orderly centre.[5] For the first time, this and other assertions about London's changing shape in the seventeenth century will be examined using the systematic evaluation of quantitative sources to provide a new history of the Fire.

Serous fires were a common feature of London's history. The earliest recorded blaze occurred during Boudica's Revolt in 60. London suffered serious fires in 122, 798 and 982. After the Norman Conquest, fire continued to blight London, with serious fires in 1087, 1135 and 1212. There were no serious city-wide fires between 1212 and 1666, but the nature of the built environment meant a major blaze was always a possibility. Within the Walls, the risk of fire was highest in the waterfront area around London Bridge, characterised by especially densely packed housing and warehouses full of flammable goods. Derek Keene has made the point that in relative terms the 1666 Fire was not the worst to inflict London.[6] Although earlier fires destroyed higher proportions of London, none could match the scale of the destruction of 1666 until the Blitz.

In general, the early modern English urban environment was very vulnerable to fire for a number of reasons: highly flammable buildings made of wood and thatch, closely packed structures, open hearths and limited water supply and fire-fighting equipment. Fire was always a possibility – 'a remorseless engine of destruction and creation, capable of engulfing whole portions of a town, and posing a constant and serious threat to people's livelihood'.[7] As such, fires were of great interest to the public and heavily reported in Restoration newspapers.[8] Looking just at seventeenth-century England, for example, around one-third of Oxford was burned in 1644 and at least 157 houses in Warwick were fired in 1694.[9] Neither of these, nor any other early modern English blazes, approached the sheer scale of the Great Fire of London. A more useful comparison for the 1666 is other 'Great Fires' to inflict major cities. The best seventeenth-century comparisons are the Great Fires of Edo (1657) and Istanbul (1660). The Edo Fire ruined three-quarters of the city and killed about one-seventh of its population of 600,000.[10] The Istanbul Fire destroyed two-thirds of the city, razing 280,000 households and killing as many as 40,000.[11] The Great Fire of Copenhagen in 1728 was proportionally as devastating as the 1666 Fire, destroying 80 per cent of the medieval city.[12] The Chicago Fire of 1871 destroyed four square miles of the city. As in London, ambitious rebuilding visions were abandoned.[13]

This book is divided into two parts. The first will provide an overview of the Great Fire and rebuilding process. Chapter 1 will give an account of the progress of the blaze and Chapter 2 will detail the progress of the rebuilding effort. The second part will examine London and England's reaction to the disaster in as holistic a method as possible. Chapter 3 will examine the response in terms of household movement and residential structure. It will use the Hearth Tax assessment records and nominal linkage to determine how the Fire impacted on residential patterns, and how it affected individual Londoners and to what extent the Fire affected longer-term shifts in the topographic structure of the metropolis. Chapter 4 will examine the economic response to the Fire in terms of the reactions of two trade groups: London's booksellers and the Merchant Taylors' Company. This will show how these two distinct bodies reacted to the economic disruption caused by the Fire, and where they resettled. Chapter 5 will draw focus on cultural reactions to the Fire using quantitative sources. The event had major polemic value for any group that wished to use it – a disaster of this magnitude was a powerful political tool. It will examine the Fire in the context of its reaction of printed media such as poems, histories, sermons and broadsides and how perceptions of the event changed. This chapter will also use various diary, letter and memoir sources to investigate the popular reaction to the Fire.

The Great Fire of 1666 was the greatest catastrophic shock to befall the early modern metropolis. Its impact on London has been extensively studied and documented to an extent – however, its impact on *Londoners* has been overlooked until now. In addition, the broader effects of the Fire in the rest of the country, and how the rest of England perceived the disaster, will be detailed. This book will examine the social, economic and cultural impact of the Fire in terms of how individuals and communities reacted and responded to it. Using a mixture of qualitative and quantitative sources allows the study of this response to be as full as possible, and also puts the response to the Fire in the context of existing trends in early modern England.

Notes

1 D. Keene, 'Fire in London: Destruction and Reconstruction, AD 982–1676', in *Destruction and Reconstruction of Towns, Volume 1: Destruction by Earthquakes, Fire and Water*, ed. M. Körner (Bern: Paul Haupt, 1999), 189.

2 A.L. Beier and R.A.P. Finlay, 'Introduction: The Significance of the Metropolis', in *London 1500–1700: The Making of the Metropolis*, ed. A.L. Beier and R.A.P. Finlay (London and New York: Longman, 1986), 1–33.

3 J. Landers, *Death and the Metropolis: Studies in the Demographic History of London 1670–1830* (Cambridge: Cambridge University Press, 1993), 43.

4 E.A. Wrigley, 'A Simple Model of London's Importance in Changing English Society and Economy, 1650–1750', *Past and Present*, 37 (1967), 44–70.

5 V. Harding, 'City, Capital, and Metropolis: The Changing Shape of Seventeenth-Century London', in *Imagining Early Modern England: Perceptions and Portrayals of the City from Stow to Strype, 1598–1720*, ed. J.F. Merritt (Cambridge: Cambridge University Press, 2001), 128.

6 Keene, 'Fire in London', 193–9.

7 P. Borsay, 'Fire and the Early Modern Townscape', in *The English Urban Landscape*, ed. P. Waller (Oxford and New York: Oxford University Press, 2000), 110–1.

8 J. Sutherland, *The Restoration Newspaper and its Development* (Cambridge: Cambridge University Press, 1986), 78.

 9 S. Porter, 'The Oxford Fire of 1644', *Oxoniensia*, 49 (1984), 295; P. Borsay, 'A County Town in Transition: The Great Fire of Warwick, 1694', in *Provincial Towns in Early Modern England and Ireland: Change, Convergence and Divergence*, ed. P. Borsay and L. Proudfoot (Oxford: Oxford University Press for the British Academy, 2002), 154.
10 K. Ugawa, 'The Great Fire of Edo (Tokyo) in 1657', in *Destruction and Reconstruction of Towns, Volume 1: Destruction by Earthquakes, Fire and Water*, ed. M. Körner (Bern: Paul Haupt, 1999), 213–38.
11 M.D. Baer, 'The Great Fire of 1660 and the Islamization of Christian and Jewish Space in Istanbul', *International Journal of Middle East Studies*, 36 (2004), 159–75.
12 H. Gamrath, 'The Great Fire of Copenhagen in 1728', in *Destruction and Reconstruction of Towns, Volume 1: Destruction by Earthquakes, Fire and Water*, ed. M. Körner (Bern: Paul Haupt, 1999), 293–302.
13 C.M. Rosen, *The Limits of Power: Great Fires and the Process of City Growth in America* (Cambridge: Cambridge University Press, 1986).

Reference list

Baer, M.D. 'The Great Fire of 1660 and the Islamization of Christian and Jewish Space in Istanbul', *International Journal of Middle East Studies*, 36 (2004), 159–75.

Beier, A.L. and Finlay, R.A.P. 'Introduction: The Significance of the Metropolis'. In *London 1500–1700: The Making of the Metropolis*, edited by A.L. Beier and R.A.P. Finlay, 1–33. London and New York: Longman, 1986.

Borsay, P. 'Fire and the Early Modern Townscape'. In *The English Urban Landscape*, edited by P. Waller, 110–1. Oxford and New York: Oxford University Press, 2000.

Borsay, P. 'A County Town in Transition: The Great Fire of Warwick, 1694'. In *Provincial Towns in Early Modern England and Ireland: Change, Convergence and Divergence*, edited by P. Borsay and L. Proudfoot, 151–70. Oxford: Oxford University Press for the British Academy, 2002.

Gamrath, H. 'The Great Fire of Copenhagen in 1728'. In *Destruction and Reconstruction of Towns, Volume 1: Destruction by Earthquakes, Fire and Water*, edited by M. Körner, 293–302. Bern: Paul Haupt, 1999.

Harding, V. 'City, Capital, and Metropolis: The Changing Shape of Seventeenth-Century London'. In *Imagining Early Modern England: Perceptions and Portrayals of the City from Stow to Strype, 1598–1720*, edited by J.F. Merritt, 117–43. Cambridge: Cambridge University Press, 2001.

Keene, D. 'Fire in London: Destruction and Reconstruction, AD 982–1676'. In *Destruction and Reconstruction of Towns, Volume 1: Destruction by Earthquakes, Fire and Water*, edited by M. Körner, 187–211. Bern: Paul Haupt, 1999.

Landers, J. *Death and the Metropolis: Studies in the Demographic History of London 1670–1830*. Cambridge: Cambridge University Press, 1993.

Porter, S. 'The Oxford Fire of 1644', *Oxoniensia*, 49 (1984), 289–300.

Rosen, C.M. *The Limits of Power: Great Fires and the Process of City Growth in America*. Cambridge: Cambridge University Press, 1986.

Sutherland, J. *The Restoration Newspaper and its Development*. Cambridge: Cambridge University Press, 1986.

Ugawa, K. 'The Great Fire of Edo (Tokyo) in 1657'. In *Destruction and Reconstruction of Towns, Volume 1: Destruction by Earthquakes, Fire and Water*, edited by M. Körner, 213–38. Bern: Paul Haupt, 1999.

Wrigley, E.A. 'A Simple Model of London's Importance in Changing English Society and Economy, 1650–1750', *Past and Present*, 37 (1967), 44–70.

Part one

1 A brief account of the Great Fire

In 1666 around 400,000 people lived in London, making up 7.5 per cent of England's total population of 5.3 million. The historic core of the metropolis was the City of London, the area enclosed by the old Roman walls and the parishes that immediately surrounded them. For the most part it retained the same street structure it had had since medieval times. Houses and businesses were closely packed together, leaning over narrow streets and lanes. Beyond the City lay London's suburbs. By 1666 London had been growing rapidly for over a century. At least 330,000 people (net) had been added to its population from 1550 to 1650. Most of these new arrivals tended to live in low-quality, densely packed, filthy houses in yards and alleys.[1] Such residences and people were spread throughout London, although most migrants first settled in the suburbs. In the City wealthier groups tended to live in the centre with poorer residents on the riverside and near to the Walls.[2]

By the mid-seventeenth century, less than half of London lived in the City within and without the Walls. The latter areas, known as the 'liberties', were outside the boundary of the Walls but within the jurisdiction of the City. The suburbs were the most rapidly growing areas of the early modern metropolis.[3] New arrivals usually lived in the suburbs because rents tended to be lower and there were more opportunities for economic growth as guild controls were less strictly imposed.[4] The northern and southern suburbs expanded rapidly from 1560 to 1600, but thereafter increased at approximately the same rate as the City. During the seventeenth century, the main areas of growth were to the west and the east of the City.[5] Despite the fact that the City was decreasing in its share of London's population, it remained a centre of wealth, influence and prestige. It was home to many of England's wealthiest merchants, a waterside thronged with quays and wharfs, and famed commercial districts like Cheapside and the Royal Exchange. The City also included Guildhall, the ceremonial and administrative centre of civic government, dozens of livery company halls, over 100 parish churches and the gothic hulk of Old St Paul's Cathedral.

Even though the Great Fire primarily impacted the City, it is vital to have an understanding of the suburbs. Each of them developed in different ways and had distinct functions and specialisations.[6] Mirroring the City was Westminster. The two were connected by the Strand and Fleet Street. Since the mid-eleventh century Westminster had been a seat of government and administration for the Crown, as well as the location of England's Parliament and key parts of its judiciary. Westminster and the City had been geographically separate until the sixteenth century, when the fields between them were filled in. The traditional boundary between the City and Westminster was Temple Bar, which was located close to the Inns of Court, the centre of the legal profession since the late fourteenth century. By the seventeenth century the 'West End' had emerged, with nobles, gentry and professions flocking to live there. It became a centre of fashion and taste, as well as a centre of commerce and leisure. Here there were larger, more prestigious dwellings, with high concentrations of elite groups which could rival the City.[7] The West End was not only made up of grand houses for the wealthy; outside of the large developments around squares, there were still low-quality houses for poorer residents, who mainly worked in the service industry, clustered in alleys and courts.[8]

The East End was the geographical and social opposite of the western suburbs. A key boundary between the eastern suburbs and the City was the Tower of London. In the east there was a higher concentration of lower-status

Figure 1.1 Panoramic view of London by Nicolaes Visscher (c. 1666)

(Reproduced with the kind permission of the London Metropolitan Archives [City of London])

residences.[9] Development in the East End in the seventeenth century tended to be lower density than in the West End, clustering along the Thames and the major thoroughfares such as Ratcliffe Highway.[10] The most important part of the area was the Port of London, which would grow to rival Amsterdam as the most important centre of shipping and commerce in Europe. The area north of the City tended to be home to craftsmen and manufacturers. It was also the location of two open areas of ground, Moorfields and Finsbury Fields, which would play a crucial role during the Fire. Finally there were the southern suburbs. Directly opposite the City, connected by London Bridge, was Southwark, an area famed for leisure and hospitality, as well as the location of some industry. Stretching away to the east along the river were Bermondsey, Rotherhithe and Greenwich, which were all associated with shipping and related industries. There was no strict delineation between the suburbs and the City. They were linked through the movements of goods and people and social networks such as the livery companies.[11]

London and England in 1666

Six years before the Fire the Stuarts had been restored to the throne. Charles II entered London in triumph on 29 May. His regime had not been able to completely bring stability to England. A major structural problem of the Restoration was that many of the political and religious divisions that had caused the Civil Wars still existed. The balance of power between crown and Parliament continued to be a matter of dispute. Charles II's religious policies were highly divisive. The Clarendon Code had targeted nonconformists, ejecting dissenting ministers from their parishes and attempting to ensure that all members of local government conformed to the Church of England. There was suspicion at the apparent sympathy that the monarchy had for Catholics. These issues combined, with practical limitations on royal power, made Charles II's regime more precarious than it appeared.[12]

London's relationship with the Crown was uneasy. The City had played a key role in supporting the Parliamentarian cause during the Civil Wars. Many Londoners had joined Parliament's armed forces and also helped to finance the anti-Royalist forces. Although London had cautiously welcomed Charles II in 1660, disputes between him and many Londoners arose, particularly due to religious differences.[13] London's population was possibly 15 to 20 per cent nonconformist, with the heaviest concentrations in wards outside the Walls, such as Aldersgate Without, Bishopsgate Without and Cripplegate Without. The Clarendon Code had therefore subjected a significant portion of Londoners to sporadic government persecution.[14] The Crown attempted to secure the loyalty and compliance of London (and other urban areas) by purging their administration of nonconformists under the 1661 Corporation Act. Symbolic of this new regime in London was the Sir Thomas Bludworth, who had been begun his one-year term as Lord Mayor in October 1665. Bludworth, a prosperous merchant to Iberia and the Levant, was a member of the Vintners' Company. He had been arrested by the Rump Parliament, but after the Restoration was knighted for his services to the Royalist cause. He had then been named one of the two sheriffs of London before being made alderman of Aldersgate Ward in 1662, his predecessor having been removed by the Crown.[15]

In 1666 England was engaged in the Second Anglo-Dutch War, which had formally begun on 22 February 1665. Charles II hoped the conflict would galvanise support for his regime.[16] The war was certainly not unpopular in London in its initial phases. Most prominent figures in the City were mercantilists who believed that the war was necessary to achieve commercial dominance over the Dutch. The City had financed the building of the HMS *Loyal London* to express their renewed allegiance to the crown and support for the war. It was launched in June 1666. That month England had won the first major engagement of the war, defeating the Dutch fleet at Lowestoft. Financing the conflict proved challenging for England. Parliament had allocated £2.5 million for the war, although the Crown had not received all of this money because of shortfalls in taxation. In October 1665 another £1.25 million was allocated for the war. Buying provisions was proving increasingly problematic as merchants charged the Royal Navy higher prices because most of their purchases were on credit.[17] The last major action of the war before the Great Fire was Holmes' Bonfire. On 9 August 1666 Rear-Admiral Robert Holmes raided the Vlie, a channel between the Dutch islands of Terschelling and Vlieland. It was full of merchant ships, which Holmes fired, destroying over 140 vessels and £1 million worth of goods. The next day his troops landed in the village of West-Terschelling, which was looted and burned. This caused outrage in the Dutch Republic, where the Great Fire would be hailed as divine retribution for Holmes' actions.[18]

Pestilence had struck England in 1665. Bubonic plague was endemic to most large cities in seventeenth-century Europe, including London. Since the Bills of Mortality had begun to be regularly compiled in 1603 there had been only four years free from plague deaths. Occasionally serious epidemics flared up, killing thousands. The most recent outbreak in London had peaked in 1647, killing 3,597. However, in 1664 there were just four recorded plague deaths in London.[19] That year rumours of a serious form of plague in the Dutch Republic emerged in England, and all ships from there were subject to quarantine. These regulations did not prevent the plague spreading to London. The first plague deaths were recorded in December 1664 in St Giles-in-the-Fields, a parish in the western suburbs that contained some of London's poorest residences. By spring 1665 it was spreading to other parishes in the west as well as emerging in the East End. On 9 May the first plague death within the Walls was recorded, in St Mary Woolchurch Haw. The epidemic peaked that summer, with over 7,000 deaths per week.[20] It would kill at least 56,000 people in London. The death toll may have been as high as 70,000 to 100,000 if suburbs and outlying areas are included.[21] The most affected areas were the generally poorer eastern and northern suburbs. In comparison the City suffered less as many of its inhabitants could afford to flee for safer outlying areas. In total London probably lost at least one-sixth of its population due to the Plague.[22]

The Great Plague led to a grim portent of the Great Fire. One year before the Fire, City authorities used fire as a technique to try and prevent the plague, hoping the smoke would fumigate houses and eliminate the disease (like most other attempts to stop the plague it was futile). On 6 September Samuel Pepys recorded, 'I looked into the street and saw Fires burning in the street, as it is through the whole City by the Lord Mayors order'.[23] The bonfires burned for three days and nights before being extinguished by heavy rain.[24] The spectre of disease brought London to a grinding halt. John Evelyn noted on 7 September 'the streete thin of people, the shops shut up, & all in mournefull silence, as not knowing whose turne might be next'.[25] Pepys' impressions were similar, recording on 20 September 'Lord, what a sad time it is, to see no boats upon the River – and grass grow all up and down Whitehall-court – and nobody but poor wretches in the streets'.[26] By winter the plague had burnt out and the wave of mortality slowed. People returned to London and business picked up. Although there were sporadic plague deaths until that summer, it appeared London had been delivered from the blight of pestilence.

Outbreak: 2 September

The Great Fire began early on a Sunday morning. The summer had been a long, hot one, drying out the timber of London's houses to make them even more flammable than usual.[27] The blaze was sparked in the parish of St Margaret New Fish Street on Pudding Lane, a small thoroughfare close to London Bridge and Thames Street, which ran parallel to the river. It began between one and two in the morning in Thomas Farriner's bakery, which had been assessed for five hearths earlier that year.[28] Despite subsequent accounts of conspiracies and arsonists, the outbreak was purely accidental. Farriner's oven had not been fully extinguished, and it is likely that it kindled a flame in the faggots that were laid up nearby to light it the next day. Smoke roused Farriner's household. With flames blocking their way to the front door, they escaped through a garret window onto the roof. Farriner's maid was apparently unwilling to follow and was left behind, becoming the first casualty of the Fire. The flames spread to Farriner's yard, where he had stockpiled wood for his oven. In these early stages, there was nothing to distinguish this blaze from the countless others that had beset London. Its initial spread was slow, but the flames inexorably spread along Pudding Lane and to nearby Fish Street Hill. The first large building to be destroyed was the Star Inn, whose proprietor Robert Whitborn had recently been assessed for twenty-nine hearths.[29] Bludworth arrived on the scene at around 3 a.m., but at this stage the blaze did not seem to be too serious.

The area around Thames Street was particularly prone to fires. In his 1667 account of the Fire Edward Waterhouse, a fellow of the Royal Society, wrote that it was 'the lodge of all combustibles, Oyl, Hemp, Flax, Pitch, Tar, Cordage, Hops, Wines, Brandies, and other materials favourable to Fire'. The neighbourhood was full of 'narrow Streets, old Buildings all of Timber, all contiguous each to other, all stuffed with aliment for the Fire, all in the very heart of the Trade and Wealth of the City'.[30] Once the flames took hold of Thames Street, they claimed their first parish church, St Magnus the Martyr, and their first livery company hall, the Fishmongers'. At around 8 a.m. the blaze spread to London Bridge, which was crowded with buildings. Southwark was under threat. Fortunately there was a gap in the buildings one-third of the way down the bridge created by a fire that had occurred in 1632. If this had not been in place the Fire could have spread quickly south of the river. This was a stroke of fortune as Southwark was just as prone to fires as Thames Street. Indeed, Southwark experienced its own 'great fire' in 1676, when 600 buildings were burned.

Bludworth is frequently held culpable by contemporaries (as well as some later historians) for not stopping the Fire in its early stages. In truth, there was little Bludworth could have done. Fire-fighting technology of the day was primitive. The most reliable course of action was to pull houses down to create fire breaks. Bludworth was reluctant to do this, fearing legal repercussions from their owners. Gaining permission from them was difficult given that most Londoners were tenants. In addition, many of the most influential citizens of the City (who could have given Bludworth the clout and advice he needed to fight the fire) were absent, having gone into the countryside to escape the hot weather. Bludworth would have also found it difficult to rouse enough manpower to fight the flames. There were only around 800 men responsible for policing the City during the mid-seventeenth century.[31] Volunteers would have to fill the gap, but most Londoners would have been more concerned with rescuing their own possessions than aiding the Lord Mayor. As Pepys noted, that day the 'streets [were] full of nothing but people and horses and carts loaden with goods, ready to run over one another'.[32] Also acting against Bludworth was the east wind that blew the fire from Pudding Lane to Thames Street and beyond. The Anglican priest William Taswell, then a child attending Westminster School, recorded in his autobiography that the wind carried 'great flakes' up to three furlongs 'pitching upon and uniting themselves to various dry substances, set on fire houses very remote from each other'.[33] The day of the week was also crucial. The ejected minister Philip Henry had noted it was 'as if the lords controversy with london was more particularly for prophaning the holy day'.[34] Even if Sabbath-breaking was apparently rife, Sunday was still a day where it was difficult to put the machinery of local and national government into action. Had the Fire started on a workday, it is possible that a more concerted effort to fight it could have been mobilised more rapidly.

The chaos of the early stages of the Fire is captured in two manuscript sources. The Londoner Thomas Rugge recorded on 2 September in his 'diurnall' that 'the fire grew masterless: and all the energy and art of man could not make any work for it was fomented by a wind that blew the fire'.[35] John Tremayne, a Cornishman living in London, reported to his father that 'the fire began in a bakers house . . . & by reason of the narrownesse of the streets could not be stopped & the winde being very high, caused it to increase so furiously that none durst come fight it & therefore all people fled with there goods & what they could carry before it, all people mindinge more the preserves of them then to quench the fire so that in short space it grew unmasterable'.[36]

Even late on Sunday morning, much of the rest of London paid little heed to the events around Thames Street. Charles II was informed of the fire at around 11 a.m., and gave permission to pull down as many houses as possible to arrest the spread of the conflagration. Pepys ran into Bludworth on Cannon Street, bringing him the royal order, but 'To the King's message, he cried like a fainting woman, "Lord, what can I do? I am spent! People will not obey me. I have been pull[ing] down houses. But the fire overtakes us faster then we can do it"'.[37] By midday Francisco de Rapicani, an Italian serving with a suite of Swedish diplomats in London, recorded that the 'fire was spreading with such fury that it was thought that about a hundred houses were being burnt every hour'.[38]

That afternoon Charles II and his brother James, Duke of York, took the royal barge to Queenhithe to view the flames before returning to Whitehall. Figure 1.2, a Dutch print, gives an indication of the view of the riverside blaze they

Figure 1.2 View of the Great Fire seen from across the River Thames (1666)

(Reproduced with the kind permission of the London Metropolitan Archives [City of London])

would have seen. One of their closest allies, William, First Earl of Craven, was left behind to help Bludworth. A few soldiers were mobilised to assist the fire-fighting. By midnight the fire had spread 500 metres west along the Thames and pushed 100 metres north as far as Cannon Street. Even at this early stage it was already the most damaging fire to strike London in living memory – and it was only going to get worse.

The blaze spreads: 3 September

The *London Gazette* was the official journal of record for the government. On 3 September it reported 'a sudden and lamentable fire brake out in this City . . . which continues still with great violence, and hath already burnt down to the ground many houses thereabouts'. As Monday morning dawned it was clear that this fire was going to be a serious one. People across the City rushed to clear their homes of goods and valuables and then flee. That day Lady Hobart wrote to the politician Sir Ralph Verney: 'thar was never so sad a sight, nor so dolefull a cry hard, my hart is not abell to expres the tenth nay the thousenth part of it, thar is all the carts within ten mils round, & cars & drays run about night & day, & thousens of men & women carring burdens'.[39] This issue of price-gouging by carters was a common feature of contemporary reports of the Fire. News of their rapacity spread even to Cambridge, where Samuel Newton, an alderman there, noted in his diary that people were able to shift their lighter goods to fields 'but at such vast rates for carriage that 8 or 10 li for the carriage of a load of goodes was ordinarily giuen'.[40] Tremayne noted even higher prices:

> porter[s] & Coaches Cartes & carters became at such an excessive rate; that they could not be hired to cary a ladinge of goods a halfe mile & 20 l & the uncouchenable villans wrought on the peoples necessity & would doe nothinge, but at the most unreasonable rates victualls were not to be gott & many heapes of rich cloth indeed of all sortes of wealth lay trodden as dunge in the streets'.[41]

This problem was not unique to London – similar complaints of price-gouging by carters were made after the Second Great Fire of New York in 1835.[42]

Charles II decided drastic action was needed. Bludworth was removed and York placed in charge of the fire-fighting effort. The king also travelled into the City to help fight the blaze. York's main tactic was to pull down houses to create fire breaks. Using water to douse the flames was ineffective. This was because the dry weather meant that the City's water supply was reduced, and many of its wells were dry. Even if there had been water, the 'squirts' (which resembled large syringes) were not particularly effective in putting out large blazes. More soldiers were sent into London to help. York ordered that a series of command posts be set up to co-ordinate activities. Parish constables were expected to attend each one, along with 100 men.

In addition thirty soldiers were sent to each post. To provision the men £5 worth of bread, cheese and beer was placed at each post, and the crown authorized a one-shilling payment to those men who performed well. York placed influential noblemen across the City, including: John Belasyse, First Baron Belasyse; Edward Montagu, Second Earl of Manchester and Anthony Ashley Cooper, Lord Ashley (from 1672 Earl of Shaftesbury). Sailors were called in from Deptford and Woolwich to help. The crown also made sure that order continued to be kept in London. Two companies of trained bands were dispersed to guard houses in Lincoln's Inn Fields, Gray's Inn Fields, Hatton Garden and St Giles' Fields. Later these areas would be piled with goods that residents of the City had managed to carry out before they were destroyed in the Fire.[43]

Despite the best efforts of York and his men, by Monday afternoon, Evelyn saw from Bankside that the whole south part of the City was aflame from Cheapside to the Thames, and along Cornhill to Baynard Castle. Lombard Street, home of some of England's wealthiest men, was fully engulfed.[44] Next to fall was the Royal Exchange, positioned between Threadneedle Street and Cornhill. It had been opened in 1571 and was home to dozens of shops. Thomas Vincent, a Puritan minister who resided in London, recorded in his account of Plague and the Fire that 'the glory of merchants [was] now invaded with much violence . . . how quickly did it run down the galleries, filling them with flames'.[45]

Evelyn recorded the scene as night fell on Monday:

> noise & crackling & thunder of the impetuous flames, the shreeking of Women & children, the hurry of people, the fall of towers, houses & churches . . . like an hideous storme, & the air all about so hot & inflamed that at the last one was not able to approch it, so as they were force'd [to] stand still, and let the flames consume.

He also noted that the flames appeared to 'leap' from house to house and street to street.[46] This occurred because the wind spread sparks and cinder, throwing it into the air to start fires in houses that were not in the direct path of the blaze. This phenomenon of houses appearing to be set alight spontaneously would later add credence to reports that foreign agents had roamed the City during the Fire, setting blazes using fireballs and grenades. In this febrile atmosphere, by Monday foreigners were beginning to be suspected of being complicit in starting the blaze. The French and the Dutch, both at war with England, naturally bore the brunt of public suspicion. Cornelius Rietvelt, a Dutch baker residing in St Margaret Westminster, had been imprisoned at the Gatehouse in Westminster on the false rumour he had set fire to his own house. His goods had been stolen by a violent crowd, so he had no money left.[47] Many 'strangers', both Dutch and French, were apprehended.[48] Tremayne reflected some of the common sentiment in the streets of London:

we were all in armes in the beginning, it beinge certainely sd that it was a plott . . . one woman that had fireballs was drawne in peeces by the multitude & any that had but the looke of a Frenchman was taken & carried to prison or cutt & slashed & the people they were so violently bent against the French.[49]

Taswell also recorded the violence against foreigners – 'the ignorant and deluded mob, who upon the occasion were hurried away with a kind of phrenzy, vented forth their rage against the Roman Catholics and Frenchmen; imagining these incendiaries . . . had thrown red-hot balls into the houses'. He saw a blacksmith fell an innocent Frenchman with an iron bar and heard from his brother that a Frenchman was almost dismembered in Moorfields because he was carrying a chest of tennis balls people believed were fireballs.[50]

Height of destruction: 4 September

As day broke on Tuesday Cheapside was destroyed. This thoroughfare had been one of the City's main commercial districts since medieval times, famed for the sale of luxury textiles and housing several prominent goldsmiths. Fortunately for them they had had the time and the resources to be able to store their valuables in the Tower.[51] Nearby Guildhall, built in 1411, was also struck. Although seriously damaged, parts of the medieval structure survived the Fire partially intact. Realising the increasing seriousness of the situation, Charles II summoned George Monck, First Duke of Albemarle, back from his role in leading the English fleet to keep order in London. The king ordered the Lords Lieutenants of Middlesex, Surrey and Hertfordshire to draw together their county militias to prevent chaos breaking out. York also ordered them to send workmen to London to help fight the Fire.[52] More soldiers and sailors were arriving in the City to assist the fire-fighting. Charles II and York battled the flames, exposing themselves to great personal risk. Rugge recorded that 'his majesty and duke of york were at the greatest danger of the increasing fires early & late encouraging his people to work'. Common citizens also pitched in. Rugge also records that one Mr Starkey provided '13 dozen of Pails & 60 Broomes at a pinch, with was the means under God of stopping the fire at one place'.[53]

York placed himself at Temple Bar. This was a crucial area, since if the flames spread too far west they could threaten the Inns of Court, or even Westminster. It was believed that the Fleet River, which flowed into the Thames along the western side of the City, would prevent the flames spreading west. That morning, as Cheapside was being destroyed, the flames crossed over the Fleet. The major thoroughfare west, Fleet Street, was in flames. Bridewell, formerly Henry VIII's London residence but now used as a prison, hospital, school and workhouse, was seriously damaged. The other major charitable foundation that stood in the path of the Fire was Christ's

Hospital in Christchurch Greyfriars, built on the site of a medieval religious house. It had operated as a school since 1552. When the Fire arrived the school was empty, as the governors had evacuated the pupils to Islington. It was seriously damaged, but not completely destroyed. However, it did not re-open to students for fourteen months.[54]

Denizens of the western suburbs scrambled to evacuate themselves and their goods. The antiquarian Elias Ashmole, residing in the Temple, had his books sent to his cousin in Tottenham. The Lord Chancellor Edward Hyde, First Earl of Clarendon, who was living in Berkshire House in St James, wrote at the time 'we who live in the suburbs . . . fled from our lodgings, and have hardly yet recovered'.[55] Meanwhile, Rapicani and his colleagues snuck out of their lodgings in Covent Garden to move to new ones in Westminster, which they believed would be less likely to be fired. They took the precaution of being well armed, as one of their foreign roommates who had earlier snuck out to see a lady was nearly lynched by an angry crowd.[56] By Tuesday evening most of the City within the Walls and its liberties to the west were in flames. Evelyn noted in his diary that thousands of Londoners were fleeing to outlying areas. People went south to areas such as St George's Fields (an area of open ground in Southwark) as well as north to Highgate and Moorfields. Rescued possessions were piled in any available public buildings and open space. Those who could not find houses used tents, huts and hovels. They had gone 'from delicatnesse, riches & easy accommodations in stately & well furnishd houses . . . reduced to extreamest misery & poverty'.[57] Many built cheap, temporary 'sheds'. These were usually made of deal – when a Dutch mariner petitioned Charles II on 24 September for a 'free pass' to import 'Deale Boards' into London, he mentioned their 'great use . . . for the rebuilding of . . . Houses since the deplorable Fire'.[58] In Moorfields 'temporary' accommodations remained in place for nearly a decade until in May 1675 the Court of Aldermen ordered 'the demolishing of all shedds . . . erected since the Late dismall fire'.[59]

St Paul's Cathedral was Tuesday's last major casualty. This was the fourth cathedral to be built on the site – the previous three had also been burned down. The structure had suffered much since the Reformation. In 1561 its spire had been destroyed by lighting and was yet to be rebuilt. Charles I had begun restoration work. In the 1630s Inigo Jones added a new west front in the classical style. During the Interregnum, work on the cathedral stopped, and it fell into disrepair. Work restarted after the Restoration. Christopher Wren (who even proposed demolishing the cathedral) had been consulting on the work since 1661. He planned to continue Jones' work as well as add a dome to replace the tower. A national charitable collection to restore St Paul's had raised over £6,000 by 1 June 1666.[60] As part of the restoration work, the cathedral was covered in wooden scaffolding. The area of Paul's Churchyard was synonymous with the book trade.[61] The booksellers decided to put their stock in the cathedral and in St Faith under St Paul (actually in a crypt of St Paul's). They believed that the heavy stone walls would keep their books, pamphlets and manuscripts safe.[62] At around 8 p.m. the flames spread to St Paul's. The heat, helped by the ignition of the scaffolding, was so intense that the heavy stone walls crumbled. They collapsed into the crypt where the books had been stored. It was a great intellectual loss. The nonconformist Richard Baxter recorded that 'the Loss of Books was an exceeding great Detriment to the Interest of Piety of Learning'. He saw half-burned leaves of books floating in the air at his home in Acton, eight miles from St Paul's, and wrote that they were seen as distant as Windsor, twenty-four miles away.[63] For Royalists such as Dryden the burning of St Paul's was part of its purging in the aftermath of its degradation during the Civil War.[64]

Just as it appeared that the situation was hopeless, salvation arrived. At around 11 p.m. the strong easterly wind that had been fanning the flames calmed down. This meant that the fire would not spread as quickly, and prevented the inferno continuing even further into the suburbs. Contemporaries recognised this was crucial. The anonymous poem *Londoners Lamentation* ended by thanking divine mercy that the Fire did not spread to Whitehall or any of the other suburbs.[65] A further positive development occurred in the east of the City. Although the flames had mostly been driven west from Pudding Lane, they had by Tuesday night spread to Tower Street. The greatest risk was the flames spreading to the Tower, which was being used to store a large stock of gunpowder for the Royal Navy. The houses surrounding the Tower were blown up. Fortunately this created an open space so large that the fire could not spread across it. If the Tower had been kindled, it would have caused a huge explosion and the resulting flames would have made short work of the closely packed wooden houses of the East End. Evelyn noted that if the Tower had been ignited it would have 'undoubtedly not only have beaten down and destroyed all the bridge, but sunk and torn the vessels in the river, and rendered the demolition beyond all expression for several miles about the country'.[66]

The end of the fire: 5 September

Even though the wind had slackened overnight, by Wednesday morning people were still expecting the suburbs to be burned, and were preparing to flee further into neighbouring counties and villages.[67] Tremayne recorded that 'we all sopposed nothing but that the suburbs as well as Citty would be destroyed'.[68] Great numbers gathered at the fields in Islington, but there were no deputy lieutenants or justices of the peace there. That day Charles II, fearing a breakdown in order, requested that a careful watch be kept on the refugees, but also to give them a 'charitable and Christian' reception, lodging and entertainment. He then proclaimed that bread should be supplied for the people left homeless. All churches, chapels, schools and public buildings were to be opened to store people's goods. Other towns were enjoined to receive refugees from London, as well as allow them to exercise their trades during the period of crisis.[69]

The fire-fighting efforts led by York carried on, with gunpowder being used to create firebreaks more quickly. Combined with the fact that the wind had also dropped considerably, this meant the fire stopped spreading and began to die out in some places. But potential dangers remained. The flames raged fiercely around Cripplegate, threatening the area north of the Walls. Bludworth, with the personal help of Charles II and York, oversaw the pulling down of houses in the area, which prevented the flames from spreading. The Fire's final burst of activity occurred that evening around the Inns of Court, where flames threatened the Inner Temple. Once again, York distinguished himself by rushing to the scene and ensuring that the fire did not take hold there. By Wednesday night the Great Fire was effectively over.

Aftermath

The scale of the damage was immense. Evelyn walked from Whitehall to London Bridge, clambering over piles of smoking rubble: 'the people who now walked about the ruines, appeard like men in some dismal desart, or rather in some greate Citty, lay'd wast by an impetuous & cruel Enemy'.[70] In addition to St Paul's Cathedral, eighty-four parish churches were destroyed and three more were seriously damaged. Forty-four of the fifty-one livery company halls were burned down.[71] Most importantly over 13,200 houses had been destroyed.[72]

Figure 1.3 Plan of the City of London and surrounding area after the Great Fire of London by Wenceslaus Hollar (1666)

(Reproduced with the kind permission of the London Metropolitan Archives [City of London])

Bad as it had been, in truth the disaster could have been worse. Had the Fire spread further into the suburbs, London would have been denuded of even more of its housing stock, and even more people would have been made homeless. A further stroke of fortune had been that the Fire had spread fairly slowly, therefore giving people time to flee to safety. Had the Fire travelled more quickly, the death toll could have been catastrophic. In the two contemporaneous Great Fires of Edo and Istanbul thousands had died – 85,000 and 40,000, respectively. It is difficult to determine how many people died in London's Fire. The actual death toll may have been higher than the traditional figure of six, but it is likely it did not run into the hundreds. Indeed the *London Gazette* did not record a single fatality as a result of the Fire. Most of the few casualties of the Fire recorded in contemporary sources shared a similar profile – they tended to be elderly. Paul Lowell, an eighty-year-old watchmaker, refused to leave his premises in Shoe Lane and was consumed in the flames.[73] Pepys recorded that the body of an old man was found under the ruins of St Paul's – he had returned there to fetch a blanket but had been overcome by the flames. Taswell recalled seeing the burned corpse of an old woman in St Paul's.[74] The elderly were more vulnerable to the privations caused by being made homeless by the Fire. The Royalist poet and playwright James Shirley and his wife Frances died as an indirect result of the Fire. They

> were driven by the dismal conflagration . . . from their habitation near to *Fleetstreet*, into the Parish of *St. Giles in the Fields* in *Middlesex*, where being in a manner overcome with affrightments, disconsolations, and other miseries occasion'd by that fire and their losses, they both died within the compass of a natural day.[75]

In addition, had there been a high death toll in the Fire, it is likely the polemical, politically driven, accounts of the Fire produced during the Popish Plot and Exclusion Crisis (see Chapter 5, this volume) would have mentioned them in detail – they did not. Similarly, none of the petitions for charity from Londoners burnt out by the Fire mentioned the death of a spouse or family member as a result of the flames. The Fire had no significant effect on the mortality regime of early modern London, and in turn crisis mortality had no significant effect on the restructuring of the metropolis.

The effort to rebuild London will be outlined in the next chapter, but first the immediate aftermath of the Fire will be considered. A major issue was the thousands of displaced Londoners. It is difficult to calculate the exact numbers of people who left the City in the face of the Fire. Given that around half of London's population of c. 400,000 lived in the City and its liberties, it is likely that well over 100,000 people (along with as many possessions as they could transport) were effectively homeless on 6 September. Experiences differed according to wealth and social status. Rugge recorded that 'the poore fled into the next fields with their goods; the rich fled with their goods to the

Adjacent villages'.[76] Those with the most money would have been able to afford to pay people to carry their goods away from the Fire. Baxter wrote that 'the streets were crowded with People and Carts, to carry away what Goods they could get out: And they that were most active, and befriended (by their Wealth) got Carts, and saved much; and the rest lost almost all'.[77] Yet it is clear that even citizens with resources found themselves bereft after the Fire. Rapicani recorded that 'great distress among the people, and countless poor persons with nothing but a stick in their hands, who had formerly been prosperous and well-placed, were scattered here and there in the fields where they had built huts for themselves'.[78] The antiquarian Anthony Wood of Oxford succinctly summed up the situation: '[t]hose that had a house today were the next glad of an hedge or a pigstie or stable'.[79]

The early administrative reaction to the Fire showed that public disorder was expected. Paranoia had spread across England. Rumours abounded of plots. On the Isle of Wight guards were put at all docks, the names of all lodgers were taken and no stranger was allowed on the island unless someone could vouch for them. Similarly at King's Lynn and Norwich in Norfolk a strong guard was put on the town, and an inquiry was made to secure all the Dutch and French people there. In Kingston-upon-Hull the governor set a strong guard, secured suspects and put Dutch prisoners under heavy guard. As far away as Naworth in Cumberland there were great fears and Charles Howard, First Earl of Carlisle ordered the trained bands to disperse across the county. Likewise at Barnstaple in Devon the trained bands there were put on strict guard. There were also strange reports from Coventry of murdered sheep being found in the fields with only their tallow taken away, which was believed to have been used to make fireballs.[80]

The situation in London was potentially volatile – particularly as it had a long tradition of anti-alien unrest.[81] Many of the public believed foreigners had caused the Fire, and 'aliens' faced the threat of violence. On 6 September Pepys wrote that it was dangerous for any 'stranger' to walk the streets.[82] The next day Evelyn recorded that people took up weapons and fell upon any Dutch or French they met, 'without sense or reason'.[83] Robert Hubert, a French watchmaker who had lived in London, was the victim of this desire for a foreign culprit. He had been travelling from Sweden to his parents' home in Rouen when English vessels intercepted his ship, the *Maid of Stockholm*, and ordered it to divert to London, where it arrived on 31 August. Hubert was arrested after the Fire in Romford, Essex, trying to leave England. When he was questioned, Hubert stated he had thrown a fireball in Westminster. Hubert was taken to London and tried at the Old Bailey in October. He claimed he was part of a larger Papist or French conspiracy. Hubert changed his story to say that he had actually used a pole to place a fireball through Farriner's window in Pudding Lane. To prove his point he was escorted to the area that the Fire had started, where he was able to point out the site of Farriner's house (which was in fact well known to the public by then). His testimony was confused and disjointed and it is likely he had mental health problems. Later testimony from the master of his ship revealed it was impossible for Hubert to have started the Fire, as he had not gone ashore until two days after the blaze started. Nonetheless, the jury found Hubert guilty and he was sentenced to death. On 27 October he was taken to Tyburn. At the gallows he claimed to be a Catholic (he was actually a Protestant) and he received absolution from one of Queen Catherine of Braganza's confessors before being hung.[84]

Part of the difficulty the authorities faced after the Fire was the paucity of public officials to keep order. Even though great numbers had taken refuge in Islington, there were no deputy lieutenants or justices of the peace there. Likewise, there was only one constable on duty at St Giles-in-the-Fields.[85] A letter written three months after the Fire noted the dangers of the fired parts of London, noting 'many persons have been found murdered in the vaults among the ruins' after being robbed. In Westminster the Provost Marshal Gilbert Thomas complained to Charles II that 'since ye late lamentable fire in London greate numbers of fellons Robbers & other notorious offenders doe harbor resort & are received in & about ye said Citty of Westminster'.[86] There was some local resentment towards the homeless Londoners in the outlying areas. Thomas Gaddesby was a wheelwright of Islington. On 10 September a warrant for his arrest was issued, accusing him of using 'opprobrious words' towards the magistrates in Islington overseeing the distressed people there. He was apparently fined but not punished further – 'having made an example, [which] will produce a compassionate disposition towards distressed people who remain in the neighbourhood'.[87] Charles II moved to calm London. The day after the Fire ended he rode to Moorfields and addressed the crowds. He told them 'it was immediate from the hand of God, and no plot' and that he 'desired them to take no more alarms; he had strength enough to defend them from any enemy, and assured them he would, by the grace of God, live and die with them'.[88] There followed royal and mayoral proclamations that forbade men to 'disquiet themselves with rumours of tumults'.[89] Thus the 'official' line of the Great Fire emerged. The account published on 10 September in the *London Gazette* had a factual tone, emphasising the accidental nature of the disaster (as well as focusing on the role of Charles II and York). This was the public voice of authority attempting to shape the perception of the Fire – however, others would challenge it.[90]

Having taken a back seat to the Crown during the Fire, City authorities immediately took an active role in the recovery. The Court of Aldermen met at Gresham College in Bishopsgate on 6 September. The next day they ordered that Guildhall and its offices be cleared of wreckage so that it could be used to conduct City business.[91] Firstly they sought to ensure the food supply to the London and re-establish trade as soon as possible. A proclamation ordered new markets to be set up at Bishopsgate Street, Tower Hill, Smithfield and Leadenhall Street. The gardens and walks of Gresham College, spared in the Fire, were to be used instead of the Royal Exchange for trade.[92] The effort to open up the resupply of food to London appeared to have been successful – by Saturday naval biscuits sent to Moorfields were refused because the markets were operating well enough to supply the people there.[93] Next the Court of Aldermen requested that the City livery companies 'take care for the releife and succour of their respective poore during the present extremity'. They then ordered that tents be sent into Finsbury Fields for the poor without any dwellings. The bridge masters were ordered to clear all around London Bridge for the use of 'freemen who are now destitute of habitacons to have Libty of erecting shedds upon the void places on each side the Bridge to imploy themselves in there callings'.[94] There was still a desire to ensure that this temporary housing was regulated – on 19 November Bludworth ordered a search of all sheds and temporary structures built since the Fire to find out who was occupying them, and to what purpose.[95]

In the immediate aftermath of the Fire, there were two plans to help Londoners by sending food. On 11 September, William Waynflet of Southwold, Suffolk, wrote to Joseph Williamson, an important aide to Henry Benet, Baron Arlington, the Secretary of State for the Southern Department, that he knew there would 'great want' of food for the poor in London. Waynflet went on to inform Williamson that the price of cheese was low, and that if letters were sent to knights and gentlemen thereabouts, they would load a small vessel for London and the cheese could be distributed to the poor.[96] Similarly, on 6 November 1666 the Lord Lieutenant of Ireland, James Butler, First Duke of Ormond, offered to import 20,000 heads of cattle from Ireland to distressed Londoners.[97] A vote in the House of Commons decided that the cattle could not be sent to England, dead or alive.[98]

There was concern about crime. Fires in early modern London were often associated with theft, and they frequently attracted looters.[99] The Great Fire was no different. Waterhouse claimed that people came in from the suburbs to capitalise on the chaos: 'multitudes of men, and those under a loose Shire Government, and many of those single Persons, Gamesters, and others of shuffling life, or married persons, full of charge and poverty' arrived to steal and embezzle goods.[100] On 19 September there was a royal proclamation ordering all persons who had taken plate, goods and building materials from houses demolished by the Fire to return them to owners by bringing them to the armoury in Finsbury Fields where they would be kept and inventoried for eventual return to rightful owners.[101] On 26 September, goods held in other places like Southwark and Westminster were also sent to Finsbury. No goods were to be delivered from there without the order of the Common Council.[102] One month after the Fire Rugge noted that 'a General search made and many goods was found in the hands of those who under a pretense of help in the time of need and fire . . . stole away many rich Goods'.[103] On 9 October Bludworth requested that vagrants wandering through the ruins be charged and that a stocks and whipping post be set up to punish them.[104]

In spite of official worries about the possibility of public upheaval after the Fire, and reports of sporadic violence against foreigners, it seems there was no great breakdown in public order or rioting after the Fire. Waterhouse records that 'honest persons' kept order against the 'common rout'.[105] On Friday Charles II was able to order the Lord Lieutenants of Middlesex, Surrey, Kent and Hertfordshire to withdraw their militias from London, although he did request they continue to supply food and tools where possible.[106] That evening Albemarle arrived in the capital. By this stage, the danger appeared to have passed but the presence of such an experienced and influential commander may have helped to restore confidence in many. 'Rege Sincera' argued that the fact that there was no major disorder showed the loyalty and affection that Londoners felt towards the Crown, who forgot their own misery as a result of Charles II's actions and filled the streets with prayers for him.[107] Given the growing dissatisfaction with the Restoration regime, this was unlikely. Rather, the absence of any major violent disruptions showed that amongst phlegmatic Londoners popular sentiment lent more towards reconstruction rather than recrimination and focussed primarily on recovering and rebuilding.

Notes

1 W.C. Baer, 'The House-Building Sector of London's Economy, 1550–1650', *Urban History*, 39 (2012), 409–13; P. Guillery, 'Houses in London's Suburbs', in *London and Middlesex 1666 Hearth Tax*, ed. M. Davies et al. (London: British Record Society, 2014), 146.

2 R.A.P. Finlay, *Population and Metropolis: The Demography of London 1580– 1650* (Cambridge: Cambridge University Press, 1981), 70–1.

3 V. Harding, 'London and Middlesex in the 1660s', in *London and Middlesex 1666 Hearth Tax*, ed. M. Davies et al. (London: British Record Society, 2014), 26–7.

4 J.P. Ward, *Metropolitan Communities: Trade Guilds, Identity, and Change in Early Modern London* (Stanford, CA: Stanford University Press, 1997), 43.

5 R.A.P. Finlay and B. Shearer, 'Population Growth and Suburban Expansion', in *London 1500–1700: The Making of the Metropolis*, ed. A.L. Beier and R.A.P. Finlay (London and New York: Longman, 1986), 44–6.

6 T. Sakata, 'The Growth of London and Its Regional Structure in the Early Modern Period'. *Keio Economic Studies*, 38 (2001), 4–14.

7 M.J. Power, 'The Social Topography of Restoration London', in *London 1500– 1700: The Making of the Metropolis*, ed. A.L. Beier and R.A.P. Finlay (London and New York: Longman, 1986), 203–4; J.F. Merritt, *The Social World of Early Modern Westminster: Abbey, Court and Community 1525–1640* (Manchester: Manchester University Press, 2005), 144–6, 140–73.

8 G. Carr, *Residence and Social Status: The Development of Seventeenth-Century London* (New York and London: Garland, 1990), 139.

9 C. Spence, *London in the 1690s: A Social Atlas* (London: Centre for Metropolitan History, 2000), 68–70.

10 Carr, *Residence and Social Status*, 142–3.

11 J.P. Ward, 'Imagining the Metropolis in Elizabethan and Stuart London', in *The Country and the City Revisited: England and the Politics of Culture, 1550–1850*, ed. G. MacLean, D. Landry and J.P. Ward (Cambridge: Cambridge University Press, 1999), 37.

12 T. Harris, *Restoration: Charles II and His Kingdoms 1660–1685* (London: Allen Lane, 2005), 83.

13 Harding, 'London and Middlesex', 55–7.

14 T. Harris, *London Crowds in the Reign of Charles II: Propaganda and Politics from the Restoration until the Exclusion Crisis* (Cambridge: Cambridge University Press, 1987), 64–6.

15 J.R. Woodhead, *The Rulers of London 1660–1689: A Biographical Record of the Aldermen and Common Councilmen of the City of London* (London: London and Middlesex Archaeological Society, 1965), 33.

16 R. Hainsworth and C. Churches, *The Anglo-Dutch Naval Wars 1652–1674* (Stroud: Sutton, 1998), 108.

17 G. Rommelse, *The Second Anglo-Dutch War (1665–1667): Raison d'état, Mercantilism and Maritime Strife* (Hilversum: Verloren, 2006), 128–62.

18 Rommelse, *Second Anglo-Dutch War*, 162.

19 W.G. Bell, *The Great Plague in London in 1665* (1st ed. London: The Bodley Head, 1924), 5.

20 R. Rideal, *1666: Plague, War and Hellfire* (London: John Murray, 2016), 33, 92.

21 R.O. Bucholz and J.P. Ward, *London: A Social and Cultural History, 1550–1750* (Cambridge: Cambridge University Press, 2012), 313.

22 Harding, 'London and Middlesex', 35.

23 S. Pepys, *The Diary of Samuel Pepys*, ed. R. Latham and W. Matthews, 11 vols. (1st ed. London: G. Bell and Sons, 1970–83), vi, 213.

24 S. Porter, *The Great Plague of London* (3rd ed. Stroud: Amberley, 2012), 42–3.

25 J. Evelyn, *The Diary of John Evelyn*, ed. E.S. De Beer, 6 vols. (Oxford: Clarendon Press, 1955), iii, 417–18.

26 Pepys, *Diary*, vi, 233.

27 Evelyn recorded that before the Fire there had been a 'long set of faire & warm weather'. Evelyn, *Diary*, iii, 452.

28 TNA, Hearth Tax Assessment Listing, City of London and parts of Middlesex, 1666, E179/252/32, Part 4, fol. 6r.

29 TNA, E179/252/32, Part 4, fol. 5r.

30 E. Waterhouse, *A Short Narrative of the Late Dreadful Fire in London* (London: W.G. for Richard Thrale and James Thrale, 1667), 47–8.

31 P. Griffiths, *Lost Londons: Change, Crime, and Control in the Capital City, 1550–1660* (Cambridge: Cambridge University Press, 2008), 304.

32 Pepys, *Diary*, vii, 270.

33 W. Taswell, *Autobiography and Anecdotes by William Taswell, D.D*, ed. G.P. Elliott (London: Camden Society, 1853), 11.

34 P. Henry, *Diaries and Letters of Philip Henry, M.A.*, ed. M.H. Lee (London: Kegan Paul, Trench and Co, 1882), 193.

35 BL, T. Rugge, *Mercurius Politicus Redivius; or, a Collection of the Most Materiall Occurrences and Transactions in Publick Affaires, Since Anno Domini 1659, Volume II*. Additional MS 10117, 1659–72, fol. 176v.

36 LMA, Letter of John Tremayne, 1666, COL/SJ/03/014, fol. 1.

37 Pepys, *Diary*, vii, 269.

38 F. de Rapicani, 'A Foreign Visitor's Account of the Great Fire, 1666', *Transactions of the London and Middlesex Archaeological Society*, 20 (1960), 83.

39 M.M. Verney, ed., *Memoirs of the Verney Family from the Restoration to the Revolution 1660 to 1696* (London: Longmans, Green, and Co, 1899), 137.

40 S. Newton, *The Diary of Samuel Newton, Alderman of Cambridge (1662–1717)*, ed. J.E. Foster (Cambridge: Cambridge Antiquarian Society, 1890), 15–16.

41 LMA, COL/SJ/03/014, fol. 1.

42 E.G. Burrows and M. Wallace, *Gotham: A History of New York City to 1898* (Oxford: Oxford University Press, 1999), 596–7.

43 M.A.E. Green, ed., *Calendar of State Papers, Domestic Series, of the Reign of Charles II, 1666–1667* (London: Longman, Green, Longman, Roberts and Green, 1864), 94–5.

44 Evelyn, *Diary*, iii, 451.

45 T. Vincent, *God's Terrible Voice in the City* (London: G. Calvert, 1667), 54.

46 Evelyn, *Diary*, iii, 451, 453.

47 *CSPD, 1666–1667*, 95.

48 Rege Sincera, *Observations both Historical and Moral upon the Burning of London, September 1666* (London: Thomas Ratcliffe, 1667), 4.

49 LMA, COL/SJ/03/014, fol. 2.

50 Taswell, *Autobiography*, 11.

51 W.G. Bell, *The Great Fire of London* (1st ed. London: John Lane, 1920), 94.

52 *CSPD, 1666–1667*, 95, 99.

53 BL, Additional MS 10117, fol. 176v.

54 Bell, *Great Fire*, 141–3.

55 E. Ashmole, *The Diary and Will of Elias Ashmole*, ed. R.T. Gunther (Oxford: Old Ashmolean Reprints, 1927), 79; Bell, *Great Fire*, 157.

56 Rapicani, 'Foreign Visitor's Account', 84.

57 Evelyn, *Diary*, iii, 457.

58 TNA, Petition of Teunis Willemsen to the King, 24 September 1666, SP 29/172, 153.

59 LMA, Rep. 80, fol. 184r-v.

60 LMA, *Day Book of the Receipts and Payments of ye Charitable Contributions towards ye repairing of ye decays and ruins of ye Cathedral Church of St Paul London*, CLA/079/04/016.

61 J. Raven, 'St Paul's Precinct and the Book Trade to 1800', in *St Paul's: The Cathedral Church of London 604–2004*, ed. D. Keene, A. Burns and A. Saint (New Haven and London: Yale University Press, 2004), 430.

62 G. Mandelbrote, 'Workplaces and Living Spaces: London Book Trade Inventories of the Late Seventeenth Century', in *The London Book Trade: Topographies of Print in the Metropolis from the Sixteenth Century*, ed. R. Myers, M. Harris and G. Mandelbrote (London and New Castle, DE: The British Library and Oak Knoll Press, 2003), 21.

63 R. Baxter, *Reliquiae Baxterianae: Or, Mr. Richard Baxter's Narrative of the Most Memorable Passages of His Life and Times, Part 3*, ed. M. Sylvester (London: T. Parkhurst, J. Robinson, J. Lawrence and J. Dunton, 1696), 16.

64 M. McKeon, *Politics and Poetry in Restoration England: The Case of Dryden's Annus Mirabilis* (Cambridge, MA: Harvard University Press, 1975), 64.

65 R.A. Aubin, ed., *London in Flames, London in Glory: Poems on the Fire and Rebuilding of London 1666–1709* (New Brunswick, NJ: Rutgers University Press, 1943), 87–8.

66 Evelyn, *Diary*, iii, 457–8.

67 Vincent, *God's Terrible Voice*, 56.

68 LMA, COL/SJ/03/014, fol. 2.

69 *CSPD, 1666–1667*, 99–100.

70 Evelyn, *Diary*, iii, 460.

71 Bell, *Great Fire*, 338.

72 T.F. Reddaway, *The Rebuilding of London after the Great Fire* (London: Jonathan Cape, 1940), 26.

73 Rege Sincera, *Observations*, 4.

74 Pepys, *Diary*, ix, 23; Taswell, *Autobiography*, 13.

75 A. Wood, *The Life and Times of Anthony Wood, Antiquary, of Oxford, 1632–1695, Described by Himself*, ed. A. Clark, 2 vols. (Oxford: Clarendon Press for the Oxford Historical Society, 1891), ii, 262.

76 BL, Additional MS 10117, fol. 176v.

77 Baxter, *Reliquiae Baxterianae*, 16.

78 Rapicani, 'Foreign Visitor's Account', 85.

79 Wood, *Life and Times*, ii, 85.

80 *CSPD, 1666–1667*, 100–16.
81 Griffiths, *Lost Londons*, 33.
82 Pepys, *Diary*, vii, 277.
83 Evelyn, *Diary*, iii, 461–2.
84 Bell, *Great Fire*, 191–5.
85 *CSPD, 1666–1667*, 99–100, 103–4.
86 TNA, Letter from James Hickes to Williamson, 12 December 1666, SP 29/181, 76; Petition of Gilbert Thomas to the King, February 1667, SP 29/192, 70.
87 *CSPD, 1666–1667*, 114–15.
88 Bell, *Great Fire*, 318.
89 LMA, Rep. 71, fol. 168r.
90 C. Wall, *The Literary and Cultural Spaces of Restoration London* (Cambridge: Cambridge University Press, 1998), 7–8, 13.
91 LMA, Rep. 71, fol. 169v.
92 LMA, Rep. 71, fol. 168r.
93 *CSPD, 1666–1667*, 107.
94 LMA, Rep. 71, fols. 168r -169r.
95 LMA, Jour. 46, 1664–9, fol. 130v.
96 *CSPD, 1666–1667*, 115–16.
97 LMA, Rep. 72, fols. 2v-3v.
98 J. Milward, *The Diary of John Milward, Esq. Member of Parliament for Derbyshire, September, 1666 to May, 1668*, ed. C. Robbins (Cambridge: Cambridge University Press, 1938), 55.
99 Griffiths, *Lost Londons*, 147–8.
100 Waterhouse, *Short Narrative*, 26–7.
101 *CSPD, 1666–1667*, 140.
102 LMA, Jour. 46, fol. 121r.
103 BL, Additional MS 10117, fol. 179r.
104 LMA, Jour. 46, fol. 124v.
105 Waterhouse, *Short Narrative*, 26–7, 105.
106 *CSPD, 1666–1667*, 104.
107 Rege Sincera, *Observations*, 6–7.

Reference list

Primary sources

Manuscript
BL, Rugge, T. *Mercurius Politicus Redivius; or, a Collection of the Most Materiall Occurrences and Transactions in Publick Affaires, Since Anno Domini 1659, Volume II*. Additional MS 10117, 1659–72.
LMA, *Day Book of the Receipts and Payments of ye Charitable Contributions towards ye repairing of ye decays and ruins of ye Cathedral Church of St Paul London*, CLA/079/04/016.
LMA, Journal of Common Council, Jour. 46, 1664–9.
LMA, Letter of John Tremayne, COL/SJ/03/014, 1666.
LMA, Repertory of the Court of Aldermen, Rep. 71–2, 1665–7.
TNA, Hearth Tax Assessment Listing, City of London and parts of Middlesex, E179/252/32, 1666.
TNA, Letter from James Hickes to Williamson, 12 December 1666, SP 29/181, 76.
TNA, Petition of Gilbert Thomas to the King, February 1667, SP 29/192, 70.
TNA, Petition of Teunis Willemsen to the King, 24 September 1666, SP 29/172, 153.

Printed

Ashmole, E. *The Diary and Will of Elias Ashmole*, edited by R.T. Gunther. Oxford: Old Ashmolean Reprints, 1927.

Aubin, R.A., ed. *London in Flames, London in Glory: Poems on the Fire and Rebuilding of London 1666–1709*. New Brunswick, NJ: Rutgers University Press, 1943.

Baxter, R. *Reliquiae Baxterianae: Or, Mr. Richard Baxter's Narrative of the Most Memorable Passages of His Life and Times, Part 3*, edited by M. Sylvester. London: T. Parkhurst, J. Robinson, J. Lawrence and J. Dunton, 1696.

Evelyn, J. *The Diary of John Evelyn*, edited by E.S. De Beer, 6 vols. Oxford: Clarendon Press, 1955.

Green, M.A.E., ed. *Calendar of State Papers, Domestic Series, of the Reign of Charles II, 1666–1667*. London: Longman, Green, Longman, Roberts and Green, 1864.

Henry, P. *Diaries and Letters of Philip Henry, M.A.*, edited by M.H. Lee. London: Kegan Paul, Trench and Co, 1882.

Milward, J. *The Diary of John Milward, Esq. Member of Parliament for Derbyshire, September, 1666 to May, 1668*, edited by C. Robbins. Cambridge: Cambridge University Press, 1938.

Newton, S. *The Diary of Samuel Newton, Alderman of Cambridge (1662–1717)*, edited by J.E. Foster. Cambridge: Cambridge Antiquarian Society, 1890.

Pepys, S. *The Diary of Samuel Pepys*, edited by R. Latham and W. Matthews, 11 vols. 1st ed. London: G. Bell and Sons, 1970–83.

Rapicani, F. de. 'A Foreign Visitor's Account of the Great Fire, 1666', *Transactions of the London and Middlesex Archaeological Society*, 20 (1960), 76–87.

Rege Sincera. *Observations both Historical and Moral upon the Burning of London, September 1666*. London: Thomas Ratcliffe, 1667.

Taswell, W. *Autobiography and Anecdotes by William Taswell, D.D*, edited by G.P. Elliott. London: Camden Society, 1853.

Verney, M.M., ed. *Memoirs of the Verney Family from the Restoration to the Revolution 1660 to 1696*. London: Longmans, Green, and Co, 1899.

Vincent, T. *God's Terrible Voice in the City*. London: G. Calvert, 1667.

Waterhouse, E. *A Short Narrative of the Late Dreadful Fire in London*. London: W.G. for Richard Thrale and James Thrale, 1667.

Wood, A. *The Life and Times of Anthony Wood, Antiquary, of Oxford, 1632–1695, Described by Himself*, edited by A. Clark, 2 vols. Oxford: Clarendon Press for the Oxford Historical Society, 1891.

Secondary sources

Baer, W.C. 'The House-Building Sector of London's Economy, 1550–1650', *Urban History*, 39 (2012), 409–30.

Bell, W.G. *The Great Fire of London*. 1st ed. London: John Lane, 1920.

Bell, W.G. *The Great Plague in London in 1665*. 1st ed. London: The Bodley Head, 1924.

Bucholz, R.O. and Ward, J.P. *London: A Social and Cultural History, 1550–1750*. Cambridge: Cambridge University Press, 2012.

Burrows, E.G. and Wallace, M. *Gotham: A History of New York City to 1898*. Oxford: Oxford University Press, 1999.

Carr, G. *Residence and Social Status: The Development of Seventeenth-Century London*. New York and London: Garland, 1990.

Finlay, R.A.P. *Population and Metropolis: The Demography of London 1580–1650*. Cambridge: Cambridge University Press, 1981.

Finlay, R.A.P. and Shearer, B. 'Population Growth and Suburban Expansion'. In *London 1500–1700: The Making of the Metropolis*, edited by A.L. Beier and R.A.P. Finlay, 37–57. London and New York: Longman, 1986.

Griffiths, P. *Lost Londons: Change, Crime, and Control in the Capital City, 1550–1660*. Cambridge: Cambridge University Press, 2008.

Guillery, P. 'Houses in London's Suburbs'. In *London and Middlesex 1666 Hearth Tax*, edited by M. Davies, C. Ferguson, V. Harding, E. Parkinson and A. Wareham, 140–53. London: British Record Society, 2014.

Hainsworth, R. and Churches, C. *The Anglo-Dutch Naval Wars 1652–1674*. Stroud: Sutton, 1998.

Harding, V. 'London and Middlesex in the 1660s'. In *London and Middlesex 1666 Hearth Tax*, edited by M. Davies, C. Ferguson, V. Harding, E. Parkinson and A. Wareham, 25–57. London: British Record Society, 2014.

Harris, T. *London Crowds in the Reign of Charles II: Propaganda and Politics from the Restoration until the Exclusion Crisis*. Cambridge: Cambridge University Press, 1987.

Harris, T. *Restoration: Charles II and His Kingdoms 1660–1685*. London: Allen Lane, 2005.

Mandelbrote, G. 'Workplaces and Living Spaces: London Book Trade Inventories of the Late Seventeenth Century'. In *The London Book Trade: Topographies of Print in the Metropolis from the Sixteenth Century*, edited by R. Myers, M. Harris and G. Mandelbrote, 21–43. London and New Castle, DE: The British Library and Oak Knoll Press, 2003.

McKeon, M. *Politics and Poetry in Restoration England: The Case of Dryden's Annus Mirabilis*. Cambridge, MA: Harvard University Press, 1975.

Merritt, J.F. *The Social World of Early Modern Westminster: Abbey, Court and Community 1525–1640*. Manchester: Manchester University Press, 2005.

Porter, S. *The Great Plague of London*. 3rd ed. Stroud: Amberley, 2012.

Power, M.J. 'The Social Topography of Restoration London'. In *London 1500–1700: The Making of the Metropolis*, edited by A.L. Beier and R.A.P. Finlay, 199–223. London and New York: Longman, 1986.

Raven, J. 'St Paul's Precinct and the Book Trade to 1800'. In *St Paul's: The Cathedral Church of London 604–2004*, edited by D. Keene, A. Burns and A. Saint, 430–8. New Haven and London: Yale University Press, 2004.

Reddaway, T.F. *The Rebuilding of London after the Great Fire*. London: Jonathan Cape, 1940.

Rideal, R. *1666: Plague, War and Hellfire*. London: John Murray, 2016.

Rommelse, G. *The Second Anglo-Dutch War (1665–1667): Raison d'état, Mercantilism and Maritime Strife*. Hilversum: Verloren, 2006.

Sakata, T. 'The Growth of London and Its Regional Structure in the Early Modern Period', *Keio Economic Studies*, 38 (2001), 1–16.

Spence, C. *London in the 1690s: A Social Atlas*. London: Centre for Metropolitan History, 2000.

Wall, C. *The Literary and Cultural Spaces of Restoration London*. Cambridge: Cambridge University Press, 1998.

Ward, J.P. *Metropolitan Communities: Trade Guilds, Identity, and Change in Early Modern London*. Stanford, CA: Stanford University Press, 1997.

Ward, J.P. 'Imagining the Metropolis in Elizabethan and Stuart London'. In *The Country and the City Revisited: England and the Politics of Culture, 1550–1850*, edited by G. MacLean, D. Landry and J.P. Ward, 24–40. Cambridge: Cambridge University Press, 1999.

Woodhead, J.R. *The Rulers of London 1660–1689: A Biographical Record of the Aldermen and Common Councilmen of the City of London*. London: London and Middlesex Archaeological Society, 1965.

2   Rebuilding London

The Great Fire was a disaster not just for London, but for the whole nation. As the ejected minister Samuel Rolls stated, 'a great part of the strength and defence of all *England*, yea, of all the three Kingdomes, is lost and taken away, in and by the destruction of *London*'.[1] Yet there was hope. Not all of London had been burned. The Fire had only eliminated 13 to 15 per cent of London's total housing stock.[2] Thomas Vincent argued that the Fire could have been made more severe by the burning of the suburbs. As he put it: 'This Judgement of the Fire might have been more dreadful than it was: Persons are escaped; Goods and Wealth much saved; Houses standing to receive them; Trade going on'.[3]

Given the scale of the Fire, Parliament had to enact new legislation to guide the rebuilding. Parliament, which had been prorogued since 31 October 1665, re-assembled on 18 September 1666. Three days later Charles II addressed the body in the State Opening. His speech began: 'I Am very glad to meet so many of you together again . . . little time hath pass'd since we were almost in despair of having this place left to meet in'.[4] A committee in Commons met to discuss the rebuilding but after a few days of debate they were unable to determine a course of action. Charles II also set up a rebuilding committee in his Privy Council.[5] Even though the reconstruction was vital, Parliament and the king had other priorities. England was still at war and it was not going well. By the end of 1666 three-quarters of sailors were unpaid and the Crown's credit had all but dwindled away.[6] Charles II had asked Parliament for another £1.6 million. However, the conflict was becoming increasingly unpopular. Many in Parliament believed the war had been mismanaged. The mercantilists in the City who had originally supported the war now opposed it, as it had led to a rise in prices and interrupted shipping. They also believed that the nation should concentrate on helping London to recover. By early 1667 peace had become a necessity, and the war was damaging Charles II's popularity and reputation.[7] Peace negotiations with the Dutch began in the spring. With much of the English fleet laid up due to lack of funds, the Dutch launched a raid on the Medway that June. It was a humiliation for England: thirteen ships were burned and two were towed away. The event caused uproar in London. John Evelyn recorded 'the alarme was so great, as put both County and Citty in to a pan[i]que feare & consternation'.[8] The Raid showed how futile it was continuing the war. The Treaty of Breda was signed in July 1667. England and London, now at peace, could recover.

Planning and building a new City

The first building work began at Blackfriars on Thursday, 13 September 1666.[9] Although everyone desired the rebuilding to be as swift as possible, the authorities realised that it must be regulated. To that end Charles II made a declaration to London that day. At this time Parliament had not yet assembled, but it was imperative that some framework for the rebuilding be put into place as soon as possible. In the proclamation Charles II stated that those who wanted to rebuild would receive speedy direction from the Court of Aldermen. A survey would be made of the ruins and each person would have their land secured by act of Parliament. Those who built on someone else's land without permission would be punished. Measures were taken to decrease the risk of fire. New houses were to be of brick or stone, with strongly arched cellars. The streets would be wide enough to ensure easy passage, and there would be no alleys unless absolutely necessary. The quayside was to be kept clear from the rest of the City. The rebuilding of churches was to be left to the charity of 'well-disposed' persons. Charles II promised that he would part with any rights belonging to him to advance of the rebuilding.[10]

In these early weeks after the Fire there were several ambitious plans for the rebuilt capital. At this stage both Charles II and City officials were open to wholesale changes. The first concept (pictured in Figure 2.1, top) was presented on 10 September by Christopher Wren, who was the Deputy Surveyor of His Majesty's Works (he became the Surveyor of His Majesty's Works after the death of his predecessor, the Royalist poet Sir John Denham in 1669). His plan would have created an entirely new City with wide principal streets and spacious plazas. He had ambitious plans to clear the riverside from Temple to Tower, and widen the clogged and narrow Fleet into a canal. Evelyn presented his plan (Figure 2.1, bottom) to the king on 13 September, claiming this new City would be 'fitter for commerce, apter for government, sweeter for wealth, more glorious for beauty'.[11] It was similar to Wren's, although it had more open areas. Robert Hooke was the Royal Society's 'Curator of Experiments' as well as the Professor of Geometry at Gresham College. His plan, displayed to the Common Council on 21 September, imposed a strict grid system. The map-maker Richard Newcourt proposed another grid layout, although based around a series of rectangular plots, each of which enclosed a church. The soldier Captain Valentine Knight made the most daring proposal. His plan included a canal through the City to carry goods, which he claimed would have given the Crown a perpetual annual income of £223,517 10s.[12] Charles II's reaction to the plan was dramatic. Thomas Rugge recorded that 'Valentine Knight was committed prisoner by his majestys order for publishing in print certain propostions for the rebuilding london againe as if his majesty would accrue a benefit to himself'.[13]

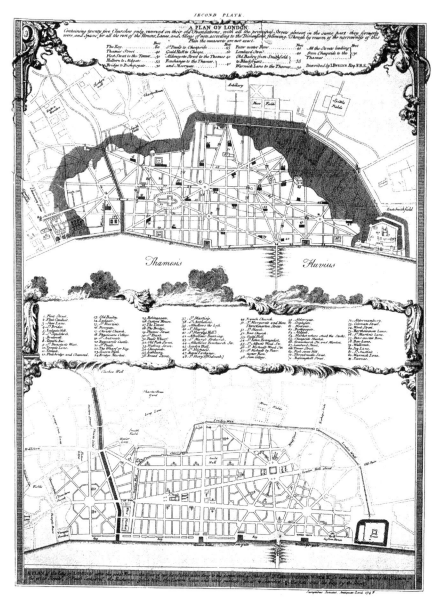

Figure 2.1 Designs for rebuilding London after the Fire by Christopher Wren and John Evelyn (1748)

(Reproduced with the kind permission of the Museum of London)

These radical plans were soon abandoned as it became clear that they were unworkable in practice. Building an entirely new street layout and determining who and how much would be compensated for any losses would have caused chaos. It would also have been too expensive for either the City or Crown to afford. Even if the plans had been imposed, Cynthia Wall argues that it was unlikely that Londoners would have been accepting of them as their cultural stubbornness made them resistant to wholesale change.[14] In terms of the structure of public space and the street layout, there was a high degree of continuity before and after the Fire. For the most part, the pre-Fire topography was retained. This meant that most of the rebuilding was left to private bodies. Abandoning an entirely new plan for London also minimised disruption to patterns of land and property holding. There would only be some minor improvements to the street layout. The rebuilding effort was pragmatic and suited London's desire to return to 'business as usual' as soon as possible – and minimise public spending.[15] Even though there was continuity in topographical structure, London would be transformed in other ways after the Fire.

City authorities, still meeting in Gresham College, began to make practical steps to prepare London for the rebuilding. On 10 September the Court of Common Council ordered the people to clear the space in front of their property. No rebuilding was to be done until this was completed. Booths were set up in every ward where occupiers of houses were required to give information about their sites and registers to be kept of people wishing to buy and sell land. A special rebuilding committee made up of aldermen and common councilmen was set up to oversee the process. Charles II appointed three 'Commissioners for Rebuilding the City of London': Wren and two prominent architects – Hugh May and Roger Pratt. On 9 October the City appointed their surveyors. The first was Hooke. The other two were Peter Mills, the City Surveyor, and his associate Edward Jerman, who provided valuable local knowledge and experience of building in London. These six men were to oversee the surveying and rebuilding of London. On 10 October the Common Council again proclaimed that the foundations of places destroyed in the Fire should be cleared, and reminded people to give their details to local officials so the survey could be completed. Clearing the streets was held up because many landlords and tenants argued over whose responsibility it was. Eventually Charles II donated £100 to pay for labourers to clear the streets. This task was accomplished by the end of the year. The planned full survey of the fired area by their occupiers or owners was never completed.[16]

The Fire of London Disputes Act received the royal assent on 8 February 1667. This established the Fire Court to mediate in disputes arising from the rebuilding. This body was necessary because property ownership in London was extremely complex. Three-quarters of London households were occupied by tenants. As many leaseholders sublet, many properties had multiple layers of rights and rents.[17] These complicated networks made the Fire Court vital, as it could cut through the various levels of ownership. The Fire Court, sitting in Clifford's Inn near Fleet Street, began hearing cases on 27 February 1667. Its first phase ended on 31 December 1668. It had been so successful that it was revived in 1670 as part of the Second Rebuilding Act, and continued to sit until 25 February 1676. On average the twenty-two judges (who did not receive a salary) heard four petitions each day. Such a pace was possible because the Fire Court operated in a streamlined fashion, with most cases being heard in just one day, and appeals rarely being granted. The Fire Court heard cases for about 20 per cent of the c. 13,200 houses destroyed in the Fire. The petitions presented to them generally related to more complex cases, where there was a dispute over who should bear the costs of rebuilding – the landlord, tenant or sub-tenant.[18] The Fire Court was a central part of the rebuilding. Had it not existed, legal wrangling could have held up the rebuilding for decades.

The Rebuilding of London Act received the Royal Assent on 8 February 1667. It aimed to achieve the 'better Regulation Uniformity and Gracefulnes of such new Buildings as shall be erected' as well as to prevent 'great and outragious Fires'. To achieve uniformity only four standardised designs of houses were allowed, depending on if they were built on by-lanes or streets, streets or lanes 'of note' or high and principal streets. New houses were to be made of brick or stone. Wood was banned from their exterior. The City was authorised to appoint surveyors to monitor the rebuilding and stake out the areas to be rebuilt. Anyone who moved their markers would be fined £10, imprisoned for three months or even 'whipped neere unto the place where the Offence shall be committed till his body be bloudy'. The City could demolish any buildings that did not meet the Act's conditions. People were given three years to rebuild. Once this term expired, the City could give a nine-month extension; after this point a jury could be appointed to value the property and the land could be sold to someone who would rebuild. The Act controlled the cost of rebuilding by appointing two judges to set the price of materials like bricks, tiles and lime, as well as the wages of workmen and labourers for hire. To further encourage the rebuilding, artificers in the building trade who came to London to work on the rebuilding within the next seven years were to be given the Freedom of the City, with the same rights and responsibilities as existing citizens. There were to be some changes to the City's street layout. No building was allowed within forty feet of the Thames (or the Fleet). Some important streets would be widened or enlarged as they 'were narrow and incommodious for Carriages and Passengers and prejudiciall to the Trade and Health of the Inhabitants'. For example Fleet Street and Cheapside were widened in places. Damages were to be paid to people who lost ground as a result. Nearly 150 streets, lanes and alleys were enlarged. Although private bodies would pay for much of the new construction, £100,000 was needed to pay for civic and ecclesiastical rebuilding. The City was around £300,000 in debt, and simply could not afford this.[19] Additional money was raised by a duty on coal, of one shilling per cauldron, brought into London, which would run until 1677.[20] The Second Rebuilding Act followed in 1670. It mainly dealt with the rebuilding of St Paul's Cathedral and parish churches and also extended the coal duty to 1687. The duty was raised to two shillings per cauldron, and would be increased to three shillings in 1677. The coal dues raised £736,804 9s 2d and provided a steady stream of income.[21] The additional legislation provided for the enlargement of streets not mentioned in the First Rebuilding Act and for more ground around public buildings like the Royal Exchange and Guildhall. To make sure that building materials and other goods could be transported to London, it fixed the rates of wharfage and cranage.[22] These pieces of legislation were wide-ranging, particularly if placed in comparison to recovery from another major urban fire. The Great Fire of Chicago (1871) destroyed four square miles of the city, spreading quickly due to dry wooden buildings and sidewalks. It caused an average of $125,000 of damage per minute it lasted and made 100,000 people homeless. As with London, plans to completely remodel the urban landscape were not realised. Unlike London, local and national governments were unable to ensure the rebuilt areas were fire-safe. Most of the new buildings in Chicago were the same densely packed wooden constructions that had caused the blaze in the first place. As a result there was a second Chicago fire in 1874 that destroyed sixty acres of the city.[23]

In early 1667 there were still 20,000 families that had not found homes.[24] It was vital that rebuilding work begin as soon as possible. Under the terms of the Rebuilding Act the City had to select surveyors to stake out the streets so construction could begin. On 13 March Mills, Hooke and Jerman were offered the job, along with another prominent City builder, John Oliver. Only Mills and Hooke accepted. Oliver offered to assist for free and was later officially sworn in as a surveyor. Mills and Hooke began staking out the streets on 27 March and completed the majority of the work in about nine weeks.[25] The rebuilding effort could finally begin in earnest. The surveyors played a valuable role in regulating construction and ensuring it was up to standard. Every prospective builder had to enter their proposed site in the Chamber of London, along with a fee of six shillings and eight pence. A surveyor viewed their foundations, and then issued the builder with a certificate detailing the plans. The first certificate was issued by Mills on 4 April, and the last by Hooke in March 1687. During their most active period, from 1667 to 1671, the City Surveyors worked at an average rate of about 2,000 surveys per year.[26]

Once the legislative and administrative framework of the rebuilding was in place, new houses sprang up. Ralph Josselin, the minister of Earls Colne in Essex, visited on 12 May 1667 and recorded that rebuilding had begun.[27] It was only in 1668 that the activity of rebuilding could be deemed to be 'general'. By spring 1668 Rolls reported that 800 houses had been rebuilt.[28] On 2 September 1671 the ejected minister Philip Henry wrote of his amazement at 'ye Strange & wonderful rebuilding of it in so short a time, which but that my eyes saw, I could hardly have believ'd'.[29] The bulk of private rebuilding was probably finished by 1671, and the majority of the rest completed by 1674.[30] The Fire gave impetus to the increasing shift away from timber toward brick.[31] This, combined with the uniform design of housing, gave the City a more continental look. Even landlords whose houses were not destroyed demolished old buildings and rebuilt new houses.[32] The Fire created a more open and clear City, but the expense of rebuilding also forced more people into overcrowded suburbs.[33] The distinction between centre and periphery was made more visible by the greater variation of building practices in the suburbs.[34]

City authorities were assiduous in enforcing the Rebuilding Act. In July 1671, the Court of Aldermen ordered that any irregular new buildings be reported.[35] In 1675 Richard Freeman of St Mary Ax was brought before the Court of Aldermen because his windows were not made of oak, he had no party walls and his house was of irregular height.[36] In May 1676 the Court of Aldermen ordered a survey of all irregular buildings. Two weeks later George Pawling, a joiner, was called before the Court. He was erecting a building on the north side of London Wall near Basinghall Street. It was found to be irregular and dangerous for fire. He was ordered to stop any building work until he met the Rebuilding Act.[37] On 21 November 1676 the Court of Aldermen declared that anyone who did not meet the conditions of the Act would face prosecution.[38] The City sought to make sure that houses were not subdivided into tenements, which were dangerous for Fire. It was especially anxious to prevent the subdividing of Essex House in the Strand, which the property developer and pioneer of fire insurance Nicholas Barbon was planning to redevelop. In spite of this opposition Barbon converted the site into various houses, tenements and shops.[39] The City was eager to prevent the construction of 'sheds' – cheap temporary housing that was highly prone to fire. In 1674 John Tombs was ordered to report to the Court of Aldermen for erecting sheds in Castle Yard, Holborn.[40]

Thomas Doolittle recorded that in 1667 there had been many small fires in the City and Southwark since the 'late dismal fire'.[41] In response to this continuing threat of fire a civic order was made on 5 November 1667. It divided the City and its liberties into four quarters. Each was to have 800 buckets and fifty ladders, whilst each parish was to have two brass squirts, twenty-four pickaxes and forty shovels. Annual reports would be made on the condition of fire-fighting equipment to the Lord Mayor. In addition the twelve largest livery companies were to each keep thirty buckets, one fire engine, six pickaxes, three ladders and two squirts whilst all others were to keep buckets and engines 'proportionable to their Abilities'. Every Alderman who had passed the office of shrievalty was to provide twenty-four buckets and one squirt; those who had not been sheriff were to provide twelve buckets and one squirt. They would be kept in their dwellings. All other principal citizens of the City were to provide buckets. Every householder on cry of fire was to place a vessel of water and a man at his door and put on a light if it was dark, at pain of a fine of twenty shillings. Every inhabitant was to have a secure place to keep ashes and embers, which would be quenched with water every night, and no gunpowder was to be kept in the City without royal permission. Constables were to look into security of hearths, stoves and ovens twice every year. If there was a fire the Lord Mayor and sheriffs were to be speedily notified by messenger and then attended by their officers. All persons would stay in their own dwelling unless ordered to, to prevent disorder. There were fines for people who did not obey the Act. Half the proceeds went to Christ's Hospital to maintain the poor children who were schooled there and half to the individual who had sued the offender.[42] Later in 1667 other steps were taken. All wooden chimneys were ordered to be pulled down and replaced with brick ones. Fire-watching was also stepped up, with people to be stationed in any steeples that still stood and 'Looking about him on all side to see if he can Espy fire, then to give the alarum by blowing the Horne, or striking the alarum Bell, be it night or day'.[43] Parishes seem to have acted on these recommendations. In 1667 St Katherine Coleman ordered 'two douzen of Buckets, wth foure Picke-Axes, & foure Shovels for publicke use & service . . . And that the old parish Hooke wth its chaine & Iron worke be repaired & amended'.[44] That year St Sepulchre Holborn paid £30 for a fire engine.[45] Care was also taken to stop the storm of paranoia that occurred after the Fire from breaking out again. Two years after the Fire, the Court of Aldermen stated that 'Care be taken for prevencon of such a Mischiefe . . . [and] punishment inflicted upon the Reporters and Dispersers of such Rumours to the Disturbance of the Quiet of the Citty'.[46] These regulations, combined with the new brick buildings, appear to have been mostly effective. There were no major conflagrations in the City after the Great Fire. The rest of London was not so fortunate. There were serious blazes outside of the City from 1666 until the end of the century, particularly in Southwark, which suffered five major fires, and Wapping, which was struck twice.[47]

Charity and the rebuilding

Charity was a major part of the recovery effort, and it was expected that worthy people who suffered as a result of the Fire should receive some kind of assistance. Evelyn noted with surprise on 7 September 1666 that when he came to the temporary camps north of the City, no one asked 'for one penny for reliefe, which to me appeard a stranger sight, than any I had yet beheld'.[48] Doolittle urged people not to think of Londoners as greater sinners, but to help them, materially and through prayer. He also reminded his readers to help the relatives that they had in London.[49] Rolls called on the nation to contribute to the recovery, as most families in England had some relative in London, either by descent or alliance.[50] On 10 October 1666 Charles II made a proclamation declaring a national charitable collection to relieve Londoners distressed by the Fire. There had already been donations made to help the post-Fire recovery. Marlborough in Wiltshire, which had suffered a serious fire in 1653, had given £50 on 27 September.[51] This collection ran until 1676, and gathered £16,487, with donations coming from parishes across England and Wales.[52]

One of the great scandals associated with the Fire concerned this brief, and the new Lord Mayor of London, Sir William Bolton, who was sworn in on 29 October 1666. At the beginning of his term he had attracted controversy by refusing to waive his right to the traditional 100 marks (£66 13s 4d) customarily presented paid to the new Lord Mayor from their company for the beautifying of his house. Bolton's company, the Merchant Taylors, wanted to excuse the gift because of the financial pressures following the Fire.[53] Bolton was accused of embezzling £1,800 later in his term. On 3 December 1667 Samuel Pepys wrote of 'the basenesse of the Late Lord Mayor, Sir W Bolton, in cheating the poor of the City (out of the collections made for the people that were burned) . . . which is the greatest piece of roguery that they say was ever found in a Lord Mayor'.[54] Bolton never admitted fault, claiming that the charge stemmed from jealousy within the City government at a royal petition to make him Surveyor General of London. On 31 May and 5 June 1667 Charles II wrote to the Court of Common Council and then the Court of Aldermen recommending Bolton for the office,[55] which he was never given. The rumours ruined Bolton. He was forced to stand down as alderman of Castle Baynard in May 1668. In response Bolton petitioned Charles II to call to account the City government for their actions. Bolton claimed that the royal petition had created 'animosity' against him and led to his being deposed 'arbitrarily & unjustly'. He added, 'ye present malice of a few [of the Court of Aldermen] . . . prodigiously shown against your Petitioner in publique reproaches, wounds ye honor of that famous Citty'.[56] Such efforts were to no avail – Bolton never again held civic office.[57] The affair still rankled. On 13 April 1673, Bolton complained of 'hard and unkind usage' from the Court of Aldermen. In response, the Court set up a committee to make Bolton 'sensible of and to acknowledge his error and impudence in charging and reflecting upon this Court'. In February 1676 Bolton again complained of legal proceedings against him in the Court of Chancery, but was advised by the Court of Aldermen to have 'a more due and becoming deportment'.[58] This was his last official attempt to protest his innocence. On 19 March 1677, Bolton petitioned the Court of Common Council for a pension, as he was 'reduced to a low Condicon and utterly unable to support himself'. He was granted three pounds per week for life.[59] The Bolton affair shows how zealously the City government sought to protect the charitable money for the sufferers of the Fire, as well as their reputation. It transcended political factions. Figures as diverse as the Tory Sir George Waterman, Lord Mayor from 1671 to 1672, and the Whig Sir Patience Ward, Lord Mayor from 1680 to 1681 (as well as being Bolton's own brother-in-law), were involved in the attempts to make Bolton admit his guilt and culpability.

Once the money collected was brought into the Chamber of London, the task of doling it out fell mostly to its chamberlain, Sir Thomas Player, who acted on the advice and orders of several bodies and individuals, especially the Court of Aldermen, various Lord Mayors and the Bishop of London.

Making sure that charity went to 'worthy' recipients was a difficult task. Richard Baxter noted that many 'lying beggars' posed as Londoners after the Fire to gain charitable help.[60] Most of the distribution of money was left to the local authorities in the City, with 58 per cent of the amount collected given to wards to disburse and 21 per cent to parishes. Larger, more populous wards and parishes received the highest sums. Areas to the west of the City received most, suggesting that many distressed Londoners fled there in the aftermath of the Fire.[61] Burned-out Londoners moved as far as St Martin-in-the-Fields. A 1666 petition to Charles II from the churchwardens there asked for £11 1s 6d for pickaxes and 'other necessities' provided (and presumably lost) during the Fire, requesting the money as it was 'parte of the poores stock who are soe numerous that [we] are not able to provide for them'. Two years later the vicar of the parish, Dr Nicholas Hardy, petitioned Charles II for a piece of royal ground to increase the size of the parish's burial ground, 'by reason not only of ye late sickening . . . but alsoe by reason of ye late sadd fyre which hath fild ye parish with Inhabitants'.[62]

The City made payments to individuals who had petitioned them, averaging £4.48, up to thirteen years after the event. The largest was £40 to widow Clara Bolton on 15 January 1668 as 'the whole remainder of her estate consisting in houses holden by Lease from the City was destroyed'.[63] Bolton's problems after the Fire were more serious. She had been granted an annual royal pension of £200 for the loyalty of her late husband and for sheltering Royalist soldiers during the Civil Wars. It had been stopped when her nephew, a Major Wood, complained that the pension had been partly for his maintenance and that Bolton had turned him and his family out of her home and wished to remarry. In 1667 Bolton claimed arrears of £500 in a petition to Charles II. Although she paid to have foundations staked out for a new house in Gracechurch Street on 9 July 1668, her financial problems continued. In 1669, she petitioned Arlington for £500 as she had mortgaged her City lands for £700 and needed to rebuild on them before the ground was seized.[64] Her case illustrates that petitioners of high social esteem who had experienced significant loss of revenue in the Fire tended to be paid higher amounts. This was a long-standing feature of early modern charity – 'respectable' people fallen on hard times were traditionally key recipients of parish pensions and payments.[65] These people had more resources to lose, and so reasoned that they would need more money to help in reconstructing their lives. Even so, the amounts they were given were dwarfed by their stated losses. Widow Elizabeth Kendall received £20 on 17 October 1667 as 'the whole estate left by her said husband consisting of goods & Merchandizes to the value of five thousand pounds was destroyed'.[66]

Widows were traditionally a major component of the 'deserving poor' and usually were a significant proportion of those given payments from the poor rates.[67] Widows were vulnerable and sometimes isolated members of the metropolitan community. Widowhood left many women in a precarious position with reduced status and resources, and more likely to become dependent on the goodwill of neighbours and the parish.[68] This is reflected in the distribution of donations from the brief. At least half of the individuals who were given money were widows. A particularly full example of the 'desolate' widow was Elizabeth Peacock, who received £10 on 5 March 1667. Peacock's

> husband & eldest sonne (in whome were her greatest hopes) being both lately dead' and 'her dwelling house . . . on Snow Hill (a faire and hardye Inne wherein she had a Terme of 4 yeares left past) had layd out and expended 800 *s* in building . . . was utterly consumed by the late dreadful fire together with her whole stocke of hay coales & beere layd in for her winter provision & alsoe all the furniture of her said home to a greate value'.

She was left with only thirty-nine shillings, five small children and 'not soe much as A stoole to sitt uppon'.[69]

Elderly unmarried women were just as vulnerable. A case in point was Frances Aske, a spinster who received £2 from the 1666 brief on 14 December 1667. Before the Fire she lived in St Dunstan in the West but 'her whole substance and maintenance . . . was utterly consumed', and she was 'now friendless & helpless aged threescore and nine years also blind (as she hath been for many years past) & under other distempers & great weakness of Body which doe not only disable her to doe anything towards her Maintenance'. The Court of Aldermen requested that in addition to this initial payment 'Aske be recommended to ye Ward of Farringdon without for a further epporcon of the money that shall bee distributed in the sd Ward for reliefe of those poore that suffered by the sd fire'.[70]

There were other avenues of charity for widows. Ann Lloyd, the widow of a groom of the royal stable, who had lost her house and all of her possessions during the Fire successfully petitioned Catherine of Braganza for a place in the alms house in Clerk's Alley, Bishopsgate Street, after the death of one of its inmates.[71] The case of another widow, Sarah Crafts, also shows how Londoners who suffered as a result of the Fire could pursue a number of charitable avenues. In 1666 she petitioned Charles II for money towards rebuilding her estate of 'houses and buildings', which had been worth around £5,000. She claimed that her family had been 'reduced to great Extremity' and was 'inforced to turne Servants and to worke hard for a poore Livelyhood'. She received £15 from the 1666 brief, as well as £10 for the relief of her father Samuel Mann, a stationer. When Crafts appeared before the Fire Court in November 1668 to petition her tenant, Thomas Fincham, a mercer, to rebuild her property in Cannon Street that she held on a long lease from the City, her circumstances had changed. She now claimed the house in Cannon Street was the 'sole livelihood' of her family. Either Crafts had lost the rest of her estate between 1666 and 1668, or she had adjusted her background for her audience. In petitions for charitable money, the greater the pre-Fire circumstances had been, the higher the payment tended to be. In the Fire Court, it appeared that judges were more likely to favour the landlord if they were of more limited circumstances. The Court eventually ordered Fincham to rebuild the house but reduced his annual rent from £35 to £15, and ordered his lease be increased by forty years.[72]

There was one payment made to a charitable foundation from the 1666 brief. On 19 June 1668, £500 was paid to Christ's Hospital because of its 'great losses' of 'bedding Apparrell furniture & household utensills . . . burnt & destroyed in the late dismall fire . . . besides a great decay of their revenue by many houses consumed & other losses'. The total value of damage done to Christ's Hospital in the Fire was over £8,000, and they lost over 100 of their rental properties.[73] The foundation also received charitable donations from individual benefactors to pay for its repair, which was completed by 1674. The other major foundation damaged during the Fire was Bridewell, which was rebuilt using money from the coal dues and charitable donations.[74]

Foundations undamaged by the Fire also suffered because they relied on rental income from properties that had been destroyed. Christ's lost half of its yearly revenue, St Bartholomew's the 'greatest part', St Thomas' a 'considerable' part and Bridewell two-thirds. Bethlehem preserved its small rental revenues, 'yet by reason of the late . . . Fire the *Hospital* is very much prejudiced in other Incomes'. The report recommended London's hospitals as 'good objects' of charity, so it is possible that charitable giving in the years after the Fire may have made up for the losses suffered to rental revenues. The smaller foundation of King Charles' Hospital, founded by Charles I for the care of fatherless children, lost half of its annual revenue of £100 because of the Fire. To make up for this, it received a royal grant of £50 in July 1669.[75] Even if London's hospitals received donations after the Fire, they still would have experienced major shortfalls in revenue, as they had lost a reliable source of income that could not be recouped until the properties were rebuilt. The Fire Court was fairly assiduous in ensuring tenants of charitable foundations rebuilt. A tavern owned by St Bartholomew's Hospital in St Nicholas' Shambles in Christchurch Greyfriars, which they had leased to Theophilus Clever for twenty-nine years and six months at £10 per annum in 1662, was ordered to be rebuilt by the Fire Court in November 1667. Clever's rent remained the same, but the lease was extended to sixty-one years. Charitable institutions tended to be under-represented in the Fire Court, as they usually offered generous terms to rebuild in order to avoid delays.[76]

Every penny counted. The governors of St Bartholomew's built shops around the hospital and leased them out. They also suspended salaries and debts and closed off some facilities.[77] Metal fixtures that had melted in the Fire were sold. In October 1666 St Margaret Lothbury sold its melted bell and lead and used it to 'keep, school and clothe a poor fatherless child (Thomas Twyne) belonging to the parish'. The next year he was apprenticed to a silk weaver.[78] Parishes were not the only ones to try to salvage wreckage. Francis Brett returned to the ruins of the eight-hearth tavern he rented on Fleet Street in St Bride Fleet Street, the Bear, and carried away a ton of iron and lead. In the Fire Court Brett claimed to be unable to rebuild; he was allowed to surrender his lease upon payment of £20 to his landlord along with the metals he had carried away.[79] Institutions needed to find temporary accommodation. The Merchant Taylors' School, which was located in Suffolk House, in the parish of St Lawrence Pountney, was completely destroyed on the first day of the Fire. While it was being rebuilt, some of the students were taught in rooms near St Andrew Undershaft. The rest were moved to the vestry house of St Katherine Cree but on the proviso that the school's usher erect a partition of boards 'to keepe his Scholars from running up and downe the church'.[80] It became progressively harder for London's livery companies to fulfil their pre-Fire charitable functions because of the costs of rebuilding their halls and the losses sustained in their housing stock.[81] Edward Waterhouse recorded that after the disaster many charities became companions with the poor in 'Misery & Poverty'.[82]

The nonconformist community had its own methods of caring for its distressed members in London. Henry Ashurst, a Presbyterian merchant famed for his philanthropy, solicited the rich abroad for help. Thomas Gouge, the ejected minister of St Sepulchre Holborn, acted as treasurer for this money, which was distributed in a weekly meeting.[83] Money for London's dissenters also came from their co-communicants across in New England. Just before the Fire the Puritan missionary John Eliot, the self-proclaimed 'Apostle to the Indians', gave his annual salary of £40 from the New England Company to needy ejected ministers in England. After the Fire assistance from the New World for England stepped up. Increase Mather, the foremost figure of American Puritanism, preached a sermon to raise contributions for 'poor saints' in England and wrote letters to ministers in London about the collections. The pastor John Davenport of New Haven in Connecticut, responding to a request from Jane Hooke, the wife of the Independent minister William Hooke, raised a fund for the assistance of ministers who had lost their homes. Conversely, when Boston suffered a fire in 1679 nonconformist congregations in London raised money for those who had lost their homes. Charitable links between Boston and London continued into the eighteenth century. When Boston suffered an even more serious fire in 1760, which affected 20 per cent of its households, merchants from London raised £3,000 for its relief.[84]

The public rebuilding

Parish churches

After the Fire, the Church of England in the City was in disarray. Only twelve parishes within the Walls were wholly unscathed. This created a shortage of places of worship. Baxter recorded, 'the peoples necessity was unquestionable: For they had none other to hear, saving a few Churches that could hold no considerable part of the people'.[85] To cater to the spiritual needs of Londoners, eight dissenting meeting houses were requisitioned and ten temporary 'tabernacles' were constructed. By 1675 eighteen more temporary churches were constructed.[86] It took time for the rebuilding of parish churches to begin. The First Rebuilding Act stated there would be no more than thirty-nine parishes rebuilt. Deciding which ones was to be carried out with the advice and consent of the Archbishop of Canterbury and the Bishop of London. However, no parishes wanted to be eliminated, and the City's parochial structure was highly complex, with multiple jurisdictions and patrons. During the wrangling over new parish boundaries empty churchyards became haunts of thievery and crime. The Second Rebuilding Act finally resolved the issue with the creation of fifty-one parish churches in the City. Some, like St Michael Cornhill, continued to exist as before the Fire. Other parishes were unified, with only one church being rebuilt. For example, St Pancras Soper Lane and All Hallows Honey Lane were joined to St Mary-le-Bow. Even if a parish did not have a church it would continue to exist, retaining its own churchwardens, officers, rates and charges.[87]

Building fifty-one new churches (as well as five more built outside of the fired area) cost £318,467 3s in coal dues.[88] There was considerable public donation. For example, in January 1669 Alice Dudley, widow of the mariner Sir Robert, bequeathed £100 for repairing the steeple of St Sepulchre Holborn. In 1678 Christopher Park Esquire presented St Michael Bassishaw with £100 to purchase new pews.[89] Wren was the director, chief architect and administrator of the effort to rebuild the City churches, but others, like Hooke or Oliver, were also involved. Construction of fourteen churches had begun by the end of 1670. The first church to be fully rebuilt was St Christopher-le-Stocks, in 1675 (the restoration of St Dunstan-in-the-East, which was just damaged, was completed in 1671). Over half of the churches were yet to begin construction by 1676. Arguments between unified parishes often held up work, as did the fact that each parish had to make a refundable deposit of £500 before construction began. There were also the usual difficulties finding building materials and workmen. Despite this, by 1683 twenty-five new churches had been created. In 1695 the parochial rebuilding was completed, when the construction of St Andrew by the Wardrobe was finished.[90]

St Paul's Cathedral

Even though St Paul's had been seriously damaged by the Fire, the original plan was just to repair it. Wren, who wanted to build an entirely new structure, fit up a temporary chapel in its ruins, where Charles II heard a sermon on the first anniversary of the Fire. When part of St Paul's collapsed on April 1668, it was decided it was too unsafe to use, and that it had to be completely demolished and rebuilt. Wren was formally given the commission in July 1669, and that year demolition of the old cathedral began. The rebuilding of St Paul's was crucial. It was the first cathedral built in England since the Reformation and would have to rival the great

Baroque buildings of continental Europe.[91] Money from coal provided a steady stream of income and paid for about five-sixths of the cost of building the cathedral.[92] The foundation of the new cathedral was laid on 21 June 1675. By 1678 work had slowed. The Exclusion Crisis made it more difficult to gain funds from Parliament for St Paul's. A Royal Commission for the Rebuilding of St Paul's was created, which could issue charitable appeals for contributions.[93] A national charitable collection for St Paul's ran from 1678 to 1686. It raised around £7,500. This sum was a fairly low total for a national brief, less than one-quarter of the 1655 collection to relieve the Vaudois, a group of Protestants in northern Italy being perse-cuted by the Duke of Savoy.[94] In 1685 Parliament allowed St Paul's to con-tinue to collect money from the coal dues until 1700, at the rate of four and a half pence per cauldron.[95] This was vital because charitable contributions were not going to be enough to pay for St Paul's – only 11.5 per cent of the rebuilding funds raised to 1685 came from briefs.[96] Coal dues financed the rest. New St Paul's had its first service in 1697, and was declared officially complete in 1711.

Civic rebuilding

The Great Fire had destroyed or damaged many major civic structures, which had to be rebuilt by the City. Fortunately, given the City's long-standing financial troubles, the coal dues financed most of this. The first major project was the restoration of Guildhall, which was completed by 1671. On 23 October 1667 Charles II laid the foundations for the new Royal Exchange, designed by Jerman and housed in an enlarged site with the number of shop spaces increased to try and cover the costs of rebuild-ing. It was fully reopened in 1671. At this point there was competition from other shopping exchanges and the City was no longer quite the thriving commercial district it had been. By 1680 many spaces were vacant. Many merchants and traders who had moved outside of the City after the Fire pre-ferred to remain there (see Chapter 4, this volume). As the City did not want to overstretch its resources, the rebuilding of civic structures was carried out gradually and not completed until 1688.[97] The City's livery companies had to finance the rebuilding of their halls themselves. By 1672 the majority of companies had new halls, but it took until 1685 for all of them to be fully re-housed.[98]

Although plans for the reconstruction of the City on a new street layout were abandoned in favour of a slight modification, there were still several important developments of public spaces. One of the most ambitious was the conversion of the Fleet into a canal useful for trade. This was finally com-pleted in October 1674. Ultimately the scheme was not a success as the canal was not heavily used, and by the mid-eighteenth century it was covered over. The plan to create a great quay along the Thames also failed in the long term. Although the City mostly enforced the ban on building within forty feet of the riverbank, they never had the resources to complete the project. In 1821 legislation repealed the restrictions on building near the Thames.[99]

The memorialisation of the Great Fire

Plans for the Fire's memorialisation were made a matter of weeks after the disaster. The First Rebuilding Act began to regulate the process by establishing an annual fast – the day of 'fasting and humiliation' was to be observed on 10 October. The Act also made provision that a column or pillar be erected near to where the Fire had began in remembrance of the event. The memorialisation of the Fire has continued into the twenty-first century. In 2016 the Fire's 350th anniversary was marked with a series of exhibitions and events. They culminated in the burning of a 400-metre-long model of seventeenth-century London on the Thames. The most visible reminders of the Fire were those in London's built environment. The most visible symbol was the Monument, pictured in Figure 2.2. It was a Wren-designed column, 202 feet high, completed in 1677. It was positioned on the site of St Margaret New Fish Street, near to where the Fire began. Initial reviews were mixed. *London's Index* (1676) stated that it was '*London*'s Standard, and proclaims/Vict'ry ore the fiercest flames'.[100] Not all reactions were so positive. A 1679 poem, sometimes attributed to John Wilmot, Second Earl of Rochester, viewed the Monument as an aberration, depicting it as a grand white elephant, a showy edifice instead of a real sense of penitence: '*Ah fools*! to dress a *Monument of woe*/In *whistling Silks*, that should in *Sackcloth*, go'.[101]

At first, the Monument reflected loyalty to the Restoration regime. Charles II appears on the bas relief on the west plinth. He is dressed in Roman garb, commanding the relief of the City. York also appears although not explicitly – he could also represent Mars or Victory. The royal cipher is inscribed on the urn on top of the column (Wren's plan to top it with a statue of Charles II never materialised). The Latin inscription on the north plinth of the base did not blame the Fire on any particular group, and described it as being part of God's will. The composer of the words was Dr Gale of St Paul's School, who worked in consultation with Hooke and Wren, and received a 'handsome piece of plate' worth ten guineas from the City for his work.[102] During the Popish Plot the Monument became a contested site, utilised by Whigs in particular. In November 1677 a crowd burnt an effigy of the Pope near the column.[103] In 1679 the Whig Charles Blount urged Londoners to go to the top of the Monument and look over the rebuilt City, and imagine the consequences of Popish tyranny.[104] This tract became the template for a print by Benjamin Harris called *A scheme of Popish cruelties* (1681) that displayed the disasters that would occur if the Popish threat was not met. The Monument, positioned on the left of the print overlooking a series of tableaux of Popish atrocities starting with the firing of London, provided a 'symbolic and explanatory grounding' for this foresight into disaster – its height allowing increased clarity of vision to truly imagine the

Figure 2.2 View of Monument's west side and adjacent buildings by William Lodge
(1676)

(Reproduced with the kind permission of the London Metropolitan Archives [City of London])

Popish threat.[105] The ultimate re-appropriation of the Monument occurred in 1680 when the Whig Lord Mayor Ward ordered a new inscription 'to be affixed . . . signifying that the Citty of London was burnt & consumed with fire by the treachery & malice of the papists'. Added to the Latin inscription in June 1681 was the line: 'Popish frenzy, which wrought such horrors, is not yet quenched'. An additional English inscription stating: 'This Pillar was sett up in Perpetuall Remembrance of that most Dreadfull Burning of this Protestant City Begun and Carried on by the Treachery and Malice of the Papists . . . in order to the carrying on their Horrid Plott; For Extirpating the Protestant Religion, and old English Liberty and Introducing Popery and Slavery' was added.[106] These words were removed during the reign of James II, but after the Glorious Revolution it was put back and remained there until 1830.[107] Even in the early eighteenth century, the Monument continued to be used as a symbol of the Popish menace. A 1720 tract urged its readers to remember the inscription on the Monument and 'let the Remembrance of SIXTY SIX be Engraven . . . on the Hearts of Posterity, to make them abhor POPERY'.[108] The highly visible Monument could not remain 'neutral' in its memorialisation of the Fire, as it was too great a tool not to be utilised.

There were three other major memorials to the Fire. The site of Farriner's house in Pudding Lane was initially viewed as something of a monument. The City Lands Committee Papers recorded that at first nothing was built on the ground 'upon a supposicon that it ought perpetually to ly wast'.[109] Upon a petition in 1676 the committee decided there was no reason why the land should not be built upon. It was declared to be worth £5 per annum, and the petitioner, Henry Freeman, was allowed to build on it. It is probable that this individual was already resident in Pudding Lane: the 1675 City Hearth Tax records a Henry Freeman on Pudding Lane in a house assessed at five hearths.[110] Like the Monument, the site on Pudding Lane was appropriated by the Whigs. In 1681, an inscription was placed on the house, stating, 'Here by the Permission of Heaven, Hell broke loose upon this Protestant City from the malicious hearts of barbarous Papists, by the hand of their Agent Hubert'.[111] The two other memorials attracted less controversy. On the south pediment of St Paul's is an engraving of a phoenix with 'RESURGAM' written underneath it. The engraving is a metaphor of the rising of London from the ruins. A more light-hearted memorial to the Fire is a small statue of a fat boy known as *The Glutton* erected in the late seventeenth century, near to Pie Corner, where the last flames of the Fire were meant to have died out. The inscription reads, 'This Boy is put up in memory for the late Fire of London occasioned by the Sin of Gluttony'. However, as the statue was placed on the corner of a tavern in an area of London well known for leisure and recreation, it is probably meant ironically. Indeed, it may have been an advertisement for an inn or cooks' shop on the site.[112] Given London's rise to global economic pre-eminence after the Fire, it is fitting that the oldest unchanged memorial to the Fire in the City was probably part of a commercial enterprise. It also hints at a third, non-politicised popular memorialisation of the

Fire, which was not recorded in contemporary media. This saw the Fire as a disaster to be sure, but one that was part of the fabric of London life, which could be overcome without excessive recrimination and blame.

Notes

1 S. Rolls, *The Burning of London in the Year 1666* (London: R.I. for Thomas Parkhurst, Nathaniel Ranew and Jonathan Robinson, 1667), part 3, 6.
2 W.C. Baer, 'Using Housing Quality to Track Change in the Standard of Living and Poverty for Seventeenth-Century London', *Historical Methods: A Journal of Quantitative and Interdisciplinary History*, 47 (2014), 7.
3 T. Vincent, *God's Terrible Voice in the City* (London: G. Calvert, 1667), 150–2.
4 PA, Manuscript Journal of the House of Lords, HL/PO/JO/1/52, Session 1666–67, fol. 14 r-v.
5 T.F. Reddaway, *The Rebuilding of London after the Great Fire* (London: Jonathan Cape, 1940), 54–5.
6 R. Hainsworth and C. Churches, *The Anglo-Dutch Naval Wars 1652–1674* (Stroud: Sutton, 1998), 156.
7 G. Rommelse, *The Second Anglo-Dutch War (1665–1667): Raison d'état, Mercantilism and Maritime Strife* (Hilversum: Verloren, 2006), 166–7, 189–91.
8 J. Evelyn, *The Diary of John Evelyn*, ed. E.S. De Beer, 6 vols. (Oxford: Clarendon Press, 1955), iii, 484.
9 W.G. Bell, *The Great Fire of London* (1st ed. London: John Lane, 1920), 216.
10 M.A.E. Green, ed., *Calendar of State Papers, Domestic Series, of the Reign of Charles II, 1666–1667* (London: Longman, Green, Longman, Roberts and Green, 1864), 121–2.
11 J. Evelyn, *London Revived: Consideration for Its Rebuilding in 1666*, ed. E.S. De Beer (Oxford: Clarendon Press, 1938), 47, 54–5.
12 *CSPD, 1666–1667*, 170.
13 BL, T. Rugge, *Mercurius Politicus Redivius; or, a Collection of the Most Materiall Occurrences and Transactions in Publick Affaires, Since Anno Domini 1659, Volume II.* Additional MS 10117, 1659–72, fol. 178v.
14 C. Wall, *The Literary and Cultural Spaces of Restoration London* (Cambridge: Cambridge University Press, 1998), 52.
15 D. Keene, 'Fire in London: Destruction and Reconstruction, AD 982–1676', in *Destruction and Reconstruction of Towns, Volume 1: Destruction by Earthquakes, Fire and Water*, ed. M. Körner (Bern: Paul Haupt, 1999), 208.
16 Reddaway, *Rebuilding of London*, 63–7.
17 W.C. Baer, 'Landlords and Tenants in London', *Urban History*, 38 (2011), 234; V. Harding, 'Real Estate: Space, Property, and Propriety in Urban England', *Journal of Interdisciplinary History*, 32 (2002), 555.
18 I. Doolittle, 'Property Law and Practice in Seventeenth-Century London', *Urban History*, 42 (2015), 206.
19 Reddaway, *Rebuilding of London*, 178–9, 191.
20 PA, Public Acts, 18&19 Charles II: An Act for Rebuilding the City of London, HL/PO/PU/1/1666/18&19C2n14, 1666.
21 Reddaway, *Rebuilding of London*, 186–7.
22 PA, Public Act, 22 Charles II, c. 11: An Act for the Rebuilding of the City of London, Uniting of Parishes and Rebuilding of the Cathedral and Parochial Churches within the Said City, HL/PO/PU/1/1670/22C2n4, 1670.
23 C.M. Rosen, *The Limits of Power: Great Fires and the Process of City Growth in America* (Cambridge: Cambridge University Press, 1986), 92–176.

24 S. Rolls, *Londons Resurrection or the Rebuilding of London* (London: W.R. for Thomas Parkhurst, 1668), 41.

25 M.A.R. Cooper, *'A More Beautiful City': Robert Hooke and the Rebuilding of London after the Great Fire* (Stroud: Sutton, 2003), 134.

26 P.E. Jones, 'New Light on the Great Fire', *Transactions of the Guildhall Historical Association*, 4 (1969), 148.

27 R. Josselin, *The Diary of Ralph Josselin*, ed. A. Macfarlane (London: Oxford University Press for the British Academy, 1976), 535.

28 Rolls, *Londons Resurrection*, 91.

29 P. Henry, *Diaries and Letters of Philip Henry, M.A.*, ed. M.H. Lee (London: Kegan Paul, Trench and Co, 1882), 242.

30 T.M.M. Baker, *London: Rebuilding the City after the Great Fire* (Chichester: Phillimore, 2000), 7.

31 I. Warren, 'Houses and Society in Restoration London: The "Great" and "Middle Sorts"', in *London and Middlesex 1666 Hearth Tax*, ed. M. Davies et al. (London: British Record Society, 2014), 131–2.

32 Baer, 'Using Housing Quality', 3–7.

33 V. Harding, 'City, Capital, and Metropolis: The Changing Shape of Seventeenth-Century London', in *Imagining Early Modern England: Perceptions and Portrayals of the City from Stow to Strype, 1598–1720*, ed. J.F. Merritt (Cambridge: Cambridge University Press, 2001), 128.

34 P. Guillery, 'Houses in London's Suburbs', in *London and Middlesex 1666 Hearth Tax*, ed. M. Davies et al. (London: British Record Society, 2014), 142, 148.

35 LMA, Rep. 78, fol. 211v.

36 LMA, Rep. 80, fol. 305v.

37 LMA, Rep. 81, fols. 199v, 215r-v.

38 LMA, Rep. 82, fols. 15v-16r.

39 LMA, Rep. 80, fols. 120v, 149r; N.G. Brett-James, 'A Speculative London Builder of the Seventeenth Century, Dr. Nicholas Barbon', *Transactions of the London and Middlesex Archaeological Society*, 6 (1933), 114–14.

40 LMA, Rep. 79, fol. 255v.

41 T. Doolittle, *Rebukes for Sin by God's Burning Anger: By the Burning of London: By the Burning of the World: By the Burning of the Wicked in Hell-Fire* (London: Dorman Newman, 1667), 59.

42 *An Act for Preventing and Suppressing of Fires within the City of London, and Liberties thereof* (London: Andrew Clark, 1677).

43 LMA, Regulations to Prevent Fires, COL/SJ/03/004, 5, 1667-8.

44 LMA, St Katherine Coleman, Vestry Minutes, GL MS 1123/1, 1659–1727, p. 16.

45 LMA, St Sepulchre Holborn, Vestry Minutes, GL MS 3149/2, 1662–83, p. 112.

46 LMA, Rep. 73, fol. 132r-v.

47 E.L. Jones et al., *A Gazetteer of English Urban Fire Disasters, 1500–1900* (Norwich: Geo Books, 1984), 17–19.

48 Evelyn, *Diary*, iii, 461.

49 Doolittle, *Rebukes for Sin*, 190–216.

50 Rolls, *Londons Resurrection*, 74–7.

51 LMA, Account Book, with Returns of the Brief and Details of Its Distribution, *Poor Sufferers by Fire in Lond*, COL/SJ/03/006, 1666.

52 J.F. Field, 'Charitable Giving and Its Distribution to Londoners after the Great Fire, 1666–1676', *Urban History*, 38 (2011), 8–9.

53 M. Davies and A. Saunders, *The History of the Merchant Taylors' Company* (Leeds: Maney, 2004), 202.

54 S. Pepys, *The Diary of Samuel Pepys*, ed. R. Latham and W. Matthews, 11 vols. (1st ed. London: G. Bell and Sons, 1970–83), viii, 562.

55 TNA, Letter from the King to the Court of Common Council, 31 May 1667, SP 29/202, 95; Letter from the King to the Court of Common Council and the Court of Aldermen, 5 June 1667, SP 29/203, 69.

56 TNA, Petition of Sir William Bolton to the King, May 1668, SP 29/240,190.

57 J.R. Woodhead, *The Rulers of London 1660–1689: A Biographical Record of the Aldermen and Common Councilmen of the City of London* (London: London and Middlesex Archaeological Society, 1965), 45.

58 LMA, Rep. 78, fols. 134v, 147r; Rep. 81, fols. 79v-80r.

59 LMA, Jour. 48, fol. 239v.

60 R. Baxter, *Reliquiae Baxterianae: Or, Mr. Richard Baxter's Narrative of the Most Memorable Passages of His Life and Times, Part 3*, ed. M. Sylvester (London: T. Parkhurst, J. Robinson, J. Lawrence and J. Dunton, 1696), 17.

61 Field, 'Charitable Giving', 13–17.

62 TNA, Petition of the Vicar and Churchwardens of St Martin-in-the-Fields to the King, 21 February 1668, SP 29/235, 33.

63 LMA, COL/SJ/03/006.

64 TNA, Petition of Clara Bolton to the King, 1667, SP 29/229, 117; Petition of Clara Bolton to Arlington, 10 July 1669, SP 29/262, 150.

65 P. Slack, *The English Poor Law 1531–1782* (Basingstoke: Macmillan, 1990), 27–8.

66 LMA, COL/SJ/03/009, 109.

67 Slack, *English Poor Law*, 27–8.

68 V.E. Brodsky, 'Widows in Late Elizabethan London: Remarriage, Economic Opportunity and Family Orientations', in *The World We Have Gained: Histories of Population and Social Structure*, ed. L. Bonfield, R.M. Smith and K. Wrightson (Oxford: Basil Blackwell, 1986), 123–4.

69 LMA, COL/SJ/03/009, 6.

70 LMA, COL/SJ/03/009, 21.

71 TNA, Petition of Ann Lloyd to the Queen, 13 September 1666, SP 29/171, 89.

72 TNA, Petition of Sarah Crafts to the King, 1666, SP 29/173, 101; LMA, COL/SJ/03/006; *Fire Court*, i, 332–3.

73 LMA, COL/SJ/03/006.

74 P. Slack, 'Hospitals, Workhouses and the Relief of the Poor in Early Modern London', in *Health Care and Poor Relief in Protestant Europe 1500–1700*, ed. O.P. Grell and A. Cunningham (London and New York: Routledge, 1997), 242.

75 TNA, *A True Report of the Great Number of Poor Children and Other Poor People Maintained in the Several Hospitals Under the Pious Care of the Lord Maior, Commonalty and Citizens of the City of London*, 8 April 1667, SP 29/196, 149; Warrant for Grant for King Charles' Hospital, July 1669, SP 29/264, 134A.

76 *Fire Court*, i, 53; Baer, 'Landlords and Tenants', 245.

77 G. Whitteridge, 'The Fire of London and St Bartholomew's Hospital', *London Topographical Record*, 20 (1952), 47–8.

78 LMA, St Margaret Lothbury, Vestry Minutes, GL MS 4352/1, 1571–1677, fol. 262r-v.

79 TNA, Hearth Tax Assessment Listing, City of London and parts of Middlesex, 1666, E179/252/32, Part 8/2, fol. 14r; *Fire Court*, i, 70–1.

80 LMA, St Katherine Cree, Vestry Minutes, GL MS 1196/1, 1639–1718, fol. 119r.

81 I.W. Archer, 'The Livery Companies and Charity in the Sixteenth and Seventeenth Centuries', in *Guilds, Society and Economy in London 1450–1800*, ed. I.A. Gadd and P.A. Wallis (London: Centre for Metropolitan History, Institute of Historical Research in association with the Guildhall Library, 2002), 23.

82 E. Waterhouse, *A Short Narrative of the Late Dreadful Fire in London* (London: W.G. for Richard Thrale and James Thrale, 1667), 79.

83 Baxter, *Reliquiae Baxterianae*, 17–18.

84 F.J. Bremer, *Congregational Communion: Clerical Friendship in the Anglo-American Puritan Community, 1610–1692* (Boston, MA: Northeastern University Press, 1994), 235–6; M. Mulcahy, 'Urban Catastrophes and Imperial Relief in the Eighteenth-Century British Atlantic World: Three Case Studies', in *Cities and Catastrophes: Coping with Emergency in European History*, ed. G. Massard-Guilbaud, H.L. Platt and D. Schott (Frankfurt: Peter Lang, 2002), 109.

85 Baxter, *Reliquiae Baxterianae*, 19.

86 M.S. Briggs, *Wren the Incomparable* (London: George Allen and Unwin, 1953), 110; R.H. Harrison, 'Temporary Churches after the Great Fire'. *Transactions of the Ecclesiological Society*, 3 (1955–6), 255–7.

87 PA, HL/PO/PU/1/1670/22C2n4.

88 Briggs, *Wren*, 110.

89 TNA, Memorandum of Charitable Giving of Alice, Duchess of Dudley, January 1669, SP 29/255, 24; LMA, St Michael Bassishaw, Vestry Minutes, MS 2598/1, pp. 70–1.

90 Bell, *Great Fire*, 310–2, 336–7.

91 J. Lang, *Rebuilding St Paul's after the Great Fire of London* (London: Oxford University Press, 1956), 35.

92 Bell, *Great Fire*, 303.

93 Lang, *Rebuilding St Paul's*, 53–62.

94 Field, 'Charitable Giving', 7–9.

95 Lang, *Rebuilding St Paul's*, 118–23.

96 D.J. Crankshaw, 'Community, City and Nation, 1540–1714', in *St Paul's: The Cathedral Church of London 604–2004*, ed. D. Keene, A. Burns and A. Saint (New Haven: Yale University Press, 2004), 60.

97 Baker, *London*, 7; W.C. Baer, 'Early Retailing: London's Shopping Exchanges, 1550–1700', *Business History*, 49 (2007), 37.

98 Reddaway, *Rebuilding of London*, 255–6.

99 Reddaway, *Rebuilding of London*, 243.

100 R.A. Aubin, ed., *London in Flames, London in Glory: Poems on the Fire and Rebuilding of London 1666–1709* (New Brunswick, NJ: Rutgers University Press, 1943), 243.

101 *Upon the Stately Structure of Bow-Church and Steeple, Burnt, an. 1666. Rebuilt, 1679, a Second Poem upon Nothing!* (London, 1679), 1.

102 LMA, Rep. 82, fol. 291r.

103 J.E. Moore, 'The Monument, or, Christopher Wren's Roman Accent', *Art Bulletin*, 80 (1998), 515.

104 C. Blount, *An Appeal from the Country to the City, for the Preservation of His Majesties Person, Liberty, Property, and the Protestant Religion* (London, 1679), 1.

105 J. Monteyne, *The Printed Image in Early Modern London: Urban Space, Visual Representation, and Social Exchange* (Aldershot: Ashgate, 2007), 198–202.

106 LMA, Jour. 49, fols. 156v, 224r.

107 F.E. Dolan, 'Ashes and "the Archive": The London Fire of 1666, Partisanship, and Proof', *Journal of Medieval and Early Modern Studies*, 31 (2001), 379–408.

108 *The True Protestant Account of the Burning of London, or, an Antidote, against the Poyson and Malignity of a Late Lying Legend, Entituled an Account of the Burning of London, &c* (London: B. Baddam for S. Popping, 1720), 12.

109 LMA, Court of Common Council: City Lands Committee Papers, COL/CC/CLC/04/001, Box 1, 1666–79, 208a.

110 TNA, Hearth Tax Assessment Listing: City of London, 1675, E179/252/23, fol. 104r.

111 LMA, Jour. 49, fol. 224r.
112 P. Ward-Jackson, *Public Sculpture of the City of London* (Liverpool: Liverpool University Press, 2003), 147–8, 372–3.

Reference list

Primary sources

Manuscript

BL, Rugge, T. *Mercurius Politicus Redivius; or, a Collection of the Most Materiall Occurrences and Transactions in Publick Affaires, Since Anno Domini 1659, Volume II*. Additional MS 10117, 1659–72.

LMA, Account Book, with Returns of the Brief and Details of Its Distribution, *Poor Sufferers by Fire in Lond*, COL/SJ/03/006, 1666.

LMA, Court of Common Council: City Lands Committee Papers, COL/CC/CLC/04/001, Box 1, 1666–79.

LMA, *Fire of London Grants of Money*, COL/SJ/03/009, 1667–75.

LMA, Journal of Common Council, Jour. 46–9, 1664–82.

LMA, Letter from Wagstaffe of the Court of Aldermen to Sir Thomas Player, MISC MSS/159/3, 1673.

LMA, Regulations to Prevent Fires, COL/SJ/03/004, 5, 1667–8.

LMA, Repertory of the Court of Aldermen, Rep. 71–82, 1665–77.

LMA, St Katherine Coleman, Vestry Minutes, GL MS 1123/1, 1659–1727.

LMA, St Katherine Cree, Vestry Minutes, GL MS 1196/1, 1639–1718.

LMA, St Margaret Lothbury, Vestry Minutes, GL MS 4352/1, 1571–1677.

LMA, St Michael Bassishaw, Vestry Minutes, MS 2598/1, 1669–1715.

LMA, St Sepulchre Holborn, Vestry Minutes, GL MS 3149/2, 1662–83.

PA, Manuscript Journal of the House of Lords, HL/PO/JO/1/52, Session 1666–67.

PA, Public Acts, 18&19 Charles II: An Act for Rebuilding the City of London, HL/PO/PU/1/1666/18&19C2n14, 1666.

PA, Public Act, 22 Charles II, c. 11: An Act for the Rebuilding of the City of London, Uniting of Parishes and Rebuilding of the Cathedral and Parochial Churches within the Said City, HL/PO/PU/1/1670/22C2n4, 1670.

TNA, *A True Report of the Great Number of Poor Children and Other Poor People Maintained in the Several Hospitals Under the Pious Care of the Lord Maior, Commonalty and Citizens of the City of London*, 8 April 1667, SP 29/196, 149.

TNA, Hearth Tax Assessment Listing, City of London and parts of Middlesex, E179/252/32, 1666.

TNA, Hearth Tax Assessment Listing, City of London and Parts of Middlesex, E179/252/23, 1675.

TNA, Letter from the King to the Court of Common Council, 31 May 1667, SP 29/202, 95.

TNA, Letter from the King to the Court of Common Council and the Court of Aldermen, 5 June 1667, SP 29/203, 69.

TNA, Memorandum of Charitable Giving of Alice, Duchess of Dudley, January 1669, SP 29/255, 24.

TNA, Petition of Ann Lloyd to the Queen, 13 September 1666, SP 29/171, 89.

TNA, Petition of Churchwardens of St Martin-in-the-Fields to the King, 1666, SP 29/173, 116.

TNA, Petition of Clara Bolton to Arlington, 10 July 1669, SP 29/262, 150.

TNA, Petition of Clara Bolton to the King, 1667, SP 29/229, 117.

TNA, Petition of Sarah Crafts to the King, 1666, SP 29/173, 101.

TNA, Petition of Sir William Bolton to the King, May 1668, SP 29/240,190.

TNA, Petition of the Vicar and Churchwardens of St Martin-in-the-Fields to the King, 21 February 1668, SP 29/235, 33.

TNA, Warrant for Grant for King Charles' Hospital, July 1669, SP 29/264, 134A.

Printed

An Act for Preventing and Suppressing of Fires within the City of London, and Liberties Thereof. London: Andrew Clark, 1677.

Aubin, R.A., ed. London in Flames, London in Glory: Poems on the Fire and Rebuilding of London 1666–1709. New Brunswick, NJ: Rutgers University Press, 1943.

Baxter, R. Reliquiae Baxterianae: Or, Mr. Richard Baxter's Narrative of the Most Memorable Passages of His Life and Times, Part 3, edited by M. Sylvester. London: T. Parkhurst, J. Robinson, J. Lawrence and J. Dunton, 1696.

Blount, C. An Appeal from the Country to the City, for the Preservation of His Majesties Person, Liberty, Property, and the Protestant Religion. London, 1679.

Doolittle, T. Rebukes for Sin by God's Burning Anger: By the Burning of London: By the Burning of the World: By the Burning of the Wicked in Hell-Fire. London: Dorman Newman, 1667.

Evelyn, J. London Revived: Consideration for Its Rebuilding in 1666, edited by E.S. De Beer. Oxford: Clarendon Press, 1938.

Evelyn, J. The Diary of John Evelyn, edited by E.S. De Beer, 6 vols. Oxford: Clarendon Press, 1955.

Green, M.A.E., ed. Calendar of State Papers, Domestic Series, of the Reign of Charles II, 1666–1667. London: Longman, Green, Longman, Roberts and Green, 1864.

Henry, P. Diaries and Letters of Philip Henry, M.A., edited by M.H. Lee. London: Kegan Paul, Trench and Co, 1882.

Josselin, R. The Diary of Ralph Josselin, edited by A. Macfarlane. London: Oxford University Press for the British Academy, 1976.

Pepys, S. The Diary of Samuel Pepys, edited by R. Latham and W. Matthews, 11 vols. 1st ed. London: G. Bell and Sons, 1970–83.

Rolls, S. The Burning of London in the Year 1666. London: R.I. for Thomas Parkhurst, Nathaniel Ranew and Jonathan Robinson, 1667.

Rolls, S. Londons Resurrection or the Rebuilding of London. London: W.R. for Thomas Parkhurst, 1668.

The True Protestant Account of the Burning of London, or, an Antidote, against the Poyson and Malignity of a Late Lying Legend, Entituled an Account of the Burning of London, &c. London: B. Baddam for S. Popping, 1720.

Upon the Stately Structure of Bow-Church and Steeple, Burnt, an. 1666. Rebuilt, 1679, a Second Poem upon Nothing!. London, 1679.

Vincent, T. God's Terrible Voice in the City. London: G. Calvert, 1667.

Waterhouse, E. A Short Narrative of the Late Dreadful Fire in London. London: W.G. for Richard Thrale and James Thrale, 1667.

Secondary sources

Archer, I.W. 'The Livery Companies and Charity in the Sixteenth and Seventeenth Centuries'. In Guilds, Society and Economy in London 1450–1800, edited by I.A. Gadd and P.A. Wallis, 15–28. London: Centre for Metropolitan History, Institute of Historical Research in Association with the Guildhall Library, 2002.

Baer, W.C. 'Early Retailing: London's Shopping Exchanges, 1550–1700', Business History, 49 (2007), 29–51.

Baer, W.C. 'Landlords and Tenants in London', Urban History, 38 (2011), 234–55.

Baer, W.C. 'Using Housing Quality to Track Change in the Standard of Living and Poverty for Seventeenth-Century London', *Historical Methods: A Journal of Quantitative and Interdisciplinary History*, 47 (2014), 1–18.

Baker, T.M.M. *London: Rebuilding the City after the Great Fire*. Chichester: Phillimore, 2000.

Bell, W.G. *The Great Fire of London*. 1st ed. London: John Lane, 1920.

Bremer, F.J. *Congregational Communion: Clerical Friendship in the Anglo-American Puritan Community, 1610–1692*. Boston, MA: Northeastern University Press, 1994.

Brett-James, N.G. 'A Speculative London Builder of the Seventeenth Century, Dr. Nicholas Barbon', *Transactions of the London and Middlesex Archaeological Society*, 6 (1933), 110–45.

Briggs, M.S. *Wren the Incomparable*. London: George Allen and Unwin, 1953.

Brodsky, V.E. 'Widows in Late Elizabethan London: Remarriage, Economic Opportunity and Family Orientations'. In *The World We Have Gained: Histories of Population and Social Structure*, edited by L. Bonfield, R.M. Smith and K. Wrightson, 122–54. Oxford: Basil Blackwell, 1986.

Campbell, J.W.P. and Bowles, R. 'The Construction of the New Cathedral'. In *St Paul's: The Cathedral Church of London 604–2004*, edited by D. Keene, A. Burns and A. Saint, 207–19. New Haven: Yale University Press, 2004.

Cooper, M.A.R. *'A More Beautiful City': Robert Hooke and the Rebuilding of London after the Great Fire*. Stroud: Sutton, 2003.

Crankshaw, D.J. 'Community, City and Nation, 1540–1714'. In *St Paul's: The Cathedral Church of London 604–2004*, edited by D. Keene, A. Burns and A. Saint, 45–70. New Haven: Yale University Press, 2004.

Davies, M. and Saunders, A. *The History of the Merchant Taylors' Company*. Leeds: Maney, 2004.

Dolan, F.E. 'Ashes and "the Archive": The London Fire of 1666, Partisanship, and Proof', *Journal of Medieval and Early Modern Studies*, 31 (2001), 379–408.

Doolittle, I. 'Property Law and Practice in Seventeenth-Century London', *Urban History*, 42 (2015), 202–24.

Field, J.F. 'Charitable Giving and Its Distribution to Londoners after the Great Fire, 1666–1676', *Urban History*, 38 (2011), 3–23.

Guillery, P. 'Houses in London's Suburbs'. In *London and Middlesex 1666 Hearth Tax*, edited by M. Davies, C. Ferguson, V. Harding, E. Parkinson and A. Wareham, 140–53. London: British Record Society, 2014.

Hainsworth, R. and Churches, C. *The Anglo-Dutch Naval Wars 1652–1674*. Stroud: Sutton, 1998.

Harding, V. 'City, Capital, and Metropolis: The Changing Shape of Seventeenth-Century London'. In *Imagining Early Modern England: Perceptions and Portrayals of the City from Stow to Strype, 1598–1720*, edited by J.F. Merritt, 117–43. Cambridge: Cambridge University Press, 2001.

Harding, V. 'Real Estate: Space, Property, and Propriety in Urban England', *Journal of Interdisciplinary History*, 32 (2002), 549–69.

Harrison, R.H. 'Temporary Churches after the Great Fire', *Transactions of the Ecclesiological Society*, 3 (1955–6), 251–8.

Jones, E.L., Porter, S., and Turner, M., eds. *A Gazetteer of English Urban Fire Disasters, 1500–1900*. Norwich: Geo Books, 1984.

Jones, P.E. 'New Light on the Great Fire', *Transactions of the Guildhall Historical Association*, 4 (1969), 146–50.

Keene, D. 'Fire in London: Destruction and Reconstruction, AD 982–1676'. In *Destruction and Reconstruction of Towns, Volume 1: Destruction by Earthquakes, Fire and Water*, edited by M. Körner, 187–211. Bern: Paul Haupt, 1999.

Lang, J. *Rebuilding St Paul's after the Great Fire of London*. London: Oxford University Press, 1956.

McKeon, M. *Politics and Poetry in Restoration England: The Case of Dryden's Annus Mirabilis.* Cambridge, MA: Harvard University Press, 1975.

Monteyne, J. *The Printed Image in Early Modern London: Urban Space, Visual Representation, and Social Exchange.* Aldershot: Ashgate, 2007.

Moore, J.E. 'The Monument, or, Christopher Wren's Roman accent', *Art Bulletin*, 80 (1998), 498–533.

Mulcahy, M. 'Urban Catastrophes and Imperial Relief in the Eighteenth-Century British Atlantic World: Three Case Studies'. In *Cities and Catastrophes: Coping with Emergency in European History*, edited by G. Massard-Guilbaud, H.L. Platt and D. Schott, 105–21. Frankfurt: Peter Lang, 2002.

Porter, S. *The Great Fire of London.* Stroud: Sutton, 1996.

Reddaway, T.F. *The Rebuilding of London after the Great Fire.* London: Jonathan Cape, 1940.

Rideal, R. *1666: Plague, War and Hellfire.* London: John Murray, 2016.

Rommelse, G. *The Second Anglo-Dutch War (1665–1667): Raison d'état, Mercantilism and Maritime Strife.* Hilversum: Verloren, 2006.

Rosen, C.M. *The Limits of Power: Great Fires and the Process of City Growth in America.* Cambridge: Cambridge University Press, 1986.

Slack, P. *The English Poor Law 1531–1782.* Basingstoke: Macmillan, 1990.

Slack, P. 'Hospitals, Workhouses and the Relief of the Poor in Early Modern London'. In *Health Care and Poor Relief in Protestant Europe 1500–1700*, edited by O.P. Grell and A. Cunningham, 243–51. London and New York: Routledge, 1997.

Wall, C. *The Literary and Cultural Spaces of Restoration London.* Cambridge: Cambridge University Press, 1998.

Ward-Jackson, P. *Public Sculpture of the City of London.* Liverpool: Liverpool University Press, 2003.

Warren, I. 'Houses and Society in Restoration London: The "Great" and "Middle Sorts"'. In *London and Middlesex 1666 Hearth Tax*, edited by M. Davies, C. Ferguson, V. Harding, E. Parkinson and A. Wareham, 121–39. London: British Record Society, 2014.

Whitteridge, G. 'The Fire of London and St Bartholomew's Hospital', *London Topographical Record*, 20 (1952), 47–8.

Woodhead, J.R. *The Rulers of London 1660–1689: A Biographical Record of the Aldermen and Common Councilmen of the City of London.* London: London and Middlesex Archaeological Society, 1965.

Part two

3   Household movement after the Great Fire

The Great Fire caused the largest dislocation of London's residential structure in its history until the Blitz nearly three centuries later. Londoners
whose houses were destroyed were forced to restructure their residential
environments. This chapter examines how this restructuring occurred after
the Fire, and the extent to which the disaster changed individual residential
structures across the socio-economic spectrum. This illuminates patterns of
early modern metropolitan neighbourhood migration. Mobility was a key
feature of the population structure of seventeenth-century London. Most
Londoners moved several times over their lives. Residential change was
socially selective. Poorer Londoners were more mobile, whilst tradesmen
and master craftsmen tended to be more stable, as they needed to be in the
same location for customers to find them.[1] Some of these moves were the
result of lifecycle events – service, apprenticeship, marriage and so forth,
but many would have been based on economic considerations – the desire
for larger trading premises perhaps. Jeremy Boulton's study of seventeenth-
century Southwark showed that 20 per cent of householders moved within
one year, and only 24 per cent stayed in the same house for ten years.[2] There
was a trend towards persistence within the same district, with people moving within the same neighbourhood.[3]

After the Fire the burned-out Londoners faced the choice of returning
to their old residences or permanently settling elsewhere. The majority of
Londoners were tenants and many were sub-tenants. Technically, this meant
that they had an obligation to rebuild after the Fire as part of their 'covenant to maintain'. The Fire Court had been established to resolve disputes
between landlords and tenants that arose during the rebuilding. It did not
coerce tenants who could not afford it to rebuild their houses and sub-
tenants were often given leeway. Tenants could not completely escape their
legal obligation to their landlords. This did not extend to having to finance
the rebuilding completely. Tenants were frequently allowed to surrender their
leases – almost always after some payment to their landlord, usually in the
form of arrears in rent or a cash settlement. Gervaise Byfield, a skinner, the
tenant of a property in Walbrook leased from the sub-tenant of the owner,
was freed by the Court on 4 July 1667 of all obligations on the property

upon payment of two months arrears of rent.[4] Not all lease surrenders were so straightforward. Anthony Selby, a salter, leased a property on New Fish Street Hill in St Margaret New Fish Street from Widow Elizabeth Robinson. He was granted a twenty-five-year lease in March 1666, but refused to rebuild because he claimed the house had lost twelve feet in frontage when the new foundations were staked out. He sought compensation of £100 for the cellars and vaults that he had added remaining on the property. The Court decreed that Selby pay Robinson £120 for the surrender of the lease. In a fairly unusual event, Selby appealed the decision on 10 June 1667, but the original decision was upheld and he was ordered to pay Robinson £5 for the inconvenience.[5] Theoretically, the Fire Court could have limited residential movement, but its decisions did not constrain those who were unable or unwilling to rebuild, allowing them to resettle elsewhere. Conversely, the Fire Court protected landlords, as it ensured that if the tenant was able to rebuild, they could be forced to do so, or else compensate the landlord fully. The destruction of a house did not destroy all of its value to its owner.

Many tenants may simply not have wanted to return to their pre-Fire residences. This was because rebuilding a property was a complicated process, lengthened by regulations and bureaucracy. More importantly, not all tenants could afford to rebuild. Although the regulations of the Rebuilding Act were effective in making houses more fire-proof, it made building them more expensive as only brick could be used. Stephen Porter, using a sample of judgments of the Fire Court, estimated that the average cost of rebuilding a house was £516,[6] a substantial sum. It could often be far more than this. William Hawkins claimed that the cost of rebuilding his 'great messuage' on St Nicholas' Lane in St Nicholas Acons, which he rented from the Clothworkers' Company, was £3,000.[7] Finding the resources to rebuild was made more difficult by the economic disruption the Fire caused. Furthermore, those who had been burnt out had to pay inflated rents in the surviving area of London while it was being rebuilt. London rents tended to be higher than the rest of the country, and the further rent rises after the Fire were huge burden for many.[8] Samuel Rolls commented in 1667 that landlords, presumably of houses that had not been destroyed, demanded excessive rents in the months after the Fire.[9] Even the master of chancery, Sir Nathaniel Hobart, faced eviction from his home in Chancery Lane, which had survived the Fire, because his landlord wanted to raise his rent.[10] In addition there was usually a fine upon starting a lease at a new property – this amount varied considerably depending on the need of the lessor for cash. The costs of furnishing a new house had to be considered. Roger Kempe claimed before the Fire Court that he was unable to rebuild and return to his former residence in Walbrook because he had already spent £200 'settling in another place'.[11]

Londoners deciding to rebuild faced other practical problems. Reconstruction could not begin in earnest until April 1667, when the staking out of properties was finished. The post-Fire widening or enlarging of some thoroughfares in the City discouraged some people from building. Richard Utber refused to rebuild his eight-hearth messuage on the Poultry in St Mary Colechurch (at an estimated cost of £550) because 'some part of the site had been taken away for widening the street'. The Fire Court allowed Utber to surrender his lease in return for paying his landlord £50.[12] Likewise, Thomas Boys refused to rebuild his five-hearth house on Fleet Street in St Bride Fleet Street because its site had been reduced by half because of the widening of the street. He was allowed to surrender and his neighbour, Robert Busby, agreed to rebuild on the remaining ground.[13] Furthermore, everyone faced difficulties in supply of material and labour, despite Parliament's attempts to free up some trading restrictions. The City government attempted to remedy this: on 7 November 1666 'to incourage the more free & plentifull making of Brick' the City Lands Committee granted a City tenant in the parish of St Giles-in-the-Fields the right to dig and cut up her land to make brick.[14] In spite of such efforts, the price of building materials would surely have gone up after the Fire. It eventually took until early 1668 for the rebuilding to be fully under way.[15] Despite these difficulties and disagreements most of the destroyed houses had been rebuilt by 1671, and the remainder by 1674.[16]

Many Londoners did not return to their pre-Fire residence and often moved away from the City altogether. The initial lack of enthusiasm of rebuilding was such that the autumn after the Fire, a London relative of the landowner Sir Ralph Verney wrote to him that 'ground goes even a begging, & there is soe much to be sold that it becomes every day cheaper than the other'.[17] Civic government recognised this and attempted to prevent new building outside of the Walls to encourage repopulation of the City. In 1671 the City Lands Committee denied Mr Colegrave the right to build on a parcel of land in Moorfields, as they did not want to give

> any Encouragement or Countenance . . . for that purpose . . . [as] there are already too many Buildings in the Out parts of this Citty which Entertaine Tradesmen & Inhabitants while other Buildings & Tenements in the body of the Citty stayd empty and unimployed.[18]

The next year the Court of Aldermen asserted that 'the buildings or shedds in Moorefeilds or other places in or about this Citty' were prejudicial to the present welfare of the City, as many houses therein were still uninhabited.[19] On 23 March 1673, the Court of Aldermen declared that due to the 'great mischiefes too visibly attending this Citty in the multitude of Buildings of late yeares erected in the Suburbs in all places round the Citty', the Bailiff of Southwark was to take care to indict all such people who erected any new houses without having laid them on four acres of ground, according to the 1588 Erection of Cottages Act. The Court also declared that the buildings erected between Whitechapel and Mile End, as well as in Spitalfields, would be likewise prosecuted.[20]

Ultimately such efforts were not effective. By the 1670s remaining outside of the City may have been more attractive. As a result of the rebuilding regulations and perhaps a lack of enthusiasm to build there, there was a reduction in the total number of houses in the fired areas after 1666. Walter Bell estimates that c. 9,000 new houses were built to replace the c. 13,200 that were destroyed in the Fire.[21] After the post-Fire price spike subsided, rents outside of the Walls tended to be lower than within. Land outside and around London tended to be relatively cheap compared to that in the centre.[22] In 1672, the City government, in a petition to Parliament, claimed that there were over 3,000 empty houses and unbuilt tofts in the City and liberties – representing one-sixth of its area.[23] That year, a committee was set up to 'consider of all expedients that may conduce to the better replenishing of this Citty with Inhabitants'.[24] Yet, according to the City Surveyors, by 1674 there were still 1,000 empty plots and 3,500 houses still unoccupied.[25] Ultimately the City government could not fight the long-term trend of most of London's population residing outside of the Walls. During the 1660s, just over half of London's population lived outside of the Walls; this rose to around two-thirds by 1700.[26]

Thousands of people *did* return to the City within the Walls. Despite the shift in London's population away from its traditional core, there were benefits to doing this. If individuals had enough resources to weather the short-term shock of the Fire, in the long run rebuilding may actually have led to saving money. This is because many landlords, anxious to encourage their tenants to return, offered them substantial savings if they would rebuild. A sample of 518 cases from the Fire Court where the tenant agreed to rebuild shows this. Tenants who rebuilt their properties enjoyed a mean 17.7 per cent reduction in annual rent over the course of their post-Fire lease. Such leases were usually substantially increased in length to further entice rebuilding. In real terms the savings would have been increased over time because the rent was fixed, and not adjusted for inflation. The case of John Tutt provides a dramatic example of this. In 1649 he had rented a house for £30 per annum (with a £70 fine) on Ludgate Hill in St Bride Fleet Street that was owned by the Dean and Chapter of Rochester Cathedral. When Tutt agreed to rebuild, the Fire Court fixed his new annual rent at £2, and his lease was extended to 1728.[27] When making its decisions the Fire Court took into account the pre-Fire condition of the property and even compensated tenants for improvements they had made. A little before the Fire William Cumberland had spent £500 repairing the 'greatly decayed' timbers of the old house he rented on Old Fish Street in St Nicholas Olave. When Cumberland agreed to rebuild, his rent was halved and thirteen years were added to his lease.[28] Occasionally tenants rebuilt their house but did not appear to have permanently settled there after the Fire. Before the Fire Godfrey Beck, a goldsmith, answered for three hearths for his house on the north side of Little Lombard Street in St Mary Woolnoth. When he appeared before the Fire Court on 14 October 1668 he agreed to rebuild the property. His annual rent was halved to £8, and his lease, which had around two years to run, was extended to fifty-one years. Beck paid to have foundations laid out but by 1675 he had moved to a five-hearth house on Broad Street in Langbourn Ward.[29] In all likelihood tenants such as Beck took advantage of the decreased rents and increased leases awarded by the Fire Court by subletting the property at a higher rent after it was rebuilt, and then moving. Some landlords were willing to rebuild themselves, recognising the long-term benefits of doing so. Sir James Altham allowed the tenant of his property in St Mary-at-Hill, Esquire Thomas Lenthall, to surrender even though there were two years left on the lease. The Fire Court's decision commented that Altham had the resources to 'rebuild better' (at an estimated cost of £2,500) and should enjoy the 'benefit' of doing so.[30]

The Hearth Tax

Residential patterns before and after the Fire can be examined systematically, and in more detail, using London's Hearth Tax records. The Hearth Tax was a property tax collected from 1662 to 1689.[31] It subjected householders 'to an inquisitorial right of search' to determine how many hearths were liable to be taxed.[32] London was more reluctant to pay the Hearth Tax than other regions and opposition to it was prevalent there since 1662. As such, collectors made a considerable effort to control evasion and ensure as many people paid as possible. This meant that the London Hearth Tax returns were some of the most detailed and comprehensive in England, creating the first complete house-to-house surveys of London and its hinterland.[33] The most useful Hearth Tax documents for reconstructing residential patterns are the assessments, preliminary reckonings of the number of taxable hearths in each property, more likely to be accurate than records of what was paid.[34] They mostly indicated the place of residence and number of hearths. Payment was made by the occupier of a property – the owner was only liable if it was empty.[35] This distinction was crucial for London, where three-quarters of households were tenant-occupied.[36]

There are three major problems with the Hearth Tax. Firstly, due to human error and the difficulties of collecting such an intrusive tax, some assessments were incomplete.[37] Secondly, the Hearth Tax assumed that there was a link between the number of hearths and personal wealth.[38] This was not always completely true in practice. Social status or wealth cannot be 'read' directly off Hearth Tax totals. Rather, they presented a 'broad continuum' of wealth, with the rich at the top, the poor at bottom and a considerable degree of overlap in between. Also, the number of hearths does not take into account the age or condition of the house – poorer households could have a number of hearths beyond their status if their residence was old or deteriorated.[39] Although the relationship between number of hearths and wealth and social status was not linear, comparison of Hearth Tax returns to other variables has shown there was at least a rough degree of correlation between the two variables.[40] In short, the Hearth Tax probably reflected wealth and social standing to a degree.[41] The third difficulty is the problem of exemption. There were two groups exempt: those certified as exempt (usually named) and paupers.[42] Regulations concerning exactly who would be exempt from the tax were ambiguous and mutable. An amendment to the 1662 Hearth Tax legislation exempted those who did not pay church or poor rates, those whose houses were worth £1 per annum or less and those with moveable goods valued at less than £10. Kilns, furnaces and private ovens were theoretically exempt but there was often confusion over their inclusion in assessments. In 1663 an amendment required the names of all non-liable householders to be entered into assessment lists, and in 1664 exemptions ceased to be granted to those with more than two hearths. The criterion that appeared to have closest match to exemption in practice was renting a house worth £1 per annum or less. Perhaps 35 per cent of households were exempt from the Hearth Tax, containing 30 per cent of the population.[43] Not all of the central instructions were implemented with equal thoroughness. The number of hearths from exempt households was often omitted, and empty dwellings, ovens and forges were recorded inconsistently.[44]

This chapter uses two databases of Hearth Tax individual assessment lists covering both fired and non-fired areas of London. The first were mostly taken from just before the Fire but as far as possible after the 1665 Plague.[45] The second was drawn from lists made after 1672, when most of the rebuilding had been completed.[46] Due to differences in the scope and range of the assessments, not all of the areas of London covered in the database could be exactly the same for before and after the Fire.

In Table 3.1 the Hearth Tax assessment lists are compared to a contemporary listing of houses destroyed by the Fire, probably made up using existing assessments for property taxes by ward officials.[47] As the Alchin List only included houses burned in the Fire it meant that for some wards that were only partly burned (for example Farringdon Without or Bishopsgate Within), the number recorded would be considerably lower than that revealed by the Hearth Tax. In general, the number of households per area is higher in the listings from after the Fire, as when most of the pre-Fire assessments were made London was still recovering from depopulation caused by the Plague. Gaps in the coverage of the Lady Day (25 March) 1666 City Hearth Tax assessment listings may also account for some of the differences. This is due to its incomplete coverage. Eight parts of the listing are missing, which presumably contained listings covering wards such as Broad Street and Cornhill. Several parts of the assessment do not provide any information on the exact place of residence of the individuals, only providing a list of people living in the parish.[48] These accounted for some of the gaps in the 1666 Hearth Tax assessments, particularly in the wards of Farringdon Without, Bishopsgate Within and Bishopsgate Without. In comparison, the coverage for the 1675 City Hearth Tax was more complete, with the differences in the number of households recorded probably due to the effects of the Fire, rather than missing or incomplete records. The returns for the western suburbs broadly covered the same geographical area. The assessments south of the Thames covered slightly different geographical areas, with only the parishes of St Olave Southwark and St Saviour Southwark being recorded in both listings. For the eastern and northern suburbs a larger geographical area was covered in the post-Fire listings.

One of the systematic reasons for the differences in the number of households in Table 3.1 is inconsistency in the recording of exempt households. Many exempt households were included. Andrew Wareham has found that

Table 3.1 Number of households in London before and after the Fire, by City ward, c. 1666 and 1675

Ward/Area	'Alchin List'	Pre-Fire Hearth Tax	Post-Fire Hearth Tax
Aldersgate Within	245	424	247
Aldersgate Without	No data	468	1,448
Aldgate	No data	543	1,004
Bassishaw	No data	108	127
Billingsgate	No data	607	325
Bishopsgate Within	88	218	466
Bishopsgate Without	No data	0	1,863
Bread Street	No data	4	243
Bridge	No data	379	321
Broad Street	412	0	693
Candlewick	238	183	245
Castle Baynard	678	264	544
Cheap	424	335	319
Coleman Street	No data	55	583
Cordwainer	396	179	248
Cornhill	242	0	227
Cripplegate Within	738	496	654
Cripplegate Without (including St Giles without Cripplegate)	41	4,967	4,244
Dowgate	584	21	346
Farringdon Within	No data	1,098	1,099
Farringdon Without	168	2,536	4,672
Langbourn	573	417	521
Lime Street	No data	76	117
Portsoken (including St Botolph without Aldgate)	No data	3,512	3,533

(*Continued*)

Table 3.1 (Continued)

Ward/Area	'Alchin List'	Pre-Fire Hearth Tax	Post-Fire Hearth Tax
Queenhithe	614	0	362
Tower	No data	746	595
Vintry	575	35	266
Walbrook	No data	376	280
Western Suburbs (1664 & 1666, 1675)*	-	8,591	10,695
Southwark (1664x6, 1673)†	-	1,870	3,267
Eastern Suburbs (1666, 1675)‡	-	8,795	14,562
Northern Suburbs (1666, 1675)§	-	1,342	3,838
Total	**6,016**	**38,645**	**57,954**

Sources: Alchin List: *Lists (fifteen in Number) of the Inhabitants, whose Houses were destroyed in the Great Fire of 1666*, LMA, Alchin Papers Box F/no. 65 COL/AC/06/006; TNA, Hearth Tax Assessment Listing, City of London and parts of Middlesex, E179/252/32, 1666; Hearth Tax Assessment Listing, City of London and Parts of Middlesex, E179/252/23, 1675; Hearth Tax Assessment Listing, Middlesex, E179/243/380, 1674/5; Hearth Tax Assessment Listing, Surrey, E179/258/4, 1664/6; Hearth Tax Assessment Listing, Surrey, E179/188/504, 1673; Hearth Tax Assessment Listing, Westminster, E179/253/25, 1675; M. Davies et al, eds., *London and Middlesex 1666 Hearth Tax* (London: British Record Society, 2014).

Note: Wards in bold designate that the majority of the ward was fired.

* For 1664: St Margaret Westminster; For 1666: St Giles-in-the-Fields, St John the Baptist Savoy, St Mary-le-Strand, St Martin-in-the-Fields and St Paul Covent Garden; For 1675: St Clement Dane, St Giles-in-the-Fields, St John the Baptist Savoy, St Margaret Westminster, St Mary-le-Strand, St Martin-in-the-Fields and St Paul Covent Garden.

† For 1664x6: St Mary Newington, St Olave Southwark and St Saviour Southwark; For 1673: St George the Martyr Southwark, St Olave Southwark, St Saviour Southwark and St Thomas Southwark.

‡ For 1666: St Dunstan Stepney, St Leonard Shoreditch, St Mary Whitechapel and Tower Liberty; For 1675: Liberty of Norton Folgate, St Dunstan Stepney, St Katherine by the Tower, St Leonard Shoreditch and St Mary Whitechapel.

§ For 1666: St James Clerkenwell; For 1675: St Andrew Holborn and St James Clerkenwell.

in the Lady Day 1666 assessment 20.5 per cent of those listed in the City and 19.6 per cent of those listed in Westminster were 'non-paying'. However, as the listing partly relied on a roll made in 1662, when the names of non-chargeable households did not have to be recorded, it is likely that for some areas they would have been under-recorded.[49] As 16.8 per cent of the households before the Fire and 12.5 per cent afterwards were assessed for one hearth, this indicates that many smaller (and presumably poorer) households were listed. It appears that at least some of the exempt may have been included. However, it is impossible to be entirely certain if they always were. For example, perhaps not all of the parochial poor and paupers were recorded in a comprehensive and consistent fashion. As some poorer members of the community were under-recorded, the number of hearths per household may be slightly skewed upwards in the database used for this chapter.[50]

Overall patterns

The difference in the distribution of the number of hearths per household before and after the Fire, as well as between regions of London, is clear from Figures 3.1 and 3.2. Firstly, within the Walls and in the western suburbs the number of hearths per household was generally higher than other parts of

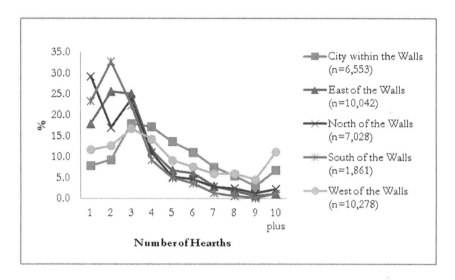

Figure 3.1 Number of hearths per household in London before the Fire (%)

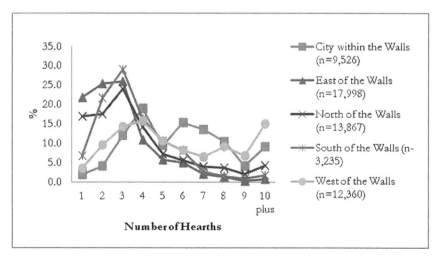

Figure 3.2 Number of hearths per household in London after the Fire (%)

London. This reflects the wealthier profile of the residents of these areas. In the City within the Walls, the proportion of households with ten or more hearths rose after the Fire from 6.8 per cent to 9.2 per cent. This was probably due to the larger size of houses in the rebuilt areas. The size of houses in the western and northern suburbs also appeared to have risen, which may reflect a desire for larger houses as well as the fact that part of the area was burned and rebuilt. In other areas of London, there was change in the numbers of hearths per household. There was an increase in the hearths per household in Southwark, but this may be due to differences in recording and some differences in the geographical coverage of the samples. The assessments for Southwark before the Fire included large numbers of paupers, which would have skewed downward the number of hearths per household. East of the Walls, there was a slight decline in the numbers of hearths per household, with more one-hearth households. This may be due to subdivision of houses as the areas coped with the influx of poorer Londoners displaced by the Fire. These people may have chosen to remain there, even after London was rebuilt. There was also a difference between male and female householders. Women generally had fewer hearths per household than men. In the City within the Walls before the Fire the mean number of hearths per female-headed household was 3.9 compared to 5.1 for males. After the Fire the figues were 5.1 and 6.0, respectively. This was because in seventeenth-century London the majority of female householders were widows, who were usually amongst the poorest and most vulnerable members of the metropolitan community.[51]

To examine the question of change in number of hearths per household more closely, twenty-four parishes with full returns for the 1666 and 1675 London Hearth Tax assessments were compared. Only a subset of parishes can be compared because the 1675 listings were mostly organised by ward rather than parish. The majority of these parishes are situated within the Walls,[52] with the exception of St Botolph without Aldgate and St Leonard Shoreditch to the east; St Bartholomew the Great, St Bartholomew the Less, St Giles without Cripplegate and St James Clerkenwell to the north; and St Bride Fleet Street, St Dunstan-in-the-West, St Giles-in-the-Fields, St Martin-in-the-Fields and St Paul Covent Garden to the west. Comparing individual parishes produced more reliable results than comparing by ward because it means that it is certain that the geographical areas being compared are identical. Unfortunately, it was not possible to accurately assess numbers of uninhabited households after the Fire for all of these parishes because the numbers of empty houses were given as a total for each ward, rather than topographically inserted into the listing.

Figure 3.3 clearly shows the effect of the Fire on the number of hearths per household. After the Fire, in the fired and rebuilt parishes in the sample, the proportion of households with more than seven hearths doubled from around 20 per cent to 40 per cent, and a general rise in the mean number of hearths per household from 4.5 to 5.9. Single- or dual-hearth households in the fired parishes decreased from just under a quarter to less than one in ten. In the parishes directly unaffected by the Fire, the

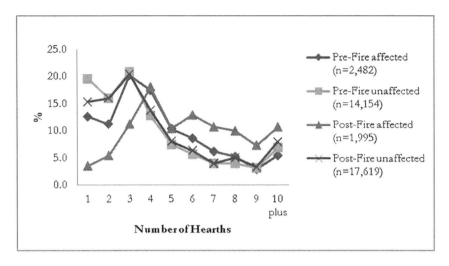

Figure 3.3 Number of hearths per household in twenty-four parishes, 1666 and 1675 (%)

distribution of the number of hearths per household was more stable. The proportion of one- or two-hearth households was about one-third before and after the Fire. There was also an increase in the mean number of hearths per household from 3.5 to 4.4. Generally in the devastated areas of London, it was likely that the rebuilt houses would have larger numbers of hearths than before the Fire.

Hearth Tax assessments recorded empty houses, which were not unusual in early modern London. Its high population turnover meant there were always significant numbers of uninhabited houses. In fact high vacancy benefitted tenants, as it forced landlords to reduce rents.[53] Assessing their geographical distribution examines an important feature of changing metropolitan housing structure in the aftermath of the Fire. Wareham shows that the Lady Day 1666 assessment reveals that nearly 40 per cent of properties in the City were empty but only 15 per cent in Westminster. This may be an exaggeration because these were working books and houses may have been listed as empty as a way of speeding up the making of the lists. However, it was clear that as a result of the Plague of 1665, many households were still empty by the next year.[54] According to the 1675 Hearth Tax assessments, the numbers of empty houses declined in the decade after the Fire. In the City within the Walls 9.7 per cent of houses were recorded as being empty, whilst in Westminster the figure was 3.5 per cent. Vacancy rates decreased across London, meaning that in 1675 just over 6 per cent of houses in the metropolis were uninhabited.

The locality of empty houses in the wards varied geographically before and after the Fire. Before the Fire empty houses were more concentrated in areas outside of the Walls. By 1675 it was the City within the Walls where uninhabited houses were more widespread. The exception was the areas within the Walls that had not been destroyed. In areas within the Walls directly unaffected by the Fire, the percentage of empty houses decreased from 9.5 to 0.1. This was such a dramatic change because these houses represented some of the few available residences in the City after the Fire and so would have been in high demand, meaning that far fewer empty households were recorded in this area. Outside of the Walls there was also a decline in vacancy rates. This reflected the houses that had been left empty as a result of the 1665 Plague, which was most serious in the poor suburban areas of London. For example, in 1666 15.8 per cent of houses in St Botolph without Aldgate were vacant, but in 1675 this had declined to 4.5 per cent. Likewise, in St Giles-in-the-Fields, also seriously affected by the Plague, the percentage of empty houses fell from 10.3 to 6.7. In addition, buildings on the periphery of the City that survived the Fire could cater for the demand for housing. The decline of uninhabited houses in areas unaffected by the Fire makes it clear that much of the residential movement out of the City may have become permanent. This suggests that perhaps the 'pull' of the City was declining, or at least was limited by the costs of building and living there. This may have been reversed by the 1690s, when vacancy levels fell in within the Walls. Over time the empty houses were filled. According to Craig Spence, by the end of the century vacancy rates in London had declined to at least 3.7 per cent.[55] The statistician Gregory King estimated in 1695 that they were slightly higher, at 5.4 per cent.[56]

The total number of houses is recorded in the sample of twenty-four parishes where there was comparable data before and after the Fire. Figure 3.4

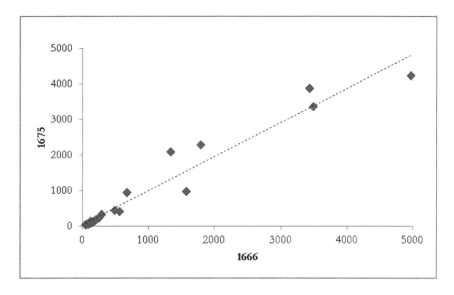

Figure 3.4 Number of households in twenty-four parishes, 1666 and 1675

shows the high level of correlation (R^2=0.950), which was statistically significant, between the total number of households recorded before and after the Fire at the parochial level. In the destroyed areas of London the total number of households did not change significantly, as most new houses were built on the same site as previous dwellings.[57] The parish with the greatest proportional reduction in houses after the Fire was St Bride Fleet Street, which recorded 1,575 households before the Fire, but only 984 afterwards. This was because a large area of this parish had still not been built on by 1675. That year's Hearth Tax assessment recorded that in the parish there were '22 great & little tofts unbuilt'.[58] The depopulation was reflected in the average numbers buried in the parish before and after the Fire. From 1660 to 1664 the mean number buried per annum was 372.6. This fell to 256.0 for the period from 1671 to 1675.[59] In suburban parishes such as St James Clerkenwell, St Giles-in-the-Fields and St Martin-in-the-Fields there were more households recorded after the Fire. Although legislation often prohibited it, property owners in the suburbs frequently subdivided houses, converted existing structures into tenements or took in lodgers. It is likely that this would have intensified in the short term at least, after the Fire, thus increasing population density in the suburbs.[60]

In summation, the Hearth Tax assessments reveal some clear overall patterns for London's household structure before and after the Fire. There was a general rise in the number of hearths per household after the Fire, reflecting a general increase in the overall size of houses. Secondly, there appears to have been a change in the geographical distribution of uninhabited houses in London, from being concentrated in the suburbs before the Fire to being concentrated in the centre afterwards. In the years around 1666, the numbers of empty houses were probably higher than average, due to the effects of plague and the Fire. Finally, in the main there appears to have been considerable continuity in the housing density of these parishes across London.

Tracing individual movement

This section explores the movement of individuals before and after the Fire, showing how individual experiences shaped residential change, and to what extent different social and geographical groups experienced common factors before and after the Fire. It places these movements in the context of overarching population trends in seventeenth-century London such as the growth of the western suburbs. To gain an understanding of this, individuals were linked between the Hearth Tax assessments for before and after the Fire. To do this, each first name and surname was assigned a percentage likelihood of it occurring based on how many times it appears in the dataset. The two values were multiplied together to give an approximate indication of the likelihood of the combination occurring by chance. All combinations with an expected likelihood of more than 0.0005 per cent were excluded to avoid any false linkages. This method excluded individuals whose first name was not listed. Many households recorded no name whatsoever – for example, for empty houses, institutions or illegible entries. This meant that there were 31,405 individuals in the pre-Fire assessments with enough information to be nominally linked (although many of them would have died in the period before 1675). In total 5.8 per cent of them could be fairly reliably linked to post-Fire assessments, with just over one-quarter of them coming from areas that had been fired. The proportion of householders was fairly consistent across London with the exception of Southwark, where only 3.2 per cent of individuals could be linked. This area was generally home to poorer and more residentially unstable people than other areas of London, making nominal linkage more problematic. These linked names showed the sequence of movement before and after the Fire. The specific nature of the recording of the place of household in the Hearth Tax also illustrated the typology of locality in terms of whether it was a street, lane, alley or yard. This indicated if any change in residence was a move upwards or downwards in terms of the relative status of locality; along with the number of hearths an individual was assessed for before and after the Fire. The Hearth Tax also gives insight into how female householders recovered from the Fire. In 1666, in the part of London the Fire had destroyed, around one in fourteen householders were women (outside of this area the proportion was far higher, at about one in five). Nominally linking women before and after the Fire was problematic as the first names of around one-third of women were not recorded in the Hearth Tax assessments (about 6 per cent of men had no first name included). There was no first name for the majority of women specifically named as widows in the London Hearth Tax assessments. However, this did not mean that all the women with first names included were *not* widows. Many would have been – in English pre-Census listings not all women who were widows were always designated as such.[61] Even so, over 200 women could be linked between the 1666 and 1675 Hearth Tax assessments.

Witness depositions from London's ecclesiastical courts were surveyed to provide an additional perspective on movement. They recorded the questions asked to witnesses to establish their social credit, and often included information about past places of residence and the amount of time spent in each location.[62] This could have been used to examine individual movement after the Fire, and indicate the duration of residence in each location. Due to gaps in the records of the Commissary and Consistory Courts of the Diocese of London from 1640 to 1669, only depositions of the Court of Arches (the appeal court for cases before all church courts in the Province of Canterbury held at Lambeth Palace) could be used. Occasionally this revealed moves after the Fire. Samuel Wheedon, testifying in the case of Isabella Metford versus John Metford on 18 December 1666, was recorded as living in St John's Street in St James Clerkenwell for the past four months, having previously lived in the parish of St Anne and St Agnes for twelve years.[63] From a three-year sample after the Fire, only eleven witnesses could be found who had lived in destroyed areas of London – not enough to be statistically useful.[64]

Residential persistence

Peter Clark argued that 1666 was a watershed in the social evolution of London: the rebuilding process created sense of 'spatial disorientation' and 'neighbourhood erosion' in the City, which was overtaken by suburban sprawl.[65] Residential movement was not unusual. Even amongst Londoners who were not fired, 67 per cent of them had moved to a different location between 1666 and 1675. The Fire made residential movement even more likely, with 87.4 per cent of those burnt out not returning to their pre-Fire address. However, many Londoners did not move after the Fire and returned to the same location ten years later. What common factors, if any, did these individuals share in choosing to return to the same address?

Around half (43 per cent) of those who remained in the same locations came from streets. Such addresses tended to be more prestigious than yards or alleys, which suggested that those who remained were of a higher social status. It also appears that individuals who did not move tended to be slightly more likely to be involved in retail. This could be the result of the fact that craftsmen could afford to be more mobile, as they did not rely on passing trade to the same extent as selling groups, and so were not tied to an address to the same degree. Ralph Box and Joseph Billers were both residents of Cheapside before the Fire. Box was a freeman of the Grocers' Company who worked as a 'druggister' and his establishment covered two rented adjacent properties (they were in different parishes – one was in St Mary Colechurch and one in St Martin Pomary, both were assessed for seven hearths on Lady Day 1666). Billers was a member of the Skinners' Company but worked as a draper and had occupied his six-hearth house on Cheapside, which lay in the parish of St Pancras Soper Lane, since 1662–3. By 1675 they had returned to Cheapside, where both were assessed for twelve hearths. It is unlikely that Box returned to exactly the same location, as he had not taken charge of rebuilding either of his rented properties, whilst it appeared that Billers did, as he paid to have the foundations of the property surveyed.[66] That both Box and Billers were freemen of two of London's 'great' livery companies further socially tied them to the City, as well as perhaps illustrating the resources they had to return, which were needed to return to an affluent address.

The cases of Box and Billers showed how residentially persistent individuals after the Fire were clustered around the most economically and socially important areas of the City. The area around St Paul's Cathedral particularly stood out, with nine in its yard and nine in nearby Paternoster Row remaining in the same location before and after the Fire. The City's major thoroughfares, such as Cheapside, Fenchurch Street, Fleet Street and Lombard Street were also likely to house individuals who returned to the same address after the Fire. Such streets housed individuals involved in retail trades, who relied on passing trade, and so would be likely to return to these areas. In comparison, the relatively poorer areas of the City, around the riverside, did not appear to have experienced the same levels of residential persistence. South of a line running roughly from Cannon Street to Bridewell, there was just one householder, Randall Richardson, who returned to the same address after the Fire. He lived in a four-hearth property on Thames Street in St Magnus the Martyr,[67] which was an important thoroughfare in itself. Superficially, the geographical location of a neighbourhood did have an effect on its likelihood of housing individuals returning to their pre-Fire addresses. The main factor in this appears to have been the socio-economic status of the neighbourhood – with the higher-status areas of the post-Fire City experiencing higher levels of residential persistence. Women were probably less likely to return to the same location after the Fire. Only one out of the nine women from the fired area who were nominally linked had returned to the same location by 1675: Mary Lammas, who remained on Staining Lane in St Mary Staining, with her number of hearths increasing from two to four.[68] London's guild regulations may also have contributed to encouraging more residential mobility for widows in particular. Even though widows of citizens inherited the freedom of the City, they were unlikely to carry on their late husband's trade after his death, due to formal (and informal) obstacles in livery company organisation.[69] So, unless they remarried quickly, they may have had no economic imperative to stay in a particular location.

Outside of the fired areas there were clear geographical differences in the stability of residential structure. As Table 3.2 shows, it was highest (over 40 per cent) in more prestigious areas like the western suburbs and the part of the City within the Walls that was not fired. Southwark and the eastern suburbs were more residentially mobile, reflecting the generally lower social status of those areas. The individuals who remained residentially stable tended to be wealthier and reside on streets. This is shown by four members of the English aristocracy who kept houses in London's western suburbs

Table 3.2 Non-movement of Londoners linked in the Hearth Tax, c. 1666 and 1675

Region of London	Total Number Linked	% of Which Did Not Move
Area Destroyed in the Fire	396	12.4
City within the Walls, unaffected by the Fire	52	40.4
East of the Walls	246	20.3
West of the Walls	385	43.6
North of the Walls	233	31.3
Southwark	48	12.5
Total	1,360	27.0

Sources: See Table 3.1.

Note: Excludes 451 individuals who were nominally linked but were not listed under a specific address.

and were assessed at the same locations in 1666 and 1675. James Compton, Third Earl of Northampton, remained in his twenty-six-hearth house on the west side of Lincoln's Inn Fields in St Giles-in-the-Fields. Robert Brudenell, Second Earl of Cardigan, kept a twenty-hearth house in nearby Portugal Row (although he refused to pay in 1666 because he claimed to have been 'out of towne that ½ year'). Oliver St John, Second Earl of Bolingbroke, did not move from his twenty-four-hearth house on Newport Street in St Martin-in-the-Fields. Close by, Robert Sidney, Second Earl of Leicester remained in his huge fifty-five-hearth mansion on the site of modern-day Leicester Square.[70] Movement within London was not unknown for its aristocratic residents. Richard Boyle, First Earl of Burlington moved from his thirty-three-hearth house in Whitefriars Precinct to a forty-one-hearth house in the more fashionable location of Portugal Street in St Martin-in-the-Fields by 1675.[71] Not all those who remained in the same location were high-status individuals. Prudence Linsey answered for one hearth for her household in Fig Tree Yard in Ratcliff Hamlet in St Dunstan Stepney in 1666 and 1675 but was exempted from payment, presumably due to her poverty.[72] Similarly, in 1666 Alice Snow was also exempted from payment for her one-hearth household on Gloucester Court in St Giles without Cripplegate and was still living at the same location in 1675.[73]

People who remained at the same address (even if they were not fired) tended to be wealthier. Just under 5 per cent of those who remained were misters, nobles or gentry compared to just under 3 per cent for those who moved. Such groups were more likely to be part of parochial or civic government – institutions that integrated individuals into the local community, creating a sense of 'belonging'. They may have also had closer social relations with their neighbours, which was important in creating a strong sense of 'loyalty' to an area. Movement at lower levels of society may have been more prevalent because they were less integrated into their pre-Fire neighbourhood, and so had fewer social ties to the place.[74]

Individual movement before and after the Fire

Even in areas directly unaffected by the Fire, the majority of linked individuals are recorded as moving, as Table 3.2 shows. Much of this movement was relatively short-distance – as most moves were generally within the same neighbourhood.[75] The proportion of residential movement was higher in areas which were destroyed by the Fire, and is similar to the proportion of Merchant Taylors who moved from areas destroyed by the Fire (see Chapter 4, this volume). The London Hearth Tax assessments, because usually they give very specific places of household, meant that Table 3.2 recorded any movement of any kind – even highly localised moves. The figures may also be a slight over-estimation because they do not take into account the remarriage of widows. In this case, the name of the householder would change to the new husband's – thus masking the residential persistence of women who remarried. For example, in 1656 the Merchant Taylor Foulke Denny leased property in Bothaw Lane in St Mary Colechurch, and was recorded as being the householder in the 1662–3 Hearth Tax. By 1666 assessments Foulke had died and his widow Mary remarried Thomas Fletcher, who occupied the house and was recorded as being the householder that year. Thus, Mary's residential persistence at the Bothaw Lane property is not revealed by the comparison of two Hearth Tax assessments.[76] Overall, the levels of residential persistence (one-third did not change residence) amongst Londoners not burnt out in the decade after the Fire match the 25 to 40 per cent rate of residential persistence calculated by Roger Finlay using parochial lists of householders. This is similar to the levels of residential persistence in seventeenth-century Southwark calculated by Boulton, where 24 per cent of the population stayed in the same house for ten years.[77] Being fired thus increased the likelihood of changing residence by roughly half.

Even if an individual from a fired area of London was recorded as not moving between 1666 and 1675, they still experienced residential change at some stage. The examination of Merchant Taylors and booksellers in the next chapter shows that returning to the same pre-Fire address, with an intervening spell in an undamaged part of London, was common. The Merchant Taylor Oliver Crumpton, a salesman based on Cannon Street in Candlewick Ward before the Fire, moved to the Minories, east of the Walls, shortly after the Fire, but had returned to Cannon Street by 1672 at the latest – or possibly earlier; he had paid to have foundations staked out in November 1667. Crumpton answered for six hearths for the Cannon Street property in 1675.[78] The bookseller George Calvert was based in Paul's Churchyard before the Fire, moved to Jewen Street in St Giles without Cripplegate after and returned to his original workplace by 1676. Linkage of the witness depositions to the Hearth Tax assessments also illustrated this. Henry Baldwin, a baker, appeared as a witness in the Court of Arches on 27 June 1667. He was recorded as living in St Ethelburga Bishopsgate but stated nine months previously (before the Fire) he had lived in St Bride Fleet Street. Baldwin returned to Fleet Street by 1675, and was recorded as living in a house with ten hearths (the high number was probably linked to his trade as a baker) on Fleet Street in that year's Hearth Tax assessment.[79] Others moved further away while London was being rebuilt. Anthony Sturt was a haberdasher and Citizen of London who lived in an eight-hearth house on the west side of Mark Lane in All Hallows Barking. Shortly before the Fire he had spent £100 in improvements (including adding a wash-house) but unfortunately part of the messuage had been blown up to stop the flames spreading east. This left his building open to the elements and required Sturt to spend £600 on repairs. On 27 June 1667, Sturt appeared as a witness at the Court of Arches. He stated that he had been resident of Mitcham in Surrey, nine miles south of the City, for the past nine months (i.e. since the Fire) and had previously lived in All Hallows Barking. Seven days earlier Sturt had appeared before the Fire Court because his landlords had refused to contribute towards the cost of rebuilding or improve the terms of his lease, which expired in 1685. It was ordered that the landlords pay Sturt £200 towards the repairs although his rent was not decreased nor was his term added to.[80] Sturt was not recorded in the 1675 Hearth Tax assessments in London. This suggests that he died before then, sublet the property or surrendered his lease (the last option is unlikely given the capital he had sunk into it).

Although such moves were common, they could still be traumatic, as the case of Abraham and Frances Browne shows. Before the Fire they ran the White Horse Inn on Lombard Street, which was assessed for eighteen hearths in 1666. Samuel Pepys visited their establishment six months before the Fire and recorded Frances was 'a very pretty woman . . . indeed' although Abraham was 'the simplest looked fellow and old that ever I saw'. Tragically in February 1667 Frances committed suicide by throwing herself into the Thames, with Pepys noting 'she hath had long melancholy upon her, and hath endeavoured to make away with herself often'. At that point they were running another establishment, the Beare Tavern, on Bridge Foot. Just over one year later Abraham had agreed to rebuild his former tavern on Lombard Street, with his rent decreased by half to £20, and his lease extended by forty years. The foundations were staked out in June 1668.[81] In the aftermath of the death of his wife, Browne was able to return to his pre-Fire address with a much reduced rent in exchange for taking on the rebuilding of the property.

The nominal linkage exercise in this chapter could not take into account the possibility of movement outside of London. Trying to take this into account using Hearth Tax assessment records would have created too large and unwieldy a dataset. The increased number of names in the sample would have made nominal linkage more problematic. Many Londoners were migrants from other areas of England who may have returned home to their kin to recover from the Fire. In addition, it should be remembered that migration to London was not always permanent.[82] The Fire may have just had the effect of speeding up a return home that was always planned. There is anecdotal evidence of people leaving London for other parts of the country after the Fire. Anthony Wood recorded that after the Fire 'several traders' from London set up shop in Oxford.[83] Unfortunately, it was not feasible to systematically recover similar cases but it was likely that this type of residential movement after the Fire was not unique. It is possible that some Londoners whose losses were particularly heavy emigrated after the Fire, or were even forced into indentured service.

Just under half of the people burnt out after the Fire had moved out of the City within the Walls by 1675. This does somewhat confirm the City government's fears that the area within the Walls may have been left depopulated were valid. After the Fire many people did leave the City for the suburbs, with female householders less likely to remain than males.

Table 3.3 Movement of nominally linked Londoners from the Hearth Tax, c. 1666 and 1675 (%)

	Region of London	Fired	Non-Fired	Total
Moved within same region of London	City within the Walls	54.0	3.5	21.2
	East of the Walls	0.0	19.5	12.7
	West of the Walls	8.6	23.0	18.0
	North of the Walls	0.0	16.9	11.0
	Southwark	0.0	4.0	2.5
Moved into different region of London	Into City within the Walls	2.9	12.3	9.0
	Eastward	10.9	6.4	8.0
	Westward	6.6	5.5	5.9
	Northward	15.1	7.5	10.2
	Southwark	1.9	1.4	1.5
	Total	100 (350)	100 (652)	100 (1,002)

Sources: See Table 3.1.

Population growth in the suburbs before the Fire had encouraged landlords and builders to create lower-cost and lower-quality units for rent.[84] In the western suburbs many of the great noble houses in this area were being divided and sub-divided after the mid-seventeenth century.[85] As a result of rebuilding regulations, such low-cost housing was not widely available in the rebuilt City. The most frequent direction of movement was to the areas north, west and east of the Walls (and was indeed even higher for women). Movement south of the river after the Fire appears to have been least common – however, it did occur. After the Fire there were temporary dwellings set up in the open spaces of St George's Fields, a mostly undeveloped area in Southwark. There was probably demand for housing there – in 1680 widow Frances Barnard petitioned the Court of Aldermen for permission to continue building a tenement there.[86]

To gain a finer sense of residential change after the Fire, individual movements amongst nominally linked Londoners who moved were more closely examined. The relative distance of residential change was identified by examining each move. Some movement was very short-distance – even to an adjacent location. Before the Fire, Posthumous Sare lived on Silver Street in St Alban Wood Street. By 1675 he had moved to Wood Street, which ran perpendicular to his former address. Likewise Gawain Corbin had resided on Fish Street Hill, meaning his house was one of the first to be destroyed on 2 September 1666. After the Fire he returned to the neighbourhood, settling on Pudding Lane, close to where the blaze had started.[87] As Table 3.4 shows, just over one-quarter of those who moved after being fired relocated to an address adjacent to their original location. When slightly longer-distance moves were examined it was revealed that 9.8 per cent of them were within the same ward, and 23.9 per cent to a neighbouring one. Women were more likely to move longer distances than men. Even if an individual had been forced to move household as a result of the Fire, it appeared that the resultant residential movement still tended to be fairly localised. Clearly, as Cynthia Wall argues, many 'Londoners figuratively as well as literally, and architecturally as well as topographically, chose rather to recreate and re-inhabit their old inconvenient spaces'.[88] This level of residential persistence was possible because the layout of London's streets, lanes and alleys remained similar after the Fire. In addition, Table 3.4 shows that movement that was not a result of the Fire also tended to be relatively close range, with only one-third of it to an area beyond neighbouring parishes or wards.

It is difficult to precisely assess the exact personal circumstances behind each individual move. Much of the movement from fired areas tended to be relatively short-distance, with just 41.2 per cent of the movement being beyond the neighbouring ward. It is possible that individuals moving longer distances across London may have moved to areas with family links.

Table 3.4 Distance of residential movement of nominally linked Londoners from the Hearth Tax, c. 1666 and 1675

	No.	% of which moved to adjacent location	% of which moved within ward or parish	% of which moved to neighbouring ward or parish	% of which moved beyond neighbouring ward or parish
Fired area	347	25.1	9.8	23.9	41.2
Within the Walls, unaffected	31	32.3	6.5	9.7	51.5
East of the Walls	196	4.1	28.1	27.0	40.8
West of the Walls	217	10.6	43.8	14.3	31.3
North of the Walls	160	13.1	38.8	12.5	35.6
Southwark	42	40.5	14.3	7.1	38.1
Total	993	16.7	25.6	19.4	38.3

Sources: See Table 3.1.

Note: For areas of London that were not in a City ward, parish boundaries were used instead.

For example, Robert Pigg, a victualler residing in St Magnus the Martyr Churchyard before the Fire, moved to Codpiece Court in St Margaret Westminster, nearby to his probable kinsman, Ralph Pigg, of Peter Street.[89] However, the Hearth Tax assessments can only show movements to areas with family on the paternal side (i.e. with the same surname). It also cannot take into account the impact of non-kin social links, which were probably more important and numerous than family links in the metropolitan context. Neighbours were the most important source of networks of social support in early modern London.[90] Social links were also formed by livery company membership, apprenticeship or even originating from the same part of the country (or indeed the world, given the metropolis's increasingly international population) before moving to London. In addition, many households were part of a network of debt and credit, which relied on a member of the local community with social credit to give someone with less credit the requisite security to carry out the loan. This mechanism became one way of forming social bonds,[91] which may have facilitated the relocation of individuals forced to move after the Fire.

Change in social standing after the Fire

The number of hearths per household, in addition to the relative prestige of an address, can be used to gain insight into the impact of the Fire on wealth and social standing of householders. Firstly, the number of hearths per household can be used as an approximate proxy for the relative wealth and social standing of the household. Although it is not a precise measure of individual wealth or status, it does serve as an approximate indicator.[92] A larger number of hearths in a household probably indicated a larger house size, although this could be skewed upwards by occupations that used forges or ovens. The second consideration was the type of address a household was situated on. Not all addresses in seventeenth-century London were equal. There was a rough gradient of desirability. For the most part, the street-front was the most favoured location, as well as the most expensive. Wealthier selling groups dominated and relied on these areas,[93] whilst poorer craftsmen and the semi-skilled had to make do with the cheaper lanes, yards, courts and alleys. Ultimately, choice of residence was dictated by commercial advantage and rent.[94] As such, change in the number of hearths and relative status of locality can be used to measure difference in social standing after the Fire.

Figure 3.5 shows the distribution of the change in the number of hearths per linked individual before and after the Fire. Unsurprisingly, Londoners whose houses were fired experienced the most change in their number of hearths, with over half losing or gaining more than one hearth. In comparison, people who came from areas that were not fired tended to be more likely to answer for the same number of hearths before and after the Fire, with just under half experiencing no change. Change in the number of hearths was

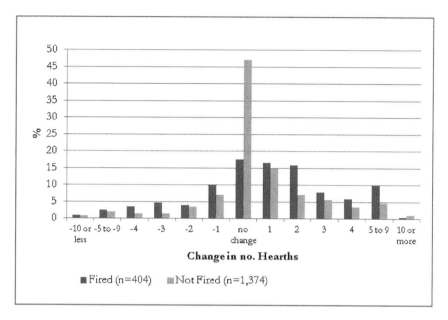

Figure 3.5 Change in number of hearths per household, c. 1666 and 1675 (%)

often associated with rebuilding a fired house, which had more hearths 63.3 per cent of the time. However, even individuals from a non-fired area who did not appear to have moved changed their number of hearths about one-quarter of the time. For example, George Westby, an upholsterer of Long Lane in St Botolph without Aldersgate, was assessed as having three hearths for his property there in 1666 but five in the same location in 1675.[95] This change in numbers of hearths even when it appeared there was no residential movement or rebuilding could be down to three factors. This could be as a result of individuals modifying or extending their households. It could be a result of a highly localised move – such as a movement within the same street. Finally, and most likely, it could show the inconsistency in the assessment of the Hearth Tax, particularly as there was a degree of confusion over which hearths were in fact liable to be taxed – particularly forges and ovens.[96] It should be remembered that the numbers of people who experienced a decline in hearths may be underestimated. Londoners who suffered a marked decline in social standing after the Fire may have been excluded from the Hearth Tax by reason of poverty, become lodgers or even left London altogether. The direction of residential movement affected the changes in numbers of hearths per household. Residential movement into two of the higher social status areas of London – the City within the Walls and the western suburbs – tended to be more associated with an increase in number of hearths. When Ward Deakes moved from Three Legg Alley in St Dunstan-in-the-West in

St Paul Covent Garden, his assessment went up from four to ten hearths.[97] Over half of the movement within the Walls was associated with an increase in number of hearths per household. The majority of movement east, north and south of the Walls tended to represent either no gain or a loss in the number of hearths per household, perhaps suggesting that the size of houses in these areas tended to be smaller, and that movement in these directions tended to represent more of a downward shift in social status. Women were less likely to experience growth in number of hearths, with just over 10 per cent increasing by more than two, compared to over one-quarter of men.

Over 90 per cent of the data for all of the linked Londoners was in the range of a loss or gain of four hearths, although there were some notable outliers. The biggest decline in number of hearths was twenty, which was experienced by one of London's aristocratic residents. George Digby, Second Earl of Bristol was a Royalist who had been forced into exile during the Interregnum. In 1666 Bristol answered for forty hearths for his mansion on Great Queen Street in St Giles-in-the-Fields. The property had been occupied by his father John, who was a Royalist supporter who died in exile in 1653. In 1644 Parliament had confiscated the house for reason of 'his treason against the Parliament and people of England'. The house had served as the official London residence of Sir Thomas Fairfax, the Parliamentary commander-in-chief. After the Restoration, the house was returned to Bristol, but in around 1667 it was acquired by William Cavendish, Third Earl of Devonshire. Bristol did not move far. His new house, in the same parish, was assessed for a mere twenty hearths in 1675, and was a short walk away on the west side of Lincoln's Inn Fields.[98] The largest absolute decline in hearths by someone who was fired was thirteen, experienced by Richard Sackville, Fifth Earl of Dorset. In 1666 his property on Salisbury Court in St Bride Fleet Street was assessed for twenty-eight hearths. Since 1629 there had been a small theatre on the grounds of the house, but it was badly damaged by Parliamentarian soldiers in 1649. Along with London's other theatres, it was re-opened after the Restoration. After the Fire a new theatre, possibly designed by Sir Christopher Wren, was built nearby, opening in 1671. Dorset himself did not remain in the same location, but moved west to a fifteen-hearth household on Drury Lane in St Giles-in-the-Fields.[99] In these cases, the decline in the number of hearths did not mean a decline in the relative status of a household. An example of a decline in the relative status of a household matching a decline in the number of hearths is provided by Praise Russell, who in 1666 was assessed for seven hearths for a house on the north side of Carter Lane in St Gregory by St Paul. By 1675 he had moved to a smaller three-hearth household in King Street, Spitalfields Hamlet in St Dunstan Stepney. This type of move, from the centre of the City to the less salubrious East End, and a smaller residence, represented a significant loss of status in the prestige of location.

The largest positive change in number of hearths was thirty-seven. Anthony Ashley Cooper, Lord Ashley had been one of the prime movers of the Restoration, was Charles II's Chancellor of the Exchequer from 1661 to 1672 and had been personally involved in the effort to battle the Fire. In 1666 his residence in the Savoy had been assessed for nineteen hearths. He was raised to Earl of Shaftesbury in 1672. Perhaps as part of his ascension, he increased the size of his house, which had fifty-six hearths in 1675.[100] By this time Shaftesbury was the main opponent of Charles II's regime as well as the chief proponent of excluding the Catholic Duke of York from the succession. Shaftesbury was imprisoned in the Tower from 1677 to 1678 and was involved in plotting against the king. Fearing prosecution for high treason, Shaftesbury fled to Amsterdam, where he died in 1683. The greatest increase in hearths for an individual who had been fired was thirteen. Henry Hothersall was a Citizen and Vintner based on Fleet Street. His tavern and messuage, the Globe, was assessed at eighteenth hearths in 1666. He had leased it from Francis Bragg Esquire in 1649 for £75 per annum plus ten gallons of 'Canary Sack' and at the time of the Fire his lease had twenty-three years to run. Hothersall wanted to rebuild but demanded a small parcel of additional land to give him access to Shoe Lane so he could bring in wine more easily. The Fire Court, which sometimes encouraged some tenants to rebuild by increasing the size of their plots, agreed to this. In addition, Hothersall was given a new lease of sixty-one years and his rent was reduced to £40 per annum. Thus Hothersall's establishment probably increased in size, as the number of hearths in his property increased to thirty-one in 1675.[101] These case studies illustrate some of the different factors surrounding change in number of hearths.

Given that there was a rough gradient of how socially desirable an address in seventeenth-century London was, it is possible to assign each type of move a rough nominal value.[102] Therefore, a move from a street to a yard is given a value of minus three, whilst a move from an alley to a lane is given a value of plus one. A move to the same type of locale is thus socially neutral and given a value of zero. However, these nominal values can be no more than estimates, as they do not take into account the relative prestige of neighbourhood. For example, Percival Gilborn moved within the parish of St Benet Sherehog from a six-hearth house on the south side of Bucklersbury, which ran off Cheapside, to a larger nine-hearth house on nearby Grocers' Alley. In comparison Grace Batchelor moved from a one-hearth house on the south side of Fenchurch Street in St Benet Gracechurch to another one-hearth house in Steile Alley, off Houndsditch in St Botolph without Aldgate, after the Fire.[103] Both these moves were given a nominal value of minus three, even though the latter move represented a greater decline in the relative prestige of address as it was associated with movement to a less prestigious area whilst the former move was very short range and presumably to a larger property. The nominal values thus can only represent a fairly broad spectrum, not a precise 'value' of the social desirability of a residential move.

Table 3.5 Changing locality of nominally linked Londoners from the Hearth Tax, c. 1666 and 1675 (%)

Pre-Fire	Post-Fire	Directly Affected by Fire	Unaffected by Fire	Total
Street	Street	17.0	14.8	15.8
	Lane	8.2	5.4	6.6
	Alley	6.6	9.0	8.0
	Yard	8.2	7.5	7.8
Lane	Street	8.9	8.0	8.4
	Lane	6.2	1.7	3.6
	Alley	3.0	3.6	3.4
	Yard	5.9	3.9	4.7
Alley	Street	7.2	9.3	8.4
	Lane	1.0	1.9	1.5
	Alley	1.6	8.3	5.4
	Yard	3.6	7.3	5.7
Yard	Street	9.5	9.5	9.5
	Lane	3.9	2.7	3.2
	Alley	2.6	3.4	3.1
	Yard	6.6	3.7	4.9
	Total	**100 (305)**	**100 (411)**	**100 (716)**

Sources: See Table 3.1.

Note: 'Rents', 'Courts' and 'Tenements' were classified with the 'Yard' group. Does not include 277 people who moved for whom there was insufficient information to determine locality.

Overall, it appears that roughly similar proportions of moves were 'positive' (34.1 per cent), 'neutral' (29.7 per cent) or 'negative' (36.2 per cent). It is striking that change in locality, rather than stability, was the norm. Over 70 per cent of residential movement was accompanied by some change in locality. As Table 3.5 shows, this was overall trend was broadly consistent regardless of whether an individual was fired or not. However, women were slightly less likely to have 'positive' moves than men. The area into which an individual moved had an impact on if was to a more desirable location. Movements south of the river appear to have been most associated with a 'downward' movement in locality, with nearly two-thirds of such moves being 'negative'. Movement into the City within the Walls from areas unaffected by the Fire appeared to have been accompanied by an increase in the relative status of a location. Sir Joseph Sheldon was a Citizen and Draper who originated from Derbyshire and was the nephew of Gilbert Sheldon, Archbishop of Canterbury. A Royalist, Sheldon later served as Lord Mayor of London from 1675 to 1676. In 1666 he answered for a household of thirty-six hearths in Half Moon Alley in St Botolph without Aldersgate, but by 1675 he had moved to one of nineteen hearths in Paul's Churchyard.

Sheldon had paid to have the foundations for his new house staked out on 24 April 1668.[104] Although he was moving to a smaller household, he was relocating from an alley to one of England's most famed commercial districts, which would have helped his trade as tallow chandler. Like many other Londoners with enough cash or credit to rebuild, Sheldon took advantage of the beneficial terms being offered for people willing to build in the fired areas of the City as an opportunity to upgrade the status of their address.

The effect of occupation and status on movement

It is axiomatic that socio-economic status would have had a significant bearing on an individual's ability to recover from the Fire. Occupation had an impact on the initial reaction to the Fire. Those in retail trades that relied on large amounts of movable goods (for example, the booksellers) would have been especially damaged as they would have almost certainly lost most of their stock. The lack and expense of carts during the Fire made it probable that tradesmen would suffer heavy losses unless they were able to pay high prices for carts. Dealers would have suffered disproportionately more from the Fire than craftsmen, whose stock of unfinished materials would have been worth less on the whole. When Daniel Berry's wharf on Cousin Lane in All Hallows the Great burned down he lost £500 of stock.[105] The vintner Richard Hilliard lost £200 in wines and goods when his establishment, the St John's Head on Chancery Lane in St Andrew Holborn, was pulled down to stop the flames spreading west.[106] As a result of the small amounts of gold and silver currency in circulation, in 1666 most Londoners did not have cash as a sizeable part of their assets. Cash compromised no more than 5 per cent of the gross assets for the 'middling sort' in early modern London. Even the wealthiest merchants' cash assets rarely exceeded £500, and this was usually in the form of plate. Investment in property was also common across all ranks of London society. If these properties were in the burned area of London, their loss was potentially disastrous. For example, Ellen Carlyle owned a nine-hearth property off Fleet Street in St Bride Fleet Street, which she leased to William Bowdler, a draper. She claimed the annual rent of £50 was the 'sole livelihood of . . . her and her children'. Bowdler could afford to rebuild, but refused to do so until he had been paid back for the goods and fixtures destroyed in the Fire. The Fire Court ordered Bowdler to rebuild. His rent remained the same but forty-two years was added to his lease and Carlyle would contribute £150, to be paid out of the rent.[107] As a result of their losses many Londoners would have been forced to borrow to finance their post-Fire recovery. Wealthier individuals and those in more prestigious occupations had easier access to credit, which was linked to an individual's personal wealth.[108] Many wealthy individuals had substantial resources in money owed to them. Sir William Turner was a wealthy woollen draper and silk merchant who was a Puritan conformist supportive of dissenters when he served as Lord Mayor from 1668 to 1669 (later he became a pro-court Tory). Before the Fire he lived in an eleven-hearth property in a 'little court' near the cathedral, and in 1675 he answered for fourteen hearths for a house in nearby Paul's Churchyard. Turner was owed £19,937 in 'bonds and other securities' up to 12 December 1666.[109] Although many of these debts may have had to be deferred or discounted as a result of the Fire, Turner would have still had a large resource to fall back on to insulate him from his losses as a result of the Fire. This is an extreme example, but it does show how wealthier Londoners were relatively economically insulated from some of the adverse effects of the Fire. Therefore, it would have been easier for richer people to either rebuild within the Walls or to move to a relatively prestigious area after the Fire.

The Lady Day 1666 Hearth Tax assessments for the City within the Walls (along with St Botolph without Aldersgate) included information about occupation at far higher rates than the other listings used for this chapter. Even so, occupations in this area were only included for 13.5 per cent of male householders (4.1 per cent were listed with some kind of social rank such as 'Mr', 'Esq', or 'gentleman') and 2.6 per cent of females. Given this low level of detail, the Hearth Taxes alone cannot be used to accurately assess London's occupational structure. However, the occupations of householders provide another prism through which the recovery from the Fire can be viewed.

The gentry and those entitled 'Mr' moved into the West End in high numbers after the Fire. Mr Deane Burgesse, a lawyer, moved west from a seven-hearth household on Ironmonger Lane in St Martin Pomary to an eight-hearth property in St Martin's Lane in the St Martin-in-the-Fields.[110] However, this group was also more likely than other groups to remain in the same location before and after the Fire. Craftsmen were generally more likely to move north or south of the Walls than dealers, and less likely to remain within the Walls. Selling groups were more reliant on being based close to customers in the City, whereas craftsmen could afford to be more mobile. Before the Fire, Francis Ellison, a merchant, and John Granes, a cooper, were both based in Marke Lane in All Hallows Staining. After the Fire, Ellison moved to nearby Blanchampleton Court whilst Granes moved east to St Katherine's Street in St Botolph without Aldgate.[111]

Case study: two neighbourhoods after the Fire

Although there had been a large degree of continuity in the street layout of the fired areas, the recovery was nonetheless disruptive in many respects, destabilising real estate and contributing to the increased fluidity of neighbourhoods.[112] To gain a greater insight into recovery from the Fire at the local level after Fire, individuals from two neighbourhoods were examined. The boundaries were chosen along parish lines, which was the principal way in which early modern Londoners referred to where they resided.[113] The first neighbourhood was positioned around St Paul's Cathedral, along the boundaries of St Gregory by St Paul's, which covered about eleven acres. The area was most associated with the book trade. It experienced high levels of residential persistence after the Fire. The second neighbourhood was positioned around Pudding Lane, where the Fire started. Its boundaries were comprised of four riverside parishes: St Michael Crooked Lane, St Magnus the Martyr, St Botolph Billingsgate and St Mary-at-Hill (whose combined area was about the same size as St Gregory by St Paul's). It included the area where the Fire had started and the approaches to London Bridge. According to the 1638 Listing of London, St Gregory by St Paul's was the wealthier area, with 34 per cent 'substantial households' compared to 22 per cent for the riverside parishes. It was also less densely populated, with 18.1 houses per acre compared to 38.4 in the riverside parishes.[114]

The Lady Day 1666 Hearth Tax assessments showed the significant difference between the two neighbourhoods. In St Gregory by St Paul's there were a total of 319 households (8.5 per cent of which were empty) assessed, compared to 472 (of which 4.4 per cent were empty) in the four riverside parishes. The mean number of hearths per household assessed before the Fire was 5.4 for St Gregory by St Paul's, and 4.5 for the riverside parishes. The largest property by number of hearths (twenty-seven) in St Gregory by St Paul's was the house of the Dean of St Paul's. There were two inns in St Gregory by St Paul's, the Bell and the Mermaid, both owned by Richard Pilley. Also resident in the parish, both in eleven-hearth households were two future Lord Mayors: the subsequently disgraced Sir William Bolton and Sir William Turner.[115] There were also substantial properties in the riverside parishes, including Thomas Ogden's of twenty-four hearths on the south side of East Cheap, as well as at least three inns – two on Fish Street Hill and one on Thames Street.[116] In the riverside parishes around one in ten of the householders were women, compared to one in twenty in St Gregory by St Paul's. Finally, 7.7 per cent of the individuals assessed in St Gregory by St Paul's had a title (from 'Mr.' upwards), compared to 2.0 per cent for the riverside parishes. Clearly, the neighbourhood around St Paul's was wealthier and more prestigious than the riverside neighbourhood in 1666.

There were twenty-five linked individuals from St Gregory by St Paul's and twenty-three from the riverside parishes. For both neighbourhoods one-third remained in their pre-Fire residence, which was higher than average for the fired areas of London. Inhabitants of both neighbourhoods moved to adjacent areas over one-third of the time. Amongst those who moved from both neighbourhoods two-thirds of St Gregory by St Paul's and four-fifths of the riverside parishes stayed in the City within the Walls. Movement east and north occurred at roughly similar levels. Movement to Southwark seems to have (unsurprisingly) been more associated with the riverside parishes. Higher proportions of movement from St Gregory by St Paul's were westward, and two of the linked individuals were traced to around the fashionable Covent Garden area, where none of the riverside group relocated to. For both neighbourhoods the average change in hearths per household was similar, at 1.4 for St Gregory by St Paul's and 1.5 for the riverside parishes. The main difference in the post-Fire movement from the two neighbourhoods appears was the relative social prestige of the move. Over two-thirds of the linked individuals from St Gregory by St Paul's increased the prestige of their locality after the Fire, whereas only one from the riverside parishes did.

A closer look at some of the moves also illustrates how the social space of the neighbourhood transcended the trauma of recovering from disaster. Two pairs of near linked individuals were near neighbours both before and after Fire. Peter Prince and Edward Wakeford lived in nearly adjacent properties on Thames Street in St Magnus the Martyr before the Fire, both relocating to nearby King's Head Court by 1675.[117] Such relationships also existed across longer moves across the metropolis. Before the Fire, Charles Hinton and Nicholas Alexander were both located on Paternoster Row. After the Fire, they moved to adjacent streets in St Paul Covent Garden: Hinton to Henrietta Street, Alexander to Bedford Street.[118] Such links are likely to be the tip of the iceberg, given how important the bonds of neighbourhood were in forming networks of social support in early modern London. It was likely that many individuals' choice of a new location after the Fire may have been influenced somewhat by the presence of a neighbour from before the Fire there.

Conclusions

The Great Fire of London significantly affected London's residential structure. This impact was not felt uniformly by all groups of society – and personal circumstances before the Fire appear to have had a significant impact on patterns of recovery after the disaster. After the Fire, the number of hearths per household in the rebuilt areas rose significantly. The average numbers of hearths did not change to such a degree in areas of London not directly affected by the Fire. There remained considerable numbers of uninhabited houses as well as unused plots of land after the Fire. Empty houses had been a part of the urban landscape before the Fire due to the 1665 Plague, but after the Fire they became more concentrated in areas not affected by the Fire. In areas not destroyed by the Fire the housing stock was more utilised – probably by those forced into moving household because of the Fire. For many Londoners burnt out by the Fire, it may have been an unattractive prospect to return to one's original place of household due to the costs of rebuilding.

The nominally linked Hearth Tax records show that movement, even amongst groups of Londoners not burnt out, was commonplace – although being burnt out did increase the proportional likelihood of moving household. More than two-thirds of individuals who were not fired moved household, whilst over 85 per cent of those burnt out moved household. However, these movements had different characteristics. Although nearly half of all movement was relatively short-distance, burnt-out groups were more likely to move longer distances. Individuals directly affected by the Fire appear to have been more likely to move into different areas of

London, although relatively few moved south of the Thames. Shifts in the relative status of a household were measured by changes in the number of hearths and in the relative prestige of the location of the household. Over half of those who were burnt out increased the number of hearths in their household. Individuals who remained within the City or who moved westward were more likely to increase the number of hearths per household. It appears the latter type of movement was thus more associated with a downward shift in house size. Changes in the typology of locality were commonplace – only around one-third of individuals moving after the Fire moved to a similar locality. Movement south and east in particular appears, again, to have been more associated with a 'downward' shift in the prestige of address, whereas other movements tended to be more likely to be 'upward'.

Closer examination of residential persistence and movement after the Fire showed that these variables were highly contingent on individual wealth and status. Individuals from relatively more socially prestigious localities appear to have been more likely to return to their pre-Fire address. This may be because the 'better sort' were more strongly integrated into local social networks, and also because they would have been more likely to have the financial resources to rebuild. However, as the case study shows, neighbourhood persistence appears to have occurred even from relatively poorer areas. They seem to have transcended the difficulties of rebuilding and been 'recreated' elsewhere in London, sometimes quite far afield from the original locality. This apparent residential stability after the Fire perhaps explains, or was resultant from, the social stability of London as a whole in the seventeenth century.[119] Londoners, in spite of their material losses after the Fire, were able to go some way in attempting to recreate their social space as it existed before the disaster.

Despite the widespread destruction that the Fire caused, the area it destroyed showed remarkable long-term stability in many respects. Gregg Carr, using a comparison of the 1638 tithe assessments and the 1695 Marriage Tax, concluded that the structure of the reconstructed City within the Walls remained fairly similar over this period, with high rents and wealth in the centre, a surrounding poorer zone and concentrations of wealth in the western limits. In addition, the distribution of substantial households was similar in 1638 compared to 1695. The basic housing statistics of the City appeared to be stable during the seventeenth century. It was in the suburbs that the greatest changes in London's population structure were experienced in the seventeenth century. The growing size of the suburbs meant there were more economic opportunities there.[120] By the beginning of the eighteenth century, the City within the Walls had a population of 70,000. In absolute terms the area's population was more or less unchanged since the Fire but in relative terms its share of London's population had declined from about one-third to one-seventh.[121]

Notes

1 R.B. Shoemaker, 'Gendered Spaces: Patterns of Mobility and Perceptions of London's Geography, 1660–1750', in *Imagining Early Modern London: Perceptions and Portrayals of the City from Stow to Strype, 1598–1720*, ed. J.F. Merritt (Cambridge: Cambridge University Press, 2001), 153, 155, 159.

2 J.P. Boulton, 'Neighbourhood Migration in Early Modern London', in *Migration and Society in Early Modern England*, ed. P. Clark and D. Souden (London: Hutchinson, 1987), 119.

3 Shoemaker, 'Gendered Spaces', 155; Boulton, 'Neighbourhood Migration', 123–4.

4 P.E. Jones, ed., *The Fire Court: Calendar to the Judgments and Decrees of the Court of Judicature Appointed to Determine Differences between Landlords and Tenants as to Rebuilding after the Great Fire*, 2 vols. (London: The Corporation of London, 1966–70), i, 145–6.

5 Jones, ed., *The Fire Court*, i, 29–30.

6 S. Porter, *The Great Fire of London* (Stroud: Sutton, 1996), 118.

7 Jones, ed., *The Fire Court*, i, 52.

8 C. Spence, *London in the 1690s: A Social Atlas* (London: Centre for Metropolitan History, 2000), 66; J.P. Boulton, 'Food Prices and the Standard of Living in London in the "Century of Revolution", 1580–1700', *Economic History Review*, 53 (2000), 462, 469, 477.

9 Rolls, *Burning of London*, part 3, 35–7.

10 M.M. Verney, ed., *Memoirs of the Verney Family from the Restoration to the Revolution 1660 to 1696* (London: Longmans, Green, and Co, 1899), 143.

11 W.C. Baer, 'The Institution of Residential Investment in Seventeenth-Century London', *Business History Review*, 76 (2002), 539; Jones, ed., *The Fire Court*, i, 144–5.

12 TNA, Hearth Tax Assessment Listing, City of London and parts of Middlesex, 1666, E179/252/32, Part 1, fol. 6v; Jones, ed., *The Fire Court*, ii, 253–4.

13 TNA, E179/252/32, Part 8/2, fol. 13v; Jones, ed., *The Fire Court*, i, 246.

14 LMA, Court of Common Council: City Lands Committee Papers, COL/CC/CLC/04/001, Box 1, 1.

15 T.F. Reddaway, *The Rebuilding of London after the Great Fire* (London: Jonathan Cape, 1940), 112, 115–16, 248.

16 T.M.M. Baker, *London: Rebuilding the City after the Great Fire* (Chichester: Phillimore, 2000), 7.

17 Verney, ed., *Memoirs of the Verney Family*, 145.

18 LMA, COL/CC/CLC/04/001, Box 1, 35.

19 LMA, Rep. 77, fol. 219v.

20 LMA, Rep. 78, fol. 126v.

21 W.G. Bell, *The Great Fire of London* (1st ed. London: John Lane, 1920), 272.

22 J.P. Ward, *Metropolitan Communities: Trade Guilds, Identity, and Change in Early Modern London* (Stanford, CA: Stanford University Press, 1997), 43; Boulton, 'Food Prices', 462, 469, 477; D. Keene, 'Growth, Modernisation and Control: The Transformation of London's Landscape, *c.* 1500-*c.* 1760', in *Two Capitals: London and Dublin 1500–1840*, ed. P. Clark and R. Gillespie (Oxford and London: Oxford University Press for the British Academy, 2001), 22.

23 GL, Broadside 20.109, *Reasons Humbly Offered to the Parliament for the Abatement of the Proportion of the Assessment upon the City of London*, 1672.

24 LMA, Rep. 78, fol. 27r.

25 Baker, *London*, 7.

26 J.P. Boulton, 'London 1540–1700', in *The Cambridge Urban History of Britain, Volume II 1540–1840*, ed. P. Clark (Cambridge: Cambridge University Press, 2000), 317; Keene, 'Growth, Modernisation and Control', 8.

27 Jones, ed., *The Fire Court*, i, 211–12.

28 Jones, ed., *The Fire Court*, i, 250–1.

29 Jones, ed., *The Fire Court*, ii, 272; TNA, E179/252/32, Part 3, fol. 3r; Hearth Tax Assessment Listing, City of London and parts of Middlesex, 1674/5, E179/243/380, fol. 84r.

30 Jones, ed., *The Fire Court*, i, 72.

31 More Detailed Accounts of the Hearth Tax's History Can Be Found in: C.D. Chandaman, *The English Public Revenue, 1660–1688* (Oxford: Clarendon Press, 1975), 77–109; T. Arkell, 'Printed Instructions for Administering the Hearth Tax', in *Surveying the People: The Interpretation and Use of Document Sources for the Study of Population in the Later Seventeenth Century*, ed. K. Schürer and T. Arkell (Oxford: Leopard's Head Press, 1992), 38–64.

32 Chandaman, *English Public Revenue*, 8.

33 E. Parkinson, 'The Administration of the Hearth Tax in Metropolitan London and Middlesex', in *London and Middlesex 1666 Hearth Tax*, ed. M. Davies et al. (London: British Record Society, 2014), 58, 72; V. Harding, 'London and Middlesex in the 1660s', in *London and Middlesex 1666 Hearth Tax*, ed. M. Davies et al. (London: British Record Society, 2014), 26.

34 J. Patten, 'The Hearth Taxes, 1662–1689', *Local Population Studies*, 7 (1971), 15.

35 Parkinson, 'Administration of the Hearth Tax', 58.

36 W.C. Baer, 'Landlords and Tenants in London, 1550–1700', *Urban History*, 38 (2011), 234.

37 T. Arkell, 'The Incidence of Poverty in England in the Later Seventeenth Century', *Social History*, 12 (1987), 30.

38 M.J. Power, 'The Social Topography of Restoration London', in *London 1500–1700: The Making of the Metropolis*, ed. A.L. Beier and R.A.P. Finlay (London and New York: Longman, 1986), 212; M.J. Braddick, *The Nerves of State: Taxation and the Financing of the English State, 1558–1714* (Manchester: Manchester University Press, 1996), 102.

39 C. Husbands, 'Hearths, Wealth and Occupations: An Exploration of the Hearth Tax in the Later Seventeenth Century', in *Surveying the People: The Interpretation and Use of Document Sources for the Study of Population in the Later Seventeenth Century*, ed. K. Schürer and T. Arkell (Oxford: Leopard's Head Press, 1992), 75; W.C. Baer, 'Housing the Poor and Mechanick Class in Seventeenth-Century London', *London Journal*, 25 (2000), 24.

40 M. Spufford, 'The Scope of Local History, and the Potential of the Hearth Tax Returns', *The Local Historian*, 30 (2000), 204; Husbands, 'Hearths, Wealth and Occupations', 73–4; N. Goose, 'How Accurately Do the Hearth Tax Returns Reflect Wealth? A Discussion of Some Urban Evidence', *Local Population Studies*, 67 (2001), 55.

41 T. Arkell, 'Identifying Regional Variations from the Hearth Tax', *The Local Historian*, 33 (2003), 165; J. Langton, 'Residential Patterns in Pre-Industrial Cities: Some Case Studies from Seventeenth-Century Britain', *Transactions of the Institute of British Geographers*, 65 (1975), 8.

42 Patten, 'Hearth Taxes', 18.

43 Arkell, 'Incidence of Poverty', 32–6, 46.

44 Arkell, 'Identifying Regional Variations', 152.

45 The listings used were: TNA, E179/252/32; Royal Subsidy Listing, Westminster, 1664, E179/143/385; Hearth Tax Assessment Listing, Surrey, 1664/6, E179/258/4, 1664/6. These were supplemented by additional listings in the printed version of the 1666 Hearth Tax in M. Davies et al., eds., *London and Middlesex 1666 Hearth Tax* (London: British Record Society, 2014).

46 The listings used were: TNA, E179/243/380; Hearth Tax Assessment Listing, Surrey, 1673, E179/188/504; Hearth Tax Assessment Listing, Westminster, 1675, E179/253/25.

47 LMA, *Lists (Fifteen in Number) of the Inhabitants, Whose Houses Were Destroyed in the Great Fire of 1666*, Alchin Papers Box F/no. 65 COL/AC/06/006.

48 St Sepulchre Holborn, St Ethelburga Bishopsgate, St Helen Bishopsgate, St Andrew Undershaft, St Katherine Cree, St James Dukes Place, Holy Trinity Minories and St Andrew Holborn.

49 A. Wareham, 'The Hearth Tax and Empty Properties in London on the Eve of the Great Fire', *The Local Historian*, 41 (2011), 279, 285.

50 Power, 'Social Topography', 200–1.

51 I. Doolittle, 'Property Law and Practice in Seventeenth-Century London', *Urban History*, 42 (2015), 213.

52 They are: All Hallows Staining, St Alban Wood Street, St Alphage London Wall, St Andrew Hubbard, St Antholin Budge Row, St George Botolph Lane, St Katherine Coleman, St Mary Aldermanbury, St Mary Magdalen Milk Street, St Mary-at-Hill, St Mary-le-Bow, St Michael Wood Street and St Olave Hart Street.

53 W.C. Baer, 'Using Housing Quality to Track Change in the Standard of Living and Poverty for Seventeenth-Century London', *Historical Methods: A Journal of Quantitative and Interdisciplinary History*, 47 (2014), 14.

54 Wareham, 'Hearth Tax', 285–6.

55 Spence used the 1693–4 property assessment for his calculations. Spence, *London in the 1690s*, 58–9.

56 J. Thirsk and J.P. Cooper, eds., *Seventeenth-Century Economic Documents* (Oxford: Clarendon Press, 1972), 771, 793.

57 Baker, *London*, 12.

58 TNA, E179/252/23, fol. 95v.

59 By 1676–80, the mean number of burials per annum in St Bride Fleet Street was 355.6 – a return to pre-Fire levels, and a reflection of the resettlement of the parish. T. Birch, ed., *A Collection of the Yearly Bills of Mortality, from 1657 to 1758 Inclusive* (London: A. Millar, 1759), 54–63, 78–97.

60 Baer, 'Housing the Poor', 13, 21–2, 28–30.

61 A.L. Erickson, 'Marital Status and Economic Activity: Interpreting Spinsters, Wives, and Widows in Pre-Census Population Listings', Cambridge Working Papers in Economic and Social History, number 7, 2012. Accessed 31 January 2017, www.econsoc.hist.cam.ac.uk/docs/CWPESH%20number%207%207%20July%202012.pdf, 12–13.

62 P. Earle, *A City Full of People: Men and Women of London 1650–1750* (London: Methuen, 1994), xii.

63 LPL, Court of Arches Depositions 1665–1668, MS Film 147, Eee 2, fol. 208r.

64 Of these, five moved north just after the Fire, three moved east, two moved west and one moved south.

65 P. Clark, 'The Multi-Centred Metropolis: The Social and Cultural Landscapes of London, 1600–1840', in *Two Capitals: London and Dublin 1500–1840*, ed. P. Clark and R. Gillespie (Oxford and London: Oxford University Press for the British Academy, 2001), 241.

66 TNA, E179/252/32, Part 1, fol. 6v, Part 16, fols. 2r, 6r; E179/252/23, fols. 88r, 89r; D. Keene and V. Harding, *Historical Gazetteer of London before the Great Fire: Cheapside; Parishes of All Hallows Honey Lane, St Martin Pomary, St Mary Le Bow, St Mary Colechurch and St Pancras Soper Lane* (London: Centre for Metropolitan History, 1987), 187–96, 475–85, 782–90.

67 TNA, E179/252/32, Part 4, fol. 3r; E179/252/23, fol. 89v.

68 TNA, E179/252/32, Part 11/1, fol. 23r; E179/252/23, fol. 70r.

69 V.E. Brodsky, 'Widows in Late Elizabethan London: Remarriage, Economic Opportunity and Family Orientations', in *The World We Have Gained: Histories of Population and Social Structure*, ed. L. Bonfield, R.M. Smith and K. Wrightson (Oxford: Basil Blackwell, 1986), 142–3.

70 *London and Middlesex 1666 Hearth Tax*, 1136, 1216; TNA, E179/143/370, fol. 25v; E179/253/25, fols. 16r, 17r.

71 TNA, 179/252/32, Part 8/1, fol. 6r; E179/253/25, fol. 20r.

72 *London and Middlesex 1666 Hearth Tax*, 1473; TNA, E179/143/370, fol. 41v.

73 *London and Middlesex 1666 Hearth Tax*, 1304; TNA, E179/143/370, fol. 58r.

74 I.W. Archer, *The Pursuit of Stability: Social Relations in Elizabethan London* (Cambridge: Cambridge University Press, 1991), 58–9, 74; J.P. Boulton, *Neighbourhood and Society: A London Suburb in the Seventeenth Century* (Cambridge: Cambridge University Press, 1987), 247.

75 Boulton, 'Neighbourhood Migration', 123–4; Shoemaker, 'Gendered Spaces', 155.

76 Keene and Harding, *Historical Gazetteer*, 421–5.

77 R.A.P. Finlay, *Population and Metropolis: The Demography of London 1580–1650*. Cambridge: Cambridge University Press, 1981, 46–7; Boulton, 'Neighbourhood Migration', 119.

78 GL, Records of the Merchant Taylors' Company: Registers of Apprentice Bindings, MS 34038/14, fol. 277; 34038/15, fol. 337; P. Mills and J. Oliver, *The Survey of the Building Sites in the City of London after the Great Fire of 1666*, ed. P.E. Jones, 5 vols. (London: London Topographical Society, 1962–7), i, 20; TNA, E179/252/23, fol. 106r. That part of Cannon Street was missing from the Lady Day 1666 assessment.

79 LPL, MS Film 147, Eee 2, fol. 455r; TNA, E179/252/23, fol. 91v.

80 LPL, MS Film 147, Eee 2, fol. 454v; TNA, E179/252/32, fol. 16r; Jones, ed., *The Fire Court*, i, 38.

81 TNA, E179/252/32, Part 3, fol. 4r; S. Pepys, *The Diary of Samuel Pepys*, ed. R. Latham and W. Matthews, 11 vols. (1st ed. London: G. Bell and Sons, 1970–83), vii, 68; viii, 82; Jones, ed., *The Fire Court*, i, 270.

82 E.A. Wrigley, 'A Simple Model of London's Importance in Changing English Society and Economy, 1650–1750', *Past and Present*, 37 (1967), 44–70; M.J. Kitch, 'Capital and Kingdom: Migrations to Later Stuart London', in *London 1500–1700: The Making of the Metropolis*, ed. A.L. Beier and R.A.P. Finlay (London and New York: Longman, 1986), 224–51; S.R. Smith, 'The Social and Geographical Origins of the London Apprentices, 1630–1660', *Guildhall Miscellany*, 4 (1973), 195–206.

83 A. Wood, *The Life and Times of Anthony Wood, Antiquary, of Oxford, 1632–1695, Described by Himself*, ed. A. Clark, 5 vols. (Oxford: Clarendon Press for the Oxford Historical Society, 1891–1907), 2, 86.

84 Baer, 'Landlords and Tenants', 237.

85 L. Stone, 'Residential Development of the West End of London in the Seventeenth Century', in *After the Reformation: Essays in Honor of J. H. Hexter*, ed. B.C. Malament (Philadelphia, PA: University of Pennsylvania Press, 1980), 194; R.M. Smuts, 'The Court and Its Neighbourhood: Royal Policy and Urban Growth in the Early Stuart West End', *Journal of British Studies*, 30 (1991), 126.

86 J. Evelyn, *The Diary of John Evelyn*, ed. E.S. De Beer, 6 vols. (Oxford: Clarendon Press, 1955), iii, 457; LMA, Rep. 85, fol. 142v.

87 TNA, E179/252/32, Part 6, fol. 10r; Part 4, fol. 7v; E179/252/23, fols. 99r, 90v.

88 C. Wall, *The Literary and Cultural Spaces of Restoration London* (Cambridge: Cambridge University Press, 1998), 51.

89 TNA, E179/252/32, Part 4, fol. 3v; E179/253/25, fol. 11r; E179/253/25, fol. 8v.

90 Boulton, *Neighbourhood and Society*, 47, 261.

91 C. Muldrew, *The Economy of Obligation: The Culture of Credit and Social Relations in Early Modern England* (Basingstoke: Macmillan, 1998), 95, 109–10, 138.

92 Husbands, 'Hearths, Wealth and Occupations', 75; Spufford, 'Scope of Local History', 204.

93 W.C. Baer, 'Early Retailing: London's Shopping Exchanges, 1550–1700', *Business History*, 49 (2007), 31.

94 Power, 'Social Topography', 210–2.

95 TNA, E179/252/32, Part 11, fol. 7r; E179/252/23, fol. 30v.

96 Arkell, 'Incidence', 33.

97 TNA, E179/252/32, Part 8/1, fol. 1v; E179/253/25, fol. 24r.

98 *London and Middlesex 1666 Hearth Tax*, 1138; TNA, E179/143/370, fol. 25v; Riley and Gomme, eds., *Survey of London: Volume 5, St Giles-in-The-Fields, Pt II*, 43–52.

99 TNA, E179/252/32, Part 8/2, fol. 28r; E179/143/370, fol. 26r.

100 *London and Middlesex 1666 Hearth Tax*, 1109; TNA, E179/143/370, fol. 21v.

101 Jones, ed., *The Fire Court*, i, 82–3; TNA, E179/252/32, fol. 25v; E179/243/380, fol. 95v.

102 Street=4; Lane=3; Alley=2; Yard, Court, Rents or Tenement=1.

103 TNA, E179/252/32, Part 3, fol. 11r, Part 19, fol. 6v; E179/252/23, fols. 47r, 89r.

104 TNA, E179/252/32, Part 11, fol. 8r; E179/252/23, fol. 76r; Mills and Oliver, *Survey*, i, 61; J.R. Woodhead, *The Rulers of London 1660–1689: A Biographical Record of the Aldermen and Common Councilmen of the City of London* (London: London and Middlesex Archaeological Society, 1965), 147.

105 Despite his losses Berry paid £700 to rebuild, and in return received a 25 per cent reduction in rent and an additional thirty-eight years on his lease. Jones, ed., *The Fire Court*, i, 134–5.

106 Hilliard had died by 1668 but his executors agreed to rebuild the property in exchange for an additional thirty-eight years on the lease. Jones, ed., *The Fire Court*, i, 262–1.

107 Bowdler remained on Fleet Street. In 1675 he was assessed for eight hearths for a house there. TNA, E179/252/32, Part 8/2, fol. 27v; E179/252/23, fol. 91v; Jones, ed., *The Fire Court*, 20–1.

108 Muldrew, *Economy of Obligation*, 98, 153; P. Earle, *The Making of the English Middle Class: Business, Society and Family Life in London, 1660–1730* (London: Methuen, 1989), 121; R.G. Grassby, 'English Merchant Capitalism in the Late Seventeenth Century: The Composition of Business Fortunes', *Past and Present*, 46 (1970), 90; Baer, 'Institution of Residential Investment', 518.

109 Woodhead, *Rulers of London*, 166; G.S. De Krey, *London and the Restoration, 1659–1683* (Cambridge: Cambridge University Press, 2005), 108, 312; GL, Sir William Turner, Stock Books, 1662–71, MS 5109/2, fol. 24v.

110 TNA, E179/252/32, Part 16, fol. 7v; E179/253/25, fol. 18v.

111 TNA, E179/252/32, Part 2/2, fol. 18r-v; E179/252/23, fol. 10r; E179/143/370, fol. 20r.

112 Wall, *Literary and Cultural Spaces*, 59–60.

113 Archer, *Pursuit of Stability*, 83.

114 Finlay, *Population and Metropolis*, 168–170.

115 TNA, E179/252/32, Part 5/3, fols. 18fr- 25v.

116 TNA, E179/252/32, Part 2/1, fols. 1r-2v; Part 4, fols. 3r-4v; Part 18, fols. 36v-41v.

117 TNA, E179/252/32, Part 4, fol. 4v; E179/252/23, fol. 90r.

118 TNA, E179/252/32, Part 5/3, fol. 18r; E179/253/25, fol. 23r.

119 Boulton, 'London 1540–1700', 327.

120 G. Carr, *Residence and Social Status: The Development of Seventeenth-Century London* (New York and London: Garland, 1990), 63, 90–1, 99, 106; Ward, *Metropolitan Communities*, 43.

121 L.D. Schwarz, *London in the Age of Industrialisation: Entrepreneurs, Labour Force and Living Conditions, 1700–1850* (Cambridge: Cambridge University Press, 1992), 7.

Reference list

Primary sources

Manuscript

GL, Broadside 20.109, *Reasons Humbly Offered to the Parliament, for the Abatement of the Proportion of the Assessment upon the City of London*, 1672.
GL, Records of the Merchant Taylors' Company: Registers of Apprentice Bindings, MS 34038/13–16, 1647–80.
GL, Sir William Turner, Stock Books, MS 5109/2, 1662–71.
LMA, Court of Common Council: City Lands Committee Papers, COL/CC/CLC/04/001, Box 1, 1666–79.
LMA, *Lists (Fifteen in Number) of the Inhabitants, Whose Houses Were Destroyed in the Great Fire of 1666*, Alchin Papers Box F/no. 65 COL/AC/06/006.
LMA, Repertory of the Court of Aldermen, Rep. 71–85, 1665–80.
LPL, Court of Arches Depositions 1665–1668, MS Film 147, Eee 2.
TNA, Hearth Tax Assessment Listing, City of London and Parts of Middlesex, E179/252/32, 1666.
TNA, Hearth Tax Assessment Listing, City of London and Parts of Middlesex, E179/252/23, 1675.
TNA, Hearth Tax Assessment Listing, Middlesex, E179/243/380, 1674/5.
TNA, Hearth Tax Assessment Listing, Surrey, E179/188/504, 1673.
TNA, Hearth Tax Assessment Listing, Surrey, E179/258/4, 1664/6.
TNA, Hearth Tax Assessment Listing, Westminster, E179/253/25, 1675.
TNA, Royal Subsidy Listing, Westminster, E179/143/385, 1664.

Printed

Birch, T., ed. *A Collection of the Yearly Bills of Mortality, from 1657 to 1758 Inclusive*. London: A. Millar, 1759.
Davies, M., Ferguson, C., Harding, V., Parkinson, E., and Wareham, A., eds. *London and Middlesex 1666 Hearth Tax*. London: British Record Society, 2014.
Evelyn, J. *The Diary of John Evelyn*, edited by E.S. De Beer, 6 vols. Oxford: Clarendon Press, 1955.
Jones, P.E., ed. *The Fire Court: Calendar to the Judgments and Decrees of the Court of Judicature Appointed to Determine Differences between Landlords and Tenants as to Rebuilding after the Great Fire*, 2 vols. London: The Corporation of London, 1966–70.
Mills, P. and Oliver, J. *The Survey of the Building Sites in the City of London after the Great Fire of 1666*, edited by P.E. Jones, 5 vols. London: London Topographical Society, 1962–7.
Pepys, S. *The Diary of Samuel Pepys*, edited by R. Latham and W. Matthews, 11 vols. 1st ed. London: G. Bell and Sons, 1970–83.
Rolls, S. *The Burning of London in the Year 1666*. London: R.I. for Thomas Parkhurst, Nathaniel Ranew and Jonathan Robinson, 1667.
Thirsk, J. and Cooper, J.P., eds. *Seventeenth-Century Economic Documents*. Oxford: Clarendon Press, 1972.
Verney, M.M., ed. *Memoirs of the Verney Family from the Restoration to the Revolution 1660 to 1696*. London: Longmans, Green, and Co, 1899.
Wood, A. *The Life and Times of Anthony Wood, Antiquary, of Oxford, 1632–1695, Described by Himself*, Volume 2, edited by A. Clark. Oxford: Clarendon Press for the Oxford Historical Society, 1891.

Secondary sources

Archer, I.W. *The Pursuit of Stability: Social Relations in Elizabethan London*. Cambridge: Cambridge University Press, 1991.

Arkell, T. 'The Incidence of Poverty in England in the Later Seventeenth Century', *Social History*, 12 (1987), 23–47.

Arkell, T. 'Printed Instructions for Administering the Hearth Tax'. In *Surveying the People: The Interpretation and Use of Document Sources for the Study of Population in the Later Seventeenth Century*, edited by K. Schürer and T. Arkell, 38–64. Oxford: Leopard's Head Press, 1992.

Arkell, T. 'Identifying Regional Variations from the Hearth Tax', *The Local Historian*, 33 (2003), 148–74.

Baer, W.C. 'Housing the Poor and Mechanick Class in Seventeenth-Century London', *London Journal*, 25 (2000), 13–39.

Baer, W.C. 'The Institution of Residential Investment in Seventeenth-Century London', *Business History Review*, 76 (2002), 515–51.

Baer, W.C. 'Early Retailing: London's Shopping Exchanges, 1550–1700', *Business History*, 49 (2007), 29–51.

Baer, W.C. 'Landlords and Tenants in London, 1550–1700', *Urban History*, 38 (2011), 234–55.

Baer, W.C. 'Using Housing Quality to Track Change in the Standard of Living and Poverty for Seventeenth-Century London', *Historical Methods: A Journal of Quantitative and Interdisciplinary History*, 47 (2014), 1–18.

Baker, T.M.M. *London: Rebuilding the City after the Great Fire*. Chichester: Phillimore, 2000.

Bell, W.G. *The Great Fire of London*. 1st ed. London: John Lane, 1920.

Boulton, J.P. *Neighbourhood and Society: A London Suburb in the Seventeenth Century*. Cambridge: Cambridge University Press, 1987.

Boulton, J.P. 'Neighbourhood Migration in Early Modern London'. In *Migration and Society in Early Modern England*, edited by P. Clark and D. Souden, 107–49. London: Hutchinson, 1987.

Boulton, J.P. 'Food Prices and the Standard of Living in London in the "Century of Revolution", 1580–1700', *Economic History Review*, 53 (2000), 455–92.

Boulton, J.P. 'London 1540–1700'. In *The Cambridge Urban History of Britain, Volume II 1540–1840*, edited by P. Clark, 315–46. Cambridge: Cambridge University Press, 2000.

Braddick, M.J. *The Nerves of State: Taxation and the Financing of the English State, 1558–1714*. Manchester: Manchester University Press, 1996.

Brodsky, V.E. 'Widows in Late Elizabethan London: Remarriage, Economic Opportunity and Family Orientations'. In *The World We Have Gained: Histories of Population and Social Structure*, edited by L. Bonfield, R.M. Smith and K. Wrightson, 122–54. Oxford: Basil Blackwell, 1986.

Chandaman, C.D. *The English Public Revenue 1660–1688*. Oxford: Clarendon Press, 1975.

Clark, P. 'The Multi-Centred Metropolis: The Social and Cultural Landscapes of London, 1600–1840'. In *Two Capitals: London and Dublin 1500–1840*, edited by P. Clark and R. Gillespie, 239–56. Oxford and London: Oxford University Press for the British Academy, 2001.

De Krey, G.S. *London and the Restoration, 1659–1683*. Cambridge: Cambridge University Press, 2005.

Doolittle, I. 'Property Law and Practice in Seventeenth-Century London', *Urban History*, 42 (2015), 202–24.

Earle, P. *The Making of the English Middle Class: Business, Society and Family Life in London, 1660–1730*. London: Methuen, 1989.

Earle, P. *A City Full of People: Men and Women of London, 1650–1750*. London: Methuen, 1994.

Erickson, A.L. 'Marital Status and Economic Activity: Interpreting Spinsters, Wives, and Widows in Pre-Census Population Listings', Cambridge Working Papers in Economic and Social History, number 7, 2012. Accessed 31 January 2017, www.econsoc.hist.cam.ac.uk/docs/CWPESH%20number%207%20July%202012.pdf.

Finlay, R.A.P. *Population and Metropolis: The Demography of London 1580–1650*. Cambridge: Cambridge University Press, 1981.

Goose, N. 'How Accurately Do the Hearth Tax Returns Reflect Wealth? A Discussion of Some Urban Evidence', *Local Population Studies*, 67 (2001), 44–63.

Grassby, R.G. 'English Merchant Capitalism in the Late Seventeenth Century: The Composition of Business Fortunes', *Past and Present*, 46 (1970), 87–107.

Harding, V. 'London and Middlesex in the 1660s'. In *London and Middlesex 1666 Hearth Tax*, edited by M. Davies, C. Ferguson, V. Harding, E. Parkinson and A. Wareham, 25–57. London: British Record Society, 2014.

Husbands, C. 'Hearths, Wealth and Occupations: An Exploration of the Hearth Tax in the Later Seventeenth Century'. In *Surveying the People: The Interpretation and Use of Document Sources for the Study of Population in the Later Seventeenth Century*, edited by K. Schürer and T. Arkell, 65–77. Oxford: Leopard's Head Press, 1992.

Keene, D. 'Growth, Modernisation and Control: The Transformation of London's Landscape, *c.* 1500–*c.* 1760'. In *Two Capitals: London and Dublin 1500–1840*, edited by P. Clark and R. Gillespie, 7–37. Oxford and London: Oxford University Press for the British Academy, 2001.

Keene, D. and Harding, V. *Historical Gazetteer of London before the Great Fire: Cheapside; Parishes of all Hallows Honey Lane, St Martin Pomary, St Mary Le Bow, St Mary Colechurch and St Pancras Soper Lane*. London: Centre for Metropolitan History, 1987.

Kitch, M.J. 'Capital and Kingdom: Migrations to Later Stuart London'. In *London 1500–1700: The Making of the Metropolis*, edited by A.L. Beier and R.A.P. Finlay, 224–51. London and New York: Longman, 1986.

Langton, J. 'Residential Patterns in Pre-Industrial Cities: Some Case Studies from Seventeenth-Century Britain', *Transactions of the Institute of British Geographers*, 65 (1975), 1–27.

Muldrew, C. *The Economy of Obligation: The Culture of Credit and Social Relations in Early Modern England*. Basingstoke: Macmillan, 1998.

Parkinson, E. 'The Administration of the Hearth Tax in Metropolitan London and Middlesex'. In *London and Middlesex 1666 Hearth Tex*, edited by M. Davies, C. Ferguson, V. Harding, E. Parkinson and A. Wareham, 58–76. London: British Record Society, 2014.

Patten, J. 'The Hearth Taxes, 1662–1689', *Local Population Studies*, 7 (1971), 14–27.

Porter, S. *The Great Fire of London*. Stroud: Sutton, 1996.

Power, M.J. 'The Social Topography of Restoration London'. In *London 1500–1700: The Making of the Metropolis*, edited by A.L. Beier and R.A.P. Finlay, 199–223. London and New York: Longman, 1986.

Reddaway, T.F. *The Rebuilding of London after the Great Fire*. London: Jonathan Cape, 1940.

Riley, E. and Gomme, L., eds. *Survey of London: Volume 5, St Giles-in-The-Fields, Pt II*. London: London County Council, 1914.

Shoemaker, R.B. 'Gendered Spaces: Patterns of Mobility and Perceptions of London's Geography, 1660–1750'. In *Imagining Early Modern London: Perceptions and Portrayals of the City from Stow to Strype, 1598–1720*, edited by J.F. Merritt, 144–65. Cambridge: Cambridge University Press, 2001.

Smith, S.R. 'The Social and Geographical Origins of the London Apprentices, 1630–1660', *Guildhall Miscellany*, 4 (1973), 195–206.

Smuts, R.M. 'The Court and Its Neighbourhood: Royal Policy and Urban Growth in the Early Stuart West End', *Journal of British Studies*, 30 (1991), 117–49.

Spence, C. *London in the 1690s: A Social Atlas*. London: Centre for Metropolitan History, 2000.

Spufford, M. 'The Scope of Local History, and the Potential of the Hearth Tax Returns', *The Local Historian*, 30 (2000), 202–21.

Stone, L. 'The Residential Development of the West End of London in the Seventeenth Century'. In *After the Reformation: Essays in Honor of J. H. Hexter*, edited by B.C. Malament, 167–212. Philadelphia, PA: University of Pennsylvania Press, 1980.

Wall, C. *The Literary and Cultural Spaces of Restoration London*. Cambridge: Cambridge University Press, 1998.

Ward, J.P. *Metropolitan Communities: Trade Guilds, Identity, and Change in Early Modern London*. Stanford, CA: Stanford University Press, 1997.

Wareham, A. 'The Hearth Tax and Empty Properties in London on the Eve of the Great Fire', *The Local Historian*, 41 (2011), 278–92.

Woodhead, J.R. *The Rulers of London 1660–1689: A Biographical Record of the Aldermen and Common Councilmen of the City of London*. London: London and Middlesex Archaeological Society, 1965.

Wrigley, E.A. 'A Simple Model of London's Importance in Changing English Society and Economy, 1650–1750', *Past and Present*, 37 (1967), 44–70.

4   London's economic topography after the Great Fire

In 1666 London was firmly at the heart of England's economy and becoming one of the most important centres of trade in Europe. London was the focus of land and sea transport networks and had a buoyant supply of labour and migrants who brought new ideas and streams of investment. The metropolis had grown to such prominence and size because it monopolised a number of functions. Most importantly, it was both England's seat of government and largest port. These two institutions, port and court, were the two largest foci of employment in London.[1] The metropolis was at the centre of the legal and medical professions as well as being the nation's most prominent centre of retail and consumption. The service sector, however, was not as large as manufacturing, which remained a vital part of London's economy. Early modern London was in the vanguard of industry in England, as well as being the largest and most diverse centre of production in England and perhaps even Europe.[2] At the time of the Fire, industry in London focussed on long-standing trades like brewing, metalworking and woollens as well as newer ones like the manufacture of silks, hats, glass and paper.[3] Much of this was to cater to the huge demand of the metropolis itself, as well as for national and international markets.[4] Despite the attention given to other areas of England, London too would play a major role in the Industrial Revolution. Increasingly, though, London lost simpler elements of manufacturing to provincial industrial centres and replaced it with the production of more sophisticated, high-quality finished goods and luxuries.[5] However, even in the early nineteenth century it employed more of the metropolitan workforce than the service sector, making London the largest manufacturing city by population in England (and thus the world).[6]

There was significant variation in London's economic topography. The City was strongly focussed on dealing and selling. There was some small-scale manufacturing there, mostly in side streets and alleys, but it tended to focus on the final stage of production.[7] Larger-scale manufacturing clustered in suburban areas, where it employed over two-thirds of the workforce. Textiles were the most important sector of metropolitan manufacturing, particularly areas like St Giles without Cripplegate and Spitalfields (then part of St Dunstan Stepney). However, there were few factories or large-scale works in London. Suburban areas were also highly geared to the transport sector. Land carriage was important in the northern and southern suburbs and shipping and related industries were mostly based in the East End. The West End was an important centre of services and professions catering to the needs of its elite residences. Increasingly it was becoming a more important commercial centre than the City.[8]

Given the Great Fire's destructiveness, it had the potential to seriously damage London's economy – particularly as it followed on from a damaging outbreak of disease and coincided with a foreign conflict. The Fire had made tens of thousands of Londoners homeless and severely disrupted metropolitan society. In 1666 London's economic activity was still inextricably bound to the household in many places, meaning that almost every house destroyed was potentially a workplace damaged and a business disrupted. The Fire destroyed a significant amount of London's economic fabric and trading stock. 'Rege Sincera' estimated the total losses were £7,335,000.[9] London's economic growth was a major component of national economic growth.[10] Therefore, the potential loss of wealth after the Fire was not just London's, it was also England's. Contemporaries were aware of this. A letter from Norwich written shortly after the Fire recorded that the people there were 'at their wits ends knowing not how to carry on trade bey the Reason of the sad fier at London'. Samuel Rolls wrote in 1667 that 'a great part of the strength and defence of all *England*, yea, of all the three Kingdomes, is lost and taken away, in and by the destruction of *London*'.[11] The Fire forced a major short-term disruption and redistribution of London's economic topography, as tradesmen and merchants attempted to reconstruct their economic lives. Examining London's economic recovery demonstrates how the metropolitan economy responded to crisis.

Not all Londoners recovered from the Fire. Many suffered from heavy debts in the aftermath of the disaster. In 1667 Edward Waterhouse called for the immediate payment of the debts of those made homeless by Fire, as many were ruined because they had no credit in the aftermath of the Fire.[12] This initiative never happened. Those owed money by the Crown had to resort to petitioning Charles II for payment. The jeweller John Le Roy requested £357 owed for a diamond ring that he had made for the king's mistress, Barbara Palmer, Countess of Castlemaine in November 1664. Prompt payment would ensure 'him self and family from ruine'. Similarly the vintner Elizabeth Proctor petitioned Charles II for payment of £600 furnished on the royal account by the Prussian ambassador in 1662, stressing the great losses she had suffered in the Fire.[13] Many were desperate enough to accept a loss on money owed to them. Samuel Pepys recorded in his diary on 5 May 1667 people were selling bills dating from before the Fire at a 35 per cent to 40 per cent loss.[14] The vintner Captain John Wadlow, who kept the Sun on Bartholomew Court behind the Royal Exchange, claimed to have had lost all of his stock in the Fire, leaving him unable to 'satisfy Bills of Exchange and mainteyne his Credit'. Wadlow overcame this and rebuilt and enlarged his establishment, which was assessed at thirty-one hearths in 1675.[15] Sir James Bunce, claimed that the Fire had 'consumed almost all . . . of his much impoverished and languishing Estate which did support and mainteyne himselfe, his Wife, and numerous Family' and that if his petition (for assignment of £5,776 owed him by Excise) was not granted he would be 'imprisoned, his Credit Estate wife and Children irreparably ruined'.[16] The destruction of houses devastated personal fortunes. Investment in property or leases was a common method of hedging against inflation. Wealthy Londoners usually held reserves of urban property as a major proportion of their fortune. Amongst the middling sort, around one-quarter of households had real estate investments, representing 21 per cent of their total wealth. Groups of lower social status also invested in real estate in the same proportions but it tended to count for higher proportions of their total wealth.[17] As such, the Fire could devastate estates and as most houses were held by multiple leases and sub-leases, all of which could be readily bought and sold, the destruction of a single house could damage multiple individuals. Some were able to weather the storm of the Fire. On 12 September 1666, Richard Pierce, who had been yeoman of the palace kitchen, petitioned Charles II for the right to trade in the livery hall of the Cooks' Company near Aldersgate, which had survived, claiming he had lost £4–5,000 as a result of the Fire. Three days later, Charles II wrote to the Cooks' Company asking them to allow Pierce to use their hall until 'it shall please God to restore him by his . . . industry to a condition of building . . . (a) Dwelling of his owne'. This gave Pierce the chance to reconstruct his business. On 28 August 1667 he paid for the setting out of foundations at his old house on Cannon Street in St Swithin London Stone, where he had been assessed for twelve hearths. He was still there in 1675, and slightly increased the size (or number of ovens) of his property, as the Hearth Tax assessed him for thirteen hearths.[18]

Economic disruption continued during the 1670s. In 1672, the City petitioned Parliament for a reduction in its taxation. The basis of this claim was that one-sixth of the City and its liberties remained unbuilt or uninhabited as well as the 'withdrawing . . . of several Inhabitants, to the Increase of Trade where they are gone and the Loss of it within the City'.[19] The City's government was so concerned with promoting economic growth after the Fire that in 1673 the freedom was granted to any person who would build in an empty plot in an area affected by Fire.[20] On 8 June 1675, the Court of Aldermen ordered that Peter Vandenanker 'having built severall houses in the Late ruines of this Citty and himself inhabited in one of them shall admitted into the freedome of this Citty by redempcon in the Company of Haberdashers'. The City paid his entry fine of forty-six shillings and eight pence.[21] That year Vandenanker was assessed for seven hearths for his property on Fenchurch Street, Langbourn Ward.[22] A 1675 pamphlet urging Charles II to grant more relief to London recorded that many of its inhabitants still laboured under the ill effects of the Fire. They faced the merciless fury of their Creditors upon them; where of the Prisons about *London* are severe Testimonies; as if they had been Men markt out by Divine vengeance . . . because of Debt, without any reflection upon the inevitable Hand of God that disabled them.[23]

Many, in the City government in particular, felt that the economic recovery was still incomplete nearly a decade after the Fire.

Examining the changes in the spatial distribution of metropolitan businesses shows what effect the Fire had on London's economic topography, and how this lasted. It shows how the Fire contributed to longer-term trends in metropolitan topography, in particular the growth of London in the western suburbs.[24] The place of business was a vital decision for Londoners, and highly important to their economic lives, as Michael Power points out – 'choice of residence was probably dictated by considerations of commercial advantage and rent, the two inextricably intertwined'.[25] In the aftermath of the Fire, the resettlement of London's traders and merchants was a vital and well-discussed issue. It is mentioned in William Wycherley's *Love in a Wood*, first performed at the Theatre Royal on Bridges Street by the Kings Company in spring 1671. In the play's first scene, Lady Flippant, the widowed sister of the lecherous Alderman Gripe says to Mrs Joyner of her search for a husband:

> 'Tis well known no woman breathing could use more industry to get her a husband than I have. Has not my husband's scutcheon walked as much ground as the citizens' signs since the fire, that no quarter of the town might be ignorant of the widow Flippant?'[26]

London's manufacturers, traders and merchants faced a stark decision after the Fire. The cost of rebuilding was prohibitive for many. Even if an individual did not take on the rebuilding themselves, they often had to pay compensation to their former landlord. There were also costs attached to moving elsewhere. To continue their economic lives at the same address as before the Fire was clearly not a straightforward decision, as it had to be weighed up against the expense of returning there, as well as the expenses already accrued in resettling immediately after the Fire. The post-Fire street layout and rebuilding regulations may have made a location less economically desirable. Many of the new houses were small and narrow because of the size of the plot. For example, John Owen refused to rebuild his house in St Mary Aldermary Churchyard because under the terms of the Rebuilding Act it would have lost two storeys, which he claimed in the Fire Court was 'too small for [his] trade'. Owen was allowed to surrender his lease upon payment of £50 to his landlord.[27]

The City government attempted to find short-term solutions for those who were burnt out. On 8 September 1666 the Court of Aldermen allowed freemen to set up sheds or tents for 'their trade and employment' anywhere outside the Wall from the Postern at Broad Street to Smithfield (this area included Moorfields). They were also allowed to set up temporary premises on any 'void ground' either side of the Bridge for a period of up to seven years. All traders formerly based in the Royal Exchange were allowed to set up shops in Gresham College.[28] Shops set up around St Bartholomew's Hospital provided a short-term solution.[29] Moorfields was the main area of these temporary premises. On 5 February 1667 citizens that had moved to Moorfields were granted permission to erect a turnpike 'to convey in Carts their goods to & from their respective houses'.[30] By April 1667 Pepys recorded houses there two storeys high 'and like to stand, and . . . become a place of great trade till the City be built'.[31] In October 1667 the Scottish jurist Sir John Lauder recorded in Moorfields there was 'a new street wheirin dwells thosse that ware burnt out in the fire. They pay wery dear for their ground and it is but to stand til they rebuild their houses again in the city'.[32] In 1673 the City government began the process of clearing Moorfields. The City Lands Committee recorded its dire condition, with the grounds spoiled, and the gates and walls 'much decayed'. It stated that there had previously been 'many considerable Citizens, who are now returned into the Citty, and in the Room of them Remain for the most part publique and scandalous houses'.[33] The Court of Aldermen ordered all 'Shedds shops and other buildings which have . . . been erected (since the late dreadfull fire) in Smithfield Moorfields and other void places within the said Citty and Libertyes thereof to taken downe and removed' by 1674. Those who built sheds without permission or exceeded their ground allowed would have to take them down by the end of June that year. Several people vacated their plots, leaving the ground spoiled. They had also left behind mess and debris despite the fact that 'every Proprietor [there] . . . did covenant and agree to Restore'. In July 1674 the Court of Aldermen ordered all sheds remaining in Moorfields to be demolished, and in May 1675 ordered 'the demolishing of all shedds . . . erected since the Late dismall fire'.[34] Clearly, many traders stayed in these temporary premises for a considerable period of time. Despite the long-term problems of allowing traders to set up temporary shops in some areas around London, there is no doubt that in the short term, the initiative would have had a major benefit. Despite being burnt out, traders could continue to operate close to their original markets, and perhaps more importantly, could begin to trade again fairly quickly after the disaster without having the time or expense of finding a new premises.

The first source used in examining the economic changes in London after the Fire are the apprenticeship binding records of the Merchant Taylors. Apprenticeship and the guild system in general were in relative 'decline' in the later seventeenth century. As guild controls disintegrated, it became less necessary to serve an apprenticeship in order to work or set up an independent business. Company membership was also in relative decline over the seventeenth century – probably less than one-quarter of adult male Londoners were company members in the 1660s.[35]

The migration field of London apprentice migrants diminished over the seventeenth century, as many parents preferred local apprenticeships or eschewed the practice altogether.[36] Apprenticing a child to a City livery company, especially a prestigious one like the Merchant Taylors, represented a significant capital investment. Yet many people were still willing to make it even during the later seventeenth century. This was because the freedom of the City and livery company membership still retained importance, as it allowed an individual to trade freely throughout London, and was also vital if one wanted to embark on any kind of political career in metropolitan civic government.[37] The breakdown in guild controls mostly affected the end of apprenticeships, rather than their beginning. As policing guild controls became more difficult, and the area of inspection of guild controls grew larger and more densely populated, apprentices could leave their masters without serving a full term and gaining the freedom through service and trade independently without being a full member of a livery company.[38] Binding records occur at the start of a guild career and so were not affected by this trend. Apprenticeships were still an important part of economic training, as they were the starting point of the vast majority of livery company members' careers. Around 90 per cent of the Merchant Taylor masters in the 1652–66 sample became freemen as a result of service, the rest either through patrimony or redemption.

The Merchant Taylors' apprenticeship records, unlike the vast majority of other London livery companies, included information on the place of business of the master in its apprenticeship binding records. The Merchant Taylors were one of the largest and most influential livery companies in London, and one of the twelve 'great companies'. They were also an economically diverse company in terms of the occupations of its members, with its connection to its original craft becoming increasingly tenuous.[39] Therefore, an examination of the Merchant Taylors illuminates a broader cross-section of the economy than just the textile industry. Most of the apprenticeship binding records also recorded the exact trade of the master, showing if the Fire had any effect on occupation. The sample was selected from the fourteen years (two complete terms of the standard length of an apprenticeship) before and after September 1666: 1652 to 1680. This sampling method may not include some of the poorer members of the company who chose not to take on any apprentices because they could not afford the associated costs of housing and training.

The second occupational group examined in this chapter is booksellers. London, and Paul's Churchyard in particular, was the centre of the book trade in England, and the ubiquity of bookselling there was frequently noted by visitors. The capital investment and uncertainty of public taste made bookselling generally high risk.[40] The Fire was a disaster outside even the normal bounds of uncertainty, and had a damaging impact on the trade nationwide, as London's booksellers traded across the country. For example, Chetham's Library in Manchester, whose agent in London was Robert

Littlebury of Little Britain in St Botolph without Aldersgate, did not receive any books until June 1669 – nearly three years after the Fire.[41] Booksellers were the single trade group most damaged by the Fire. A not atypical example is found in the petitions for relief from the money collected in the brief for Londoners distressed by the Fire. The bookseller Philemon Stephens the Elder of St Paul's Church Yard complained of 'the great losse that he had sustained by the late dreadfull fire, to his utter undoing, as alsoe of his Age, & greate charge of Wife & Children'.[42] On 5 October 1666, Pepys estimated that £150,000 worth of books were destroyed in St Faith's (a figure also arrived at by his contemporary Waterhouse), and he was also concerned it might lead to a rise in prices.[43] The London book trade was central to England's consumption of printed material and so was a highly significant feature of the metropolitan economy and English cultural life in the later seventeenth century in general.

The booksellers provided a stark contrast to the Merchant Taylors. They were a smaller group. There were at least 150 (or perhaps as many as 250) book shops and stalls in London in the seventeenth century, and although this number was probably on the increase over the century, it was nowhere near as many as the numbers of Merchant Taylors.[44] The booksellers were a far more homogenous group than the Merchant Taylors, certainly in terms of occupation. Not all booksellers, however, dealt only in books. Joseph Moxon, of the Atlas on Ludgate Hill, was also a globe and instrument maker, as well as the supplier of Pepys' globes both at home and in the Navy Office. The booksellers were less variegated in their locations across London, bookselling having a highly specialised topography.[45] Although in the later seventeenth century the London book trade expanded to be more topographically diverse as merchants followed wealthy customers westward and the significance of areas such as Fleet Street and Temple grew,[46] the Merchant Taylors, in comparison, were still far more spread out across London (and beyond).

Using livery company records for the booksellers would have produced inaccurate and unrepresentative data. Although the Stationers' Company was responsible for much of the administration of the metropolitan book trade, not all booksellers were members. Increasingly, booksellers were members of other livery companies or none at all. In 1684 there were booksellers from thirteen other livery companies, including at least one Merchant Taylor, James Magnes of Covent Garden.[47] The method used to chart the topography of the booksellers in London was a search of the *English Short Title Catalogue* for all books published in London in the years 1663–5, 1667–9 and 1676–8. From this, the place of business of the bookseller was extracted from the information on the frontispiece. Books from 1666 were not used as it could not be specified if the book was published before or after the Fire. This created a database of most of the booksellers active in London at those dates although it may not include those who specialised solely in the second-hand trade.

Overall patterns: economic topography before and after the Fire

Merchant Taylors

In absolute terms, there was a decline in the number of Merchant Taylors registering apprentices, with 3,594 in the fourteen years before the Fire and 2,162 after. The main reason for this was the 1665 Plague. It was also associated with the breakdown of guild controls in London – especially as after the Fire they were less regulated than previously. This would have made guild membership less attractive. The upheaval of the Fire may have led to masters delaying taking on the expense of an apprentice, or only taking on one apprentice, or even opting out of the apprenticeship system altogether. In addition, apprentices may also have decided to stay on with a master for longer before setting up independently. Table 4.1 shows the dramatic shift of the Merchant Taylors away from the City within the Walls.

In 1652–66 just over half of the Merchant Taylors were based in areas directly affected by the Fire. The area which experienced the greatest decline in numbers was the City within the Walls, which had been most devastated by the Fire and experienced a relative decline of 17.8 per cent. The eastern and western suburbs experienced the greatest relative growth, 5.9 per cent and 5.3 per cent, respectively. The rise in Merchant Taylors in the western suburbs was associated with the shift in commercial activity towards that area – for example, numbers based on the Strand rose from fifty to sixty-four. The expense of recovering from the Fire meant that many Londoners may have moved to less prestigious areas that they previously would not have considered. Rolls noted that many areas to the east of London were 'formerly mean', but after the Fire contained good citizens.[48] They mostly clustered in parishes close to the Walls such as St Botolph without Aldgate and Holy Trinity Minories. Before the Fire the tailor John Geary was based on Dowgate in the City, but relocated to East Smithfield, which was outside

Table 4.1 Place of business, Merchant Taylors, 1652–66, 1666–80 (%)

Region	1652–66	1666–80
City within the Walls	51.6	33.8
East of the Walls	7.4	13.3
West of the Walls	16.7	22.0
North of the Walls	15.8	19.6
Southwark	6.2	8.0
Other	2.3	3.3
Total	100 (3,532)	100 (2,119)

Source: GL, Merchant Taylors' Apprenticeship Bindings 1652–80, MS 34038/13–16.

Note: Does not include the fifty-six masters from 1652–66 and the forty-three from 1666–80 whose place of work was not specified.

of the Walls near to the Tower, after the Fire.[49] However, these figures for the eastern suburbs should be regarded as minima. It was comparatively poorer and cheaper to live in than other areas of London, and thus would have been more attractive to poorer masters, who were less likely to take on apprentices. North of the Walls, areas such as Aldersgate Street, Clerkenwell and Smithfields were the most popular for Merchant Taylors. There seems to have been no significant rise in the number of Merchant Taylors based in Moorfields. The traders there were based in sheds or tents and so would have certainly been small scale, and it is probable that the majority would have not had the need, or financial wherewithal, to take on any apprentices. As such, the sampling technique for the Merchant Taylors may underestimate the numbers of masters who moved to these temporary premises, as they may not have taken on any apprentices immediately after the Fire.

Booksellers

The Fire radically affected the geographical distribution of booksellers in London, at least in the short term. In the three years after the Fire the City within the Walls experienced a decline of 34.2 per cent after the Fire, whilst the northern suburbs experienced relative growth of 30.7 per cent. Numbers in other areas remained relatively stable. By 1676–8, as Table 4.2 shows, there was a return to the pre-Fire distribution of booksellers.

Before the Fire the main area for booksellers was around Paul's Churchyard. One-quarter of the subjects in the 1663–5 sample were based there. Booksellers north of the Walls were clustered in areas such as Little Britain and Pie Corner, less than half a mile from St Paul's, and known to be a centre of the second-hand book trade.[50] In the western suburbs, the main areas of concentration were around Fleet Street and the Temple. In the three years after the Fire, only two of the subjects were based in Paul's Churchyard. Those remaining within the Walls were in the eastern parts

Table 4.2 Geographical distribution of London booksellers, 1663–5, 1667–9 and 1676–8 (%)

Area	1663–5	1667–9	1676–8
City within the Walls	53.1	18.9	49.4
East of the Walls	0	1.3	2.9
West of the Walls	32.5	36.0	31.2
North of the Walls	13.1	43.8	15.9
Southwark	1.3	0	0.6
Total	100 (160)	100 (153)	100 (170)

Source: *English Short Title Catalogue.*

of the City that had not been fired, around Bishopsgate Street or Gresham College – the latter location was where the Royal Exchange had been relocated to whilst its replacement was being built. The area north of the walls was the biggest recipient of fired booksellers, in particular, around Little Britain, where over one-quarter of the sample were based. The profile west of the walls is similar to 1663–5, with most booksellers based around Temple and Fleet Street.

In 1676–8 sample there was a return to the pre-Fire distribution. There are slightly more booksellers based to the north and east of the Walls, but the differences were not significant. Paul's Churchyard re-established itself as the main concentration of booksellers, although it experienced a relative decline of 7.4 per cent compared to its numbers in 1663–5. This decline is due to the decreasing numbers of stalls in the area, which were replaced with shops, meaning that the concentration of booksellers declined. The Fire only temporarily reversed St Paul's status as major bookselling area. Giles Mandelbrote concludes that St Paul's probably began to recover its dominance of the book trade from 1670 on. Although Little Britain still had the densest concentration of booksellers north of the Walls, the proportion of booksellers in the sample based there decreased 16.7 per cent from 1667–9 to 1676–8. The numbers based there fell away after the 1660s as Paul's re-established itself.[51] Again, the area around Fleet Street and Temple remained the most common areas for booksellers in the western suburbs.

Some booksellers did not survive the dislocations and damage caused by the Fire. Joshua Kirton of Paul's Churchyard had been Pepys' regular bookseller from at least 1660. Kirton, like many other booksellers, lost most of his stock during the Fire, and built up debts afterwards. On 5 October 1666 a kinsman of Kirton's told Pepys that Kirton was 'utterly undone . . . and made 2 or 3000*l* worse then nothing, from being worth 7 or 8000*l*'. On 11 November 1667, Pepys recorded: 'This day I hear Kirton my bookseller, poor man, is dead; I believe of grief for his losses by the fire'.[52] Pepys, however, had a 'new bookseller' within six months of Kirton's death: John Starkey of Temple Bar. On 30 September 1666, John Ogilby, the publisher and cartographer, in a petition to Charles II asking for leave to import printing paper from France, duty free, wrote that he lost £3,000 worth of stock in the Fire.[53] Samuel Gellibrand was based at the Golden Ball on Paul's Churchyard, which like many other booksellers was on the site of the Bishop of London's Palace. Gellibrand claimed to have lost at least £1,700 because of the Fire. He received £10 in relief from the brief for distressed Londoners on 26 February 1667. Gellibrand must have found some additional money, because on 30 May 1668 he appeared before the Fire Court stating that he would rebuild 'upon just encouragement' from his landlord, Humphrey Henchman, the Bishop of London. Gellibrand's annual rent (£1) remained the same, but forty years was added to his lease, which would now expire in 1742. According to the Hearth Tax Gellibrand was still based there in 1675.

At least five other booksellers from Paul's Churchyard who rented from the Bishop appeared before the Fire Court – all had their leases lengthened in return for rebuilding.[54] Relations between Henchman and the booksellers were not always so straightforward. Pepys' recording of a conversation on 14 January 1668 with one of his 'new booksellers', John Martin (of Paul's Churchyard before the Fire and Temple Bar afterward), encapsulates some of the problems of booksellers wishing to return to Paul's Churchyard faces. Pepys noted,

> most of the booksellers do design to fall a-building again the next year; but he says that the Bishop of London doth use them most basely, worse than any other landlords, and say he will be paid to this day the rent, or else he will not come to treat with them for the time to come; and will not, on that condition neither, promise them anything how he will use them.[55]

Booksellers operating two outlets did occur, but only one example of this was found. Henry Mortlock operated in Westminster both before and after the Fire. Sometime after 1669, he opened another shop in Paul's Churchyard. Evidence in Pepys' diary suggests that this was not unique. Henry Herringman was one of London's most well-known and influential booksellers, publisher of the poets John Dryden; John Wilmot, Second Earl of Rochester; William Davenant and Thomas Shadwell.[56] He operated shops on New Exchange and Temple Bar. The ubiquitous Pepys visited both of them and also made Herringman a (perhaps unsuspecting) partner in his infidelities. On 18 November 1668 Pepys told one 'Mrs Willet' to leave a time and place for an assignation in a sealed envelope at Herringman's shop on New Exchange.[57]

Individual mobility after the Fire

After charting overall geographical distributions of the Merchant Taylors and the booksellers, the samples before and after the Fire were compared in order to determine individual movements (or non-movements). As has been shown in Chapter 3 (this volume), the decisions surrounding movement after the Fire were affected by a number of other considerations surrounding leases, rents and rebuilding. Rebuilding was often delayed because of problems with a landlord. Poorer traders in particular may have been 'priced out' of a return to their pre-Fire location.

The Merchant Taylors data is more numerous than the booksellers. This makes nominal linkage more difficult. Of the 3,594 Merchant Taylors in 1652–66, only 16.6 per cent could be linked with certainty in 1666–80. Of the 549 masters who could be linked both before and after the Fire, and who had sufficient information about their place of work, just over half were based in fired areas of London. Eighty per cent of the fired Merchant Taylors moved their place of work after the disaster, 3.5 per cent moved but returned to their original location and the rest did not move. Overall, the Fire led to more than half (56.8 per cent) of the Merchant Taylors moving to another area of London, although not all of these moves were permanent. However, even if a subject was based in an area of London unaffected by Fire, just under one-third moved their location after 1666. Mobility, thus, was a fairly common occurrence for even for traders not based in Fire-affected areas, although being burnt out increased the likelihood of moving.

As Table 4.3 shows, there were differences in the profiling of movement of the Merchant Taylors, according to where they moved in London and whether the move was as a result of the Fire. Movement west of the Walls was the most popular destination, followed by movement east. There are differences in the type of movement depending on if the master was based in a fired area of London. Movement outside of the Walls was more common for Merchant Taylors affected by the Fire, with movement north and west being the most popular, in particular to areas such as Holborn, Temple and Fleet Street as well as some movement into the developments in the West End like Covent Garden. Movement north was towards Holborn and Smithfield. Movement east of the Walls was particularly to areas such as the Minories and Houndsditch. Movement south of the Thames was less common. These areas were less prestigious, so the masters who relocated

Table 4.3 Movement of Merchant Taylors, 1652–66 and 1666–80 (%)

	Region of London	Fired Areas	Non-Fired Areas	Total
Moved within same region of London	City within the Walls	27.0	10.4	23.0
	North	0	0	0
	South	0	1.3	0.3
	East	0.4	14.3	3.8
	West	1.2	16.9	5.0
Moved into different region of London	Into the City within the Walls	1.2	12.9	4.1
	Northward	4.7	0	3.5
	Southward	6.2	6.5	6.3
	Eastward	24.5	14.3	22.0
	Westward	34.4	22.1	31.4
	Out of London	0.4	1.3	0.6
	Total	100 (241)	100 (77)	100 (318)

Source: See Table 4.1.

Note: Does not include seventeen masters whose moves cannot be exactly identified and the 261 who did not move.

there after the Fire may not have been able to take on any apprentices and so would not have been included in the sample. The sample also does not record any movement outside of Southwark, although there is anecdotal evidence that there was some movement of tradesmen to nearby Lambeth. A petition to the Court of Aldermen records that four dyers had moved to Lambeth and had erected stairs onto the Thames for their trade. This was technically illegal, but the dyers, due to their 'present exigency', were allowed one year's grace to remove the stairs.[58] Only four fired masters moved out of London altogether; three moved to areas on the metropolis's northern periphery (one each to Highgate, Hampstead and Islington). John Bill, a carpenter based in Lothbury before the Fire, moved nearly fifty miles east to Burnham in Essex.[59]

Movement from areas unaffected by the Fire was more likely to be more short range. Movement west still remained the most popular. Such moves occurred at high levels whether or not a master was based in a fired area of London before 1666, whilst movement to other areas was more likely to be a reaction to being burnt out. Therefore, the Fire only accelerated movement to the West End – a trend that had been ongoing for decades. There were slight differences in the likelihood of a move to a different district of London being permanent dependent on where the move was made to, and if the move originated in a fired area. Moves from fired areas were 3.8 per cent less likely to be permanent than moves from non-fired areas. This difference stems from the fact that moves after the Fire were more likely to be based on short-term considerations based on the instant loss of a property, whereas if the move came from a non-fired area it was probably more likely to be either part of a considered business strategy or at least to have come with some longer-term warning (for example, a lease ending or a reaction to changing retail demands). The decision to move back to a fired area of London could have been motivated by improved terms of lease holding to encourage movement back into rebuilt areas.

The Merchant Taylors affected by the Fire were more likely to stay in areas moved to after 1666. This may be due to the method in which the sample was collected. Taking on an apprentice was more likely to occur if the master had a settled location. Therefore, it may be that there was a short-term 'middle step' move between the Fire and the long-term residential change that could be recorded from the apprenticeship bindings. Movement back into fired areas of the City could not take place immediately after the Fire because of the process of rebuilding. As such, there would have been a period of at least one year after the Fire where it would have been impossible to move back into a workplace in a fired area of London. Secondly, movement within the Walls and west of the Walls was more likely to be permanent than other movements. These areas were generally more settled and prestigious than the areas north, east and south of the Walls, making them a more potentially lucrative and stable long-term place of business.

The booksellers were a smaller group, and so the nominal linkage exercise was more straightforward. Just under half of the 1663–5 sample could be traced to the 1667–9 sample, and just over a quarter could also be traced to the 1676–8 sample. Between 1663–5 and 1667–9 none of the twenty-eight booksellers based in areas directly unaffected by the Fire moved. Booksellers, if not for the huge disruption of the Fire, were more stable in their residence than the Merchant Taylors. Over 90 per cent of the fifty-one booksellers affected by Fire moved. Only four did not: George Hurlock of St Magnus the Martyr Church Corner, Joseph Moxon at the Atlas on Ludgate Hill and Humphrey Robinson and Samuel Gellibrand of Paul's Churchyard. Over half of those who moved went northward, to the Little Britain and Smithfield areas. These moves appear occurred fairly quickly after the Fire. A letter from two London booksellers to a Flemish dealer asking for new books to replenish their stock showed that within days of the Fire, these booksellers from St Paul's had moved on to new premises, in this case to Little Britain.[60] About one-quarter moved westward, mostly going outside of the Walls towards Fleet Street and the Strand. Those who moved eastward, about one-quarter, stayed within the City Walls, five clustering around the temporary shops in Gresham College. Only one bookseller moved outside of the Walls: Dixy Page, who moved to East Smithfield from Cornhill. It is also possible that a bookseller could operate a business in their former place of work in a fired area whilst living elsewhere. Although booksellers frequently tied workplace to dwelling, the trade did not always require a shop – many booksellers operated out of stalls and so would have had separate homes and workplaces.[61] This would mean a bookseller could operate out of a temporary stall whilst living elsewhere.

There was not a long-term change in the distribution of the London booksellers. By the 1670s the pre-Fire status quo had been re-established. To what extent is this reflected in the individual movements of the linked booksellers? Forty-three of the 1663–5 sample could be traced to the 1667–9 and 1676–8 samples. A comparison of place of work shows that the booksellers were very stable in their distribution across London. Eighteen of the booksellers linked between 1663–5 and 1676–8 were from areas unaffected by the Fire. Only one, Francis Smith, moved, relocating from Temple to Cornhill. There was a general movement back to pre-Fire topographical patterns; of the twenty-five booksellers affected by the Fire, twenty-two returned to, or near to, their pre-Fire places of work – most commonly, Paul's Churchyard. Only three booksellers remained in the same area they had moved to after being burnt out in 1666. Even if a bookseller was burnt out, it was fairly likely he would have returned to his original place of work by the 1670s, for the most part after a spell operating in a different area of London. Familiarity of location was essential, with successful sellers trading from sites with a long tradition of bookselling. Even by the 1850s booksellers continued to operate in high numbers in Paul's Churchyard.[62]

Occupational change after the Fire

The Merchant Taylors were not a homogenous company. By the seventeenth century, many of its members had diversified out of the cloth trade. The 'custom of London' meant that any freeman had the right to operate in any trade, regardless of their company. The apprenticeship bindings (mostly) recorded the exact occupation of the master. This shows the occupational structure of the company and illuminated to what extent locality affected the exact trade of a master, and to what extent the Fire may have affected the distribution of trades in the company.

Table 4.4 shows that the Merchant Taylors were involved in many different trades, although textiles remained the most significant, with over half of the company involved in either their manufacture or sale both before and after the Fire. Textiles and clothing was the largest sector of manufacturing in early modern London, accounting for around one-fifth of the workforce.[63] The occupational distribution of the Merchant Taylors differed from that of the rest of London. When comparing the occupational structure of the Merchant Taylors to Power's study of twenty parishes in 1666,[64] the distributions are statistically different. When the textile trades are excluded, the differences in the distributions are still statistically different, but they are slightly more similar. Merchant Taylors were more likely to be involved in dealing and textile occupations than the rest of London, and less likely to be involved in the victualling, building and carrying trades.

There were differences in the occupational distributions before and after the Fire. After 1666, craftsmen within the company became more diversified in their occupations, with proportionally fewer being involved in textile

Table 4.4 Occupational groups of Merchant Taylors, 1652–66 (%)

Group	1652–66	1666–80
Dealer	13.6	12.7
Dealer of Textiles	8.3	7.0
Victualler	6.6	6.6
Professional	3.5	3.0
Wood	3.2	3.8
Metal	4.9	7.8
Textile	49.6	42.5
Leather	2.6	3.9
Miscellaneous Manufacturing	3.7	5.9
Builder	2.4	5.1
Carrier	1.6	1.7
Total	100 (1,805)	100 (2,138)

Source: See Table 4.1.

manufacturing. This is in line with the long-term tendency for manufacturing to move out of the City after the mid-seventeenth century.[65] It also reflected the long-term decline in textile prices in England from the second half of the sixteenth century to the late eighteenth century.[66] These two factors combined to make textile manufacturing a less attractive prospect, and meant that other trades would have grown in relative size as new masters chose to pursue avenues outside of textiles. The main change was the increased proportion of Merchant Taylors becoming involved in the building trade. This doubled after the Fire. Clearly this was a response to the building boom after the Fire. Building in seventeenth-century London was an easy trade to enter, with small groups who worked for a limited amount of time. It was not undertaken by large firms, but by independent builders who completed a few units per year.[67] As such, it would have been straightforward for Merchant Taylors to make the occupational switch to building.

Before the Fire, the City within the Walls had a higher proportion of dealers (over one-quarter) than other areas of London (about one in seven). After the Fire, the proportion of dealers within the Walls remained constant. However, the proportion east and west of the Walls grew to one in five. This was a response to the growing population density of these areas, as well as the problems of rebuilding the fired areas of London. The proportion of craftsmen across regions of London was fairly similar before and after the Fire. The exception is Southwark, which had a higher proportion of builders and victuallers both before and after the Fire, and a higher proportion of masters involved in carrying trades. The higher proportion of victuallers was due to Southwark's important position on the southern routes into London, meaning hospitality accounted for a significant proportion of the local economy. Borough High Street, which was the main route between the South Coast and London, had a high concentration of inns to cater for travellers. Southwark's leisure attractions may also have encouraged the hospitality trades in the area. Jeremy Boulton's study of the occupational structure of seventeenth-century Southwark showed that many parts of the area had a relatively higher proportion of people working in the building and carrying trades than other parts of London.[68]

The occupations of nominally linked masters were examined to determine if occupations changed over time, and if moving shop or being burnt out had any significant effect on occupation. Occupational mobility was not uncommon. Even though the overall occupational distributions are similar both before and after the Fire, there was movement in occupations, with over 10 per cent of the linked masters changing their exact trade from 1652–66 to 1666–80. Builders and craftsmen working with wood experienced the highest levels of occupational turnover. This is unsurprising given that these trade groups were comparatively low status, low skill and probably had the cheapest manufacturing and trading stock. When Abraham Wright of St Martin-in-the-Fields changed from a carpenter to a wheelwright, it would not have required a great deal of change in stock or materials.[69]

For the most part occupational changes were in related industries. Robert Croft (of Cheapside before the Fire, and the Strand after) changed from working as a bodice seller to a bodice maker.[70] John Andrews (of Fenchurch Street before the Fire, and Bishopsgate Street Without after) changed from a linen draper to a woollen draper.[71] Some occupational changes were more dramatic, and likely a response to local market demand. Isaac Logsdon of Holborn changed his occupation from a wheelwright to a tennis court keeper – clearly catering to the leisure needs of residents of the western suburbs and the nearby Inns of Court was more lucrative than woodwork.[72] Not all occupational moves came as a result of being burnt out. Masters who changed occupations were equally likely to come from a fired area of London as a non-fired area. Changing occupation was not always accompanied by movement in workplace. Just under half of the masters who changed their occupation did not move their place of work. Table 4.5 shows London's changing occupational structure over the second half of the seventeenth and early eighteenth centuries.

A.L. Beier has used burial registers to elucidate male occupations from 1500 to 1700.[73] This was compared to a sample from the marriage registers of the chapel at the Fleet Prison. During the first half of the eighteenth century thousands of Londoners married at this location because it offered more convenience and flexibility than a parish wedding.[74] Its registers are so valuable because they are the only London-wide source of occupations that pre-date the Census. Table 4.5 compares Beier's figures from 1641–1700 to a 1710–12 sample from the Fleet that has been adjusted for the occupational

Table 4.5 London's male occupational structure, 1641–1700 and 1710–12 (%)

Group	1641–1700	1710–12
Food and Drink Production and Manufacture	15.9	7.8
Clothing and Textile Manufacture	22.7	15.8
Leather Manufacture	8.9	8.6
Metal Manufacture	8.9	6.0
Building	7.2	9.2
Other Manufactures	7.2	13.0
Dealers and Sellers	7.0	7.6
Services and Professions	9.8	13.3
Transport and Communications	7.5	14.3
Labourers	4.9	4.4

Sources: 1641–1700: A.L. Beier, 'Engine of Manufacture: the Trades of London', in *London 1500–1700: The Making of the Metropolis*, ed. A.L. Beier and R.A.P. Finlay (London and New York: Longman, 1986), 148; 1710–12: TNA, Fleet Chapels Marriage Registers, RG7/7, 10, 18, 20, 23–9.

and geographical biases of the source.[75] The Merchant Taylors' shift away from textiles was clearly part of a general decline in the importance of the sector in London that occurred over the second half of the seventeenth century. Manufacturing in general remained important and it became more diversified and less focussed on textiles. Building increased its share of the workforce. This was certainly a response to the rebuilding boom after the Fire, as well as the growth of London in the suburbs. The service sector also grew substantially during this period, increasing proportionally by half.

The impact of age

Using the freedom register of the Merchant Taylors, it was possible to approximate proxy ages, taking twenty-four as the age for gaining the freedom of the company through service or redemption and twenty-one for gaining the freedom through patrimony.[76] This provided a minimum approximation for the age at which the master was in 1666. The age at which the freedom was attained did vary, although it is unlikely it would be any older than the ages detailed above.[77] This allows the effect of age on movement before and after the Fire to be gauged. It is expected that younger members of the company would find it more difficult to recover after the disaster given the high costs of re-establishing a business in London and the relative difficulty young businessmen had in obtaining credit.[78]

Only one-third of the 1652–66 sample of Merchant Taylors could be linked to individuals in the freedom registers. Only individuals who could be linked to both before and after the Fire were examined, as this ensures that only Merchant Taylors who were actually alive and economically active after the Fire were considered. Of the 596 masters that could be accurately linked before and after the Fire, the approximate age of around 40 per cent could be calculated. The age range was broadly what one would expect, with most of the masters middle aged (over 90 per cent of the sample was between twenty-six and fifty-six). The oldest was Peter Whalley, a writing master who moved from Old Jewry to Houndsditch after the Fire. He was in his early eighties in 1666, and had gained his freedom through service in 1608.[79] The youngest was William Gibbons, a chandler based on Bishopsgate Street, who was in his early twenties and gained his freedom through patrimony from his father John in 1664.[80]

Age may have had a slight bearing on movement after 1666, although there is no significant statistical difference between the ages of the masters who moved and did not move. For those masters burnt out by the Fire, slightly higher proportions of Merchant Taylors under the age of twenty-nine moved after the Fire. In comparison, masters between the ages of thirty and forty-nine were more likely to return to their original workplace. Masters over fifty were more likely to move after the Fire. This may be a commonly occurring phenomenon in metropolitan economic life, as the group of Merchant Taylors not burnt out in 1666 has a similar profile to the masters that were burnt out. Younger Merchant Taylors may have been less economically stable and established than those in the prime of their business lives, and so may have been slightly more likely to move in order to find an effective trading site. However, to more accurately profile this economic movement, it has to be linked to geographic direction. Masters in middle age (thirty to forty-nine) were slightly more likely to remain within the Walls, whilst younger and older masters showed a slightly greater proclivity to move outside of the Walls. However, these differences are marginal. The relatively higher numbers of older masters moving east, which is possibly the most downwardly socially mobile 'direction', perhaps reflects a contemporary trend towards 'downsizing' in old age. It was usual to take on a smaller house as one got older,[81] so perhaps it is possible that this trend could be extended towards 'downsizing' in terms of geographical location. It appears that younger Merchant Taylors may have been slightly more likely to move than their older contemporaries, but the sample size was too small to make any firm conclusions about the impact of age on geographical movement in particular. Merchant Taylors under twenty-nine had a fairly different distribution of occupations compared to the older age groups in two main ways. They were far less likely to be engaged in textile-based crafts than other age groups, and far more likely to be engaged in the building trade. This reflects the flexibility of the younger masters not yet fully established in one trade and able to react to changing economic conditions – namely, the decline of the textile trade and the boom in building in London after the Fire.

The effect of the Fire on female-run businesses

Women played an important role in the metropolitan economy, and most women in London work were involved in the labour force. Custom and law meant that this role was certainly limited and tended to be mostly restricted to poorly paid, low-status occupations – particularly domestic service and needle trades.[82] The guild system was overwhelmingly masculine in identity and membership. It was almost always as the wife or widow of a master that women had the right to trade within the guild system.[83] Some female livery company members had their trading rights through service, but their numbers were usually small. Indeed, only two out of the fifty-seven female Merchant Taylors from the 1652–66 sample gained freedom through service. They were both seamstresses: Margaret Brookes of Seething Lane in All Hallows Barking and Susanna Ridley of Cheapside.[84] Thus it was mostly widows who could have operated businesses independently, as the livery company system theoretically gave widows the trading rights of their deceased husbands. In reality only widows of wealthier tradesmen were able to remain economically independent and active, but lower down the social scale, widowhood left many women in a precarious financial position, reducing their chances of economic success. Boulton's study of seventeenth-century Southwark has shown that the incidence of poverty was related to having a female head of household.[85] As such, many widows quickly remarried. This explains the low proportion of female masters in the Merchant Taylors' Company. Women accounted for only 1.6 per cent of the masters in the 1652–66 sample and 3.5 per cent in the 1666–80 sample. Proportionally more women were involved in bookselling. This was due to the fact that bookselling was a more prestigious occupation than most Merchant Taylors, meaning that the women in the trade would have had more resources and so been more likely to be able to start and sustain their independent business. The proportion of women in bookselling declined over time. For the 1663–5 group, 5 per cent of the booksellers were women, falling to 3.3 per cent in 1667–9 and 0.6 per cent in 1676–8. This decline may have been due to the increased costs of operating in London and recovering from the damages of the Fire, which would have affected women more, as they were more likely to have fewer economic resources than men.

The structure of metropolitan widowhood also contributed to fewer women operating as independent traders for an extended period of time. Remarriage in London was both commonplace and (in the national context) fairly rapid – around two-thirds of widows remarried within one year. In this case, the new husband would usually take over as the head of the business from the widow and also enjoy her trading rights. Even if a widow did not remarry, it appears that only small proportions operated their businesses for longer than a few years. Also, many did not take on apprentices, probably because of the cost involved in the process.[86] These considerations mean that it may be difficult to link significant amounts of women before and after the Fire, as they were less likely to operate businesses independently for an extended period of time, and because they tended to be more vulnerable to downward social mobility, which may have cost them out of either the apprenticeship system, or operating in London altogether.

Before the Fire, female Merchant Taylor topographic structure was similar to the overall pattern, although proportionately more women were likely to be based in Southwark. Likewise, gender did not have a statistically significant effect on economic topography after the Fire. However, there are slight differences – women continue to be more likely to be based in Southwark. As the numbers of booksellers are lower than the Merchant Taylors, it is not possible to examine the effect of gender on their topography in the same way. However, superficially, gender does not seem to make a great deal of difference, and broadly reflects the pattern for booksellers in general. The occupational structure of female Merchant Taylors was similar to the overall pattern. There was no statistical difference between the occupational structure of females and the overall structure, both before and after the Fire. However, it does appear that there were slightly higher proportions of women involved in the victualling. The similarity between female and male occupational structures in the Merchant Taylors is probably due to the fact that most females operating in the company were widows. As such, it would have been likely that they would have continued the trade of their husband, as a great deal of their economic experience and connections would have been gained in the trade of their late husband.

Conclusion: London's economic resilience

The Fire clearly had a significant effect on the topographical distribution of the metropolitan economy, although there were certainly significant differences between the two trade groups examined in this section. The booksellers, the smaller and more homogenous group, experienced more short-term disruption as a result of the Fire as its centre, Paul's Churchyard, was comprehensively gutted. However, in the long term booksellers returned to pre-Fire topographical patterns. There were slight differences in the topography of new and established booksellers, with fledging enterprises more likely to be based outside of the centre of the City than established ones. This may be in response to increasing demand in the areas outside of the City. Overall, the topography of the metropolitan booksellers appears to have been remarkably stable. The Merchant Taylors were a far larger and more diverse group than the booksellers. The Fire directly affected more than half of the company's members, forcing four out of five of the masters in fire-affected areas to move their place of work. These movements were far more likely to be long-term than for the booksellers. Overall, the Fire led to an increase in the numbers of Merchant Taylors based in the northern and eastern suburbs of London. Movement to the western suburbs occurred in response to the Fire, but it also came from non-fired areas. Clearly this was a long-term topographical trend that would have occurred whether or not the Fire had started. The same is probably not true for the growth in the proportion of Merchant Taylors operating in other suburbs of London.

Gauging the effect of the Fire on occupational changes in the Merchant Taylors showed that there was a 10 per cent occupational turnover in the company, usually between related trades. This occurred in equal measure for masters who were burnt out and those who were not, although masters burnt out who had changed occupations were more likely to move location as well. When age was considered, it was probable that younger masters were more likely to move, whether or not they were burnt out. Younger masters were more likely to take up occupations in the building trades after the Fire than older masters. The effect of the Fire on businesses run by women appears to have been similar to the effect of it on businesses run by men. Although it is probable that women traders had slightly different economic profiles to men – they were more likely to be involved in less prestigious occupations and live in relatively cheaper areas – these differences (for the sample involved) do not seem to have been statistically significant before or after the Fire.

Modern studies have shown that cities are highly robust to exogenous shocks even of immense size. Donald Davis and David Weinstein's study of the recovery of Japanese cities after World War II showed that they returned to their pre-shock function, in economic and demographic terms – 'in the aftermath of a shock, there is a strong tendency for city population, aggregate manufacturing and even the particular industries that existed prior to the shock to return to their former importance'.[87] Over time, it appears that even if the shock was of a large size, its effects tended to undo themselves eventually.[88] Similarly, in seventeenth-century England, it is clear that London was able to retain its economic pre-eminence after the Fire in spite of the destruction of its traditional core. The political arithmetician William Petty did speculate that other towns may have advanced at the expense of London, but eventually decided 'What other places may compete with it for naturall advantages?'[89] Modern economic studies have shown that geographic factors play a strong role in determining the economic activity of an area.[90] Many of London's advantages were indeed 'naturall' – for example, its geographical position and close access to sea routes. However, London's economic strength ultimately lay in the progressive centralisation of English politics, society and economy on the metropolis.[91]

The Fire spared the political centre of the metropolis – Westminster – allowing parliamentarians to come to London less than a month after the Fire. One of London's primary cultural functions was also left intact after the Fire. The only licensed theatres in England were both based in non-fired areas of London and although they had been closed as a result of the 1665 Plague, they re-opened the month after the Fire.[92] Finally, London's economic function was able to continue after the Fire because its core – shipping – was largely unaffected by the Fire. London relied strongly on foreign imports, exports and re-exports, as well as the internal coastal trade. Boulton suggests that around one-quarter of the metropolitan workforce was employed in the Port of London and ancillary trades by the early eighteenth century.[93] The wharves destroyed by the Fire around Billingsgate and Queenhithe were all rebuilt by 1670 with little or no change.[94] However, more important was the network of ports that extended from just below London Bridge two miles downriver to Limehouse. It escaped any damage as a result of the Fire.[95] Its survival and later flourishing would be crucial to London, and England's, long-term economic growth. The Port of London was the major centre of exports of finished goods from the rest of the country, and also was the main entrepôt of goods from Asia and the Americas.[96] The survival of London's shipping network meant it could continue to flourish economically whilst dealing with the dislocation caused by the Fire.

In addition to this, London remained the centre of English politics and culture and continued to attract money and talent from the rest of the country. For the wealthy and the nobility, London continued to offer leisure and access to power. For footloose labourers, attracted to the metropolis by the prospect of higher wages,[97] London was still an attractive destination, particularly as the Fire did not destroy their main area of settlement – the suburbs. As such, London's population could continue to grow in size, and pre-Fire demographic trends could continue. Ultimately, as Derek Keene points, out, 'trade was the prime force which conditioned the reordering and rebuilding of the city after the Great Fire'.[98] Elaborate rebuilding schemes were eschewed in favour of practical and quick reconstruction along the existing layout of the City. The only major change was the straightening of Cheapside, which further integrated the City.[99] The absence of a total reconstruction of London's layout, in addition to London's wholly essential place in the English economy, meant the metropolitan economy was able to recover and resume its growth and expansion. As well as this, the presence of London's suburbs as a residential outlet and legislation allowing the short-term settlement of open areas near to the City meant that economic recovery did not have to wait until the City was rebuilt. Many of the traders burnt out may have turned temporary moves into permanent ones. Pepys recorded on 27 June 1668 that when he purchased some linen at New Exchange, on the Strand, the master of the shop said that, 'his and other tradesmen's retail trade is so great here, and better than it was in London, that they believe they shall not return, nor the city be ever so great for retail as heretofore'.[100] There were means to ensure that Londoners could rebuild their businesses and economic lives as quickly as was feasibly possible to do so. Thanks to the continuation of London's economic and demographic function, they did not face a reduction in market size, and so, to an extent, could recover their pre-catastrophe equilibrium.

Notes

1 P. Earle, 'The Economy of London, 1660–1730', in *Urban Achievement in Early Modern Europe: Golden Ages in Antwerp, Amsterdam and London*, ed. P.K. O'Brien et al. (Cambridge: Cambridge University Press, 2001), 82–3; L.D. Schwarz, 'London 1700–1840', in *The Cambridge Urban History of Britain, Volume II 1540–1840*, ed. P. Clark (Cambridge: Cambridge University Press, 2000), 666.

2 A.L. Beier, 'Engine of Manufacture: The Trades of London', in *London 1500–1700: The Making of the Metropolis*, ed. A.L. Beier and R.A.P. Finlay (London and New York: Longman, 1986), 144–7; M.J. Daunton, 'Industry in London: Reflections and Revisions', *London Journal*, 21 (1996), 1.

3 Earle, 'Economy of London', 94.

4 V. Harding, 'London and Middlesex in the 1660s', in *London and Middlesex 1666 Hearth Tax*, ed. M. Davies et al. (London: British Record Society, 2014), 41.

5 Harding, 'London and Middlesex', 42–3; L.D. Schwarz, *London in the Age of Industrialisation: Entrepreneurs, Labour Force and Living Conditions, 1700–1850* (Cambridge: Cambridge University Press, 1992), 8–9, 23, 32; R.C. Michie, 'London and the Process of Economic Growth Since 1750', *London Journal*, 22 (1997), 64–5.

6 L. Shaw-Taylor, 'A Hidden Contribution to Industrialization? The Male Occupational Structure of London 1817–71'. The Occupational Structure of Britain 1379–1911, Report 3. Accessed 12 January 2017, www.campop.geog.cam.ac.uk/research/projects/occupations/abstracts/paper3.pdf.

7 Harding, 'London and Middlesex', 42–3.

8 Beier, 'Engine of Manufacture', 152–6; T. Sakata, 'The Growth of London and Its Regional Structure in the Early Modern Period', *Keio Economic Studies*, 38 (2001), 8.

9 Rege Sincera, *Observations both Historical and Moral upon the Burning of London, September 1666* (London: Thomas Ratcliffe, 1667), 16.

10 Schwarz, 'London 1700–1840', 670.

11 TNA, Letter from Robert Scrivener to James Hickes, 17 September 1666, SP 29/172, 6; S. Rolls, *The Burning of London in the Year 1666* (London: R.I. for Thomas Parkhurst, Nathaniel Ranew and Jonathan Robinson, 1667), part 3, 6.

12 E. Waterhouse, *A Short Narrative of the Late Dreadful Fire in London* (London: W.G. for Richard Thrale and James Thrale, 1667), 157–8.

13 TNA, Petition of Elizabeth Proctor to the King, 1666, SP 29/173, 114.

14 S. Pepys, *The Diary of Samuel Pepys*, ed. R. Latham and W. Matthews, 11 vols. (1st ed. London: G. Bell and Sons, 1970–83), viii, 201.

15 TNA, Petition of Captain John Wadlow to the King, 19 September 1666, SP 29/172, 42; E179/252/23, fol. 82v. While the Sun was being rebuilt Wadlow kept a tavern in Bishopsgate. Pepys, *Diary*, x, 427.

16 TNA, Petition of Sir James Bunce to the King, 7 November 1666, SP 29/177, 104.

17 R.G. Grassby, 'English Merchant Capitalism in the Late Seventeenth Century: The Composition of Business Fortunes', *Past and Present*, 46 (1970), 91; W.C. Baer, 'The Institution of Residential Investment in Seventeenth-Century London', *Business History Review*, 76 (2002), 518–19.

18 TNA, Petition of Richard Pierce to the King, 12 September 1666, SP 29/171, 67; TNA, Letter from the King to the Company of Cooks, 15 September 1666, SP 29/171, 124; P. Mills and J. Oliver, *The Survey of the Building Sites in the City of London after the Great Fire of 1666*, ed. P.E. Jones, 5 vols. (London: London Topographical Society, 1962–7), i, 20; TNA, Hearth Tax Assessment Listing, City of London and parts of Middlesex, 1666, E179/252/32, Part 3, fol. 6v; Hearth Tax Assessment Listing: City of London and Parts of Middlesex, 1675, E179/252/23, fol. 65v.

19 GL, Broadside 20.109, *Reasons Humbly Offered to the Parliament, for the Abatement of the Proportion of the Assessment upon the City of London*, 1672.

20 J.R. Kellett, 'The Breakdown of Gild and Corporation Control over the Handicraft and Retail Trade in London', *Economic History Review*, 10 (1957–8), 382.

21 LMA, Rep. 80, fol. 208v.

22 TNA, E179/252/23, fol. 85v.

23 Philanthropus Philagathus, *An Humble Remonstrance to the King & Parliament in the Behalf of Many Decayed and Decaying Citizens and Families of London, Occasioned Solely by the Dreadful Fire of That City, and Some Concurring Calamitous Events of Providence since* (London, 1675), 1–2, 4–5.

24 R.M. Smuts, 'The Court and Its Neighbourhood: Royal Policy and Urban Growth in the Early Stuart West End', *Journal of British Studies*, 30 (1991), 117–49; L. Stone, 'The Residential Development of the West End of London in the Seventeenth Century', in *After the Reformation: Essays in Honor of J. H. Hexter*, ed. B.C. Malament (Philadelphia, PA: University of Pennsylvania Press, 1980), 167–212.

25 M.J. Power, 'The Social Topography of Restoration London', in *London 1500–1700: The Making of the Metropolis*, ed. A.L. Beier and R.A.P. Finlay (London and New York: Longman, 1986), 212.

26 W. Wycherley, 'Love in a Wood (1672)', in *The Plays of William Wycherley*, ed. P. Holland (Cambridge: Cambridge University Press, 1981), act 1, scene 1, lines 18–23.

27 W.C. Baer, 'Using Housing Quality to Track Change in the Standard of Living and Poverty for Seventeenth-Century London', *Historical Methods: A Journal of Quantitative and Interdisciplinary History*, 47 (2014), 7; P.E. Jones, ed., *The Fire Court: Calendar to the Judgments and Decrees of the Court of Judicature*

Appointed to Determine Differences Between Landlords and Tenants as to Rebuilding after the Great Fire, 2 vols. (London: The Corporation of London, 1966–70), i, 228–9.

28 LMA, Rep. 71, fols. 168v-170v.

29 G. Whitteridge, 'The Fire of London and St Bartholomew's Hospital', *London Topographical Record*, 20 (1952), 47–8.

30 LMA, Rep. 72, fol. 56r.

31 Pepys, *Diary*, viii, 155.

32 J. Lauder, *Journals of Sir John Lauder, Lord Fountainhall, with His Observations on Public Affairs and Other Memoranda, 1665–1676*, ed. D. Crawford (Edinburgh: Edinburgh University Press for the Scottish History Society, 1900), 174.

33 LMA, Court of Common Council: City Lands Committee Papers, COL/CC/CLC/04/001, Box 1, 1666–79, 80.

34 LMA, Rep. 78, fol. 132v, Rep. 79, fol. 292r; Rep. 80, fol. 184r-v; COL/CC/CLC/04/001, 80.

35 Harding, 'London and Middlesex', 42.

36 J.F. Field, 'Apprenticeship Migration to London from the North-East of England in the Seventeenth Century', *London Journal*, 35 (2010), 1–21.

37 J.P. Ward, *Metropolitan Communities: Trade Guilds, Identity, and Change in Early Modern London* (Stanford, CA: Stanford University Press, 1997), 43; M. Knights, 'A City Revolution: The Remodelling of the London Livery Companies in the 1680s', *Economic History Review*, 112 (1997), 1143.

38 M. Berlin, '"Broken All in Pieces": Artisans and the Regulation of Workmanship in Early Modern London', in *The Artisan and the European Town, 1500–1900*, ed. G. Crossick (Aldershot: Scolar Press, 1997), 78.

39 M. Davies and A. Saunders, *The History of the Merchant Taylors' Company* (Leeds: Maney, 2004), 225.

40 A. Johns, 'Printing, Publishing and Reading in London, 1660–1720', in *Urban Achievement in Early Modern Europe: Golden Ages in Antwerp, Amsterdam and London*, ed. P. O'Brien et al. (Cambridge: Cambridge University Press, 200), 265; J. Raven, *The Business of Books: Booksellers and the English Book Trade 1450–1850* (New Haven: Yale University Press, 2007), 9, 98.

41 J. Raven, 'St Paul's Precinct and the Book Trade to 1800', in *St Paul's: The Cathedral Church of London 604–2004*, ed. D. Keene, A. Burns and A. Saint (New Haven and London: Yale University Press, 2004), 435; M.G. Yeo, *The Acquisition of Books by Chetham's Library, 1655–1700* (Leiden: Brill, 2011), 115. Littlebury was assessed for seven hearths in the Lady Day 1666 Hearth Tax. He remained in the same location after the Fire, and was also accessed for seven hearths in 1675. TNA, E179/252/32, Part 11, fol. 10r; E179/252/23, fol. 31r.

42 LMA, Account Book, with returns of the brief and details of its distribution, *Poor Sufferers by Fire in Lond*, COL/SJ/03/006, 1666; Stephens was assessed for five hearths for his property on the north side of Paul's Church Yard in Lady Day 1666, TNA E179/252/32, Part 5/5, fol. 34r.

43 Pepys, *Diary*, vii, 309–10; Waterhouse, *Short Narrative*, 78.

44 Johns, 'Printing, Publishing and Reading', 265.

45 G. Mandelbrote, 'From the Warehouse to the Counting-House: Booksellers and Bookshops in Late 17th-Century London', in *A Genius for Letters: Booksellers and Bookselling from the 16th to the 20th Century*, ed. R. Myers and M. Harris (Winchester and New Castle, DE: St Paul's Bibliographies and Oak Knoll Press, 1995), 50.

46 G. Mandelbrote, 'Workplaces and Living Spaces: London Book Trade Inventories of the Late Seventeenth Century', in *The London Book Trade: Topographies of Print in the Metropolis from the Sixteenth Century*, ed. R. Myers, M. Harris

and G. Mandelbrote (London and New Castle, DE: The British Library and Oak Knoll Press, 2003), 25, 38.

47 Mandelbrote, 'From the Warehouse', 51.

48 Rolls, *Burning of London*, part 3, 144–6.

49 GL, Records of the Merchant Taylors' Company: Registers of Apprentice Bindings, MS 34038/14, fol. 133; 34038/15, fol. 362.

50 Mandelbrote, 'From the Warehouse', 53. However, after the 1720s Little Britain ceased to be an important centre of book-selling. Raven, *Business of Books*, 167.

51 Mandelbrote, 'Workplaces and Living Spaces', 23–6.

52 Pepys, *Diary*, vii, 309; viii, 525.

53 M.A.E. Green, ed., *Calendar of State Papers, Domestic Series, of the Reign of Charles II, 1666–1667* (London: Longman, Green, Longman, Roberts and Green, 1864), 171.

54 LMA, *Fire of London Grants of Money, 1667–75*, COL/SJ/03/009, 5; TNA, E179/252/32, Part 5/3, fol. 19v; E179/252/23, fol. 76v; Jones, ed., *The Fire Court*, ii, 143, 146, 183–6, 322–3. The other booksellers were: James Allestry, Timothy Garthwaite, William Grantham, Edward Mann and William Miller.

55 Pepys, *Diary*, ix, 23.

56 P. Hammond, 'The Restoration Poetic and Dramatic Canon', in *The Cambridge History of the Book in Britain, Volume IV 1557–1695*, ed. J. Barnard and D.F. McKenzie (Cambridge: Cambridge University Press, 2002), 391–2.

57 Pepys, *Diary*, ix, 367.

58 LMA, Rep. 73, fol. 281r.

59 GL, MS 34038/15, fol. 283; 34038/16, fol. 61.

60 Mandelbrote, 'Workplaces and Living Spaces', 22.

61 Johns, 'Printing, Publishing and Reading', 268.

62 Raven, *Business of Books*, 155, 190, 367.

63 Beier, 'Engine of Manufacture', 147.

64 Power, 'Social Topography', 214–15.

65 J. Styles, 'Product Innovation in Early Modern London', *Past and Present*, 168 (2000), 129.

66 C. Shammas, 'The Decline of Textile Prices in England and British America Prior to Industrialization', *Economic History Review*, 47 (1994), 483–507.

67 W.C. Baer, 'The House-Building Sector of London's Economy, 1550–1650', *Urban History*, 39 (2012), 425, 430.

68 J.P. Boulton, *Neighbourhood and Society: A London Suburb in the Seventeenth Century* (Cambridge: Cambridge University Press, 1987), 64–6, 71.

69 GL, MS 34038/15, fols. 240, 339.

70 GL, MS 34038/15, fol. 258; MS 34038/16, fol. 92.

71 GL, MS 34038/15, fols. 13, 393.

72 GL, MS 34038/15, fol. 294; MS 34038/16, fol. 311.

73 Beier, 'Engine of Manufacture', 144–8. His sample is based on fifteen burial registers that included occupations, although it does not include any from the western suburbs.

74 G. Newton, 'Clandestine Marriage in Early Modern London: When, Where and Why?', *Continuity and Change*, 29 (2014), 151–80.

75 This is based on the author's work with Leigh Shaw-Taylor, which will be part of their wider study of London's changing occupational structure over the eighteenth and nineteenth centuries, forthcoming.

76 P. Earle, 'Age and Accumulation in the London Business Community', in *Business Life and Public Policy: Essays in Honour of D. C. Coleman*, ed. N. McKendrick and R.B. Outhwaite (Cambridge: Cambridge University Press, 1986), 323.

77 I.K. Ben-Amos, *Adolescence and Youth in Early Modern England* (New Haven and London: Yale University Press, 1994), 93.

78 C. Muldrew, *The Economy of Obligation: The Culture of Credit and Social Relations in Early Modern England* (Basingstoke: Macmillan, 1998), 153.

79 GL, MS 34038/15, fol. 242; MS 34038/16, fol. 216; Records of the Merchant Taylors' Company: Alphabetical Lists of Freemen, MS 34037/4, 1530–1928.

80 GL, MS 34038/15, fol. 310; MS 34038/16, fol. 105; MS 34037/2.

81 N. Goose, 'How Accurately Do the Hearth Tax Returns Reflect Wealth? A Discussion of Some Urban Evidence', *Local Population Studies*, 67 (2001), 44.

82 P. Earle, *A City Full of People: Men and Women of London, 1650–1750* (London: Methuen, 1994), 112–13, 124, 139; P. Earle, 'The Female Labour Market in London in the Late Seventeenth and Early Eighteenth Centuries', *Economic History Review*, 42 (1989), 346; A.L. Erickson, 'Married Women's Occupations in Eighteenth-Century London', *Continuity and Change*, 23 (2008), 267–9.

83 V.E. Brodsky, 'Widows in Late Elizabethan London: Remarriage, Economic Opportunity and Family Orientations', in *The World We Have Gained: Histories of Population and Social Structure*, ed. L. Bonfield, R.M. Smith and K. Wrightson (Oxford: Basil Blackwell, 1986), 141.

84 GL, MS 34037/1, 3.

85 Boulton, *Neighbourhood and Society*, 175.

86 Brodsky, 'Widows in Late Elizabethan London', 133, 143.

87 D.R. Davis and D.E. Weinstein, 'A Search for Multiple Equilibria in Urban Industrial Structure', NBER Working Paper 10252, 2004.

88 M. Bosker et al., 'Looking for Multiple Equilibria When Geography Matters: German City Growth and the WWII Shock', *Journal of Urban Economics*, 61 (2007), 167.

89 W. Petty, *The Petty Papers: Some Unpublished Writings of Sir William Petty*, ed. H.C.K. Petty-Fitzmaurice, 2 vols. (London: Constable, 1927), ii, 27–9.

90 J. Rappaport and J.D. Sachs, 'The U.S. as a Coastal Nation', Research Working Paper, Federal Reserve Bank of Kansas City, 2002.

91 A.L. Beier and R.A.P. Finlay, 'Introduction: The Significance of the Metropolis', in *London 1500–1700: The Making of the Metropolis*, ed. A.L. Beier and R.A.P. Finlah (London and New York: Longman, 1986), 5, 11–15.

92 R.D. Hume, *The Development of English Drama in the Late Seventeenth Century* (Oxford: Clarendon Press, 1976), 248.

93 J.P. Boulton, 'London 1540–1700', in *The Cambridge Urban History of Britain, Volume II 1540–1840*, ed. P. Clark (Cambridge: Cambridge University Press, 2000), 320–4.

94 J.A. Chartres, 'Trade and Shipping in the Port of London: Wiggins Key in the Later Seventeenth Century', *Journal of Transport History*, 1 (1980), 29.

95 C. Spence, *London in the 1690s: A Social Atlas* (London: Centre for Metropolitan History, 2000), 25.

96 D. Acemoglu et al., 'The Rise of Europe: Atlantic Trade, Institutional Change, and Economic Growth', *American Economic Review*, 95 (2005), 563–6; R.C. Allen, 'The British Industrial Revolution in Global Perspective: How Commerce Created the Industrial Revolution and Modern Economic Growth'. Nuffield College Research Paper, 2006. Accessed 12 January 2017, www.nuffield.ox.ac.uk/users/Allen/unpublished/econinvent-3.pdf, 7.

97 J.P. Boulton, 'Wage Labour in Seventeenth-Century London', *Economic History Review*, 49 (1996), 268–90.

98 D. Keene, 'Growth, Modernisation and Control: The Transformation of London's Landscape, *c.* 1500-*c.* 1760', in *Two Capitals: London and Dublin 1500–1840*, ed. P. Clark and R. Gillespie (Oxford and London: Oxford University Press for the British Academy, 2001), 30.

99 J. Hanson, 'Order and Structure in Urban Design: The Plans for Rebuilding London after the Great Fire of 1666', *Ekistics*, 56 (1989), 37–8.

100 Pepys, *Diary*, ix, 250. The New Exchange, on the Strand, was built in 1608–9 but rose to full prominence in the 1660s, partly as a result of the Fire. W.C. Baer, 'Early Retailing: London's Shopping Exchanges, 1550–1700', *Business History*, 49 (2007), 40–1.

Reference list

Primary sources

Manuscript
GL, Broadside 20.109, *Reasons Humbly Offered to the Parliament, for the Abatement of the Proportion of the Assessment upon the City of London*, 1672.
GL, Records of the Merchant Taylors' Company: Alphabetical Lists of Freemen, MS 34037/1–4, 1530–1928.
GL, Records of the Merchant Taylors' Company: Registers of Apprentice Bindings, MS 34038/13–16, 1647–80.
LMA, Account Book, with Returns of the Brief and Details of Its Distribution, *Poor Sufferers by Fire in Lond*, COL/SJ/03/006, 1666.
LMA, Court of Common Council: City Lands Committee Papers, COL/CC/CLC/04/001, Box 1, 1666–79.
LMA, Repertory of the Court of Aldermen, Rep. 71–82, 1665–77.
TNA, Fleet Chapels Marriage Registers, RG7/7, 10, 18, 20, 23–9, 1710–12.
TNA, Hearth Tax Assessment Listing, City of London and Parts of Middlesex, E179/252/32, 1666.
TNA, Hearth Tax Assessment Listing, City of London and Parts of Middlesex, E179/252/23, 1675.
TNA, Letter from the King to the Company of Cooks, 15 September 1666, SP 29/171, 124.
TNA, Letter from Robert Scrivener to James Hickes, 17 September 1666, SP 29/172, 6.
TNA, Petition of Captain John Wadlow to the King, 19 September 1666, SP 29/172, 42.
TNA, Petition of Elizabeth Proctor to the King, 1666, SP 29/173, 114.
TNA, Petition of John Le Roy to the King, 1666, SP 29/173, 106.
TNA, Petition of Richard Pierce to the King, 12 September 1666, SP 29/171, 67.
TNA, Petition of Sir James Bunce to the King, 7 November 1666, SP 29/177, 104.

Printed
Evelyn, J. *The Diary of John Evelyn*, edited by E.S. De Beer, 6 vols. Oxford: Clarendon Press, 1955.
Green, M.A.E., ed. *Calendar of State Papers, Domestic Series, of the Reign of Charles II, 1666–1667*. London: Longman, Green, Longman, Roberts and Green, 1864.
Jones, P.E., ed. *The Fire Court: Calendar to the Judgments and Decrees of the Court of Judicature Appointed to Determine Differences between Landlords and Tenants as to Rebuilding after the Great Fire*, 2 vols. London: The Corporation of London, 1966–70.
Lauder, J. *Journals of Sir John Lauder, Lord Fountainhall, with His Observations on Public Affairs and Other Memoranda, 1665–1676*, edited by D. Crawford. Edinburgh: Edinburgh University Press for the Scottish History Society, 1900.
Mills, P. and Oliver, J. *The Survey of the Building Sites in the City of London after the Great Fire of 1666*, edited by P.E. Jones, 5 vols. London: London Topographical Society, 1962–7.
Pepys, S. *The Diary of Samuel Pepys*, edited by R. Latham and W. Matthews, 11 vols. 1st ed. London: G. Bell and Sons, 1970–83.

Petty, W. *The Petty Papers: Some Unpublished Writings of Sir William Petty*, 2 vols., edited by H.C.K. Petty-Fitzmaurice. London: Constable, 1927.

Philanthropus Philagathus. *An Humble Remonstrance to the King & Parliament in the Behalf of Many Decayed and Decaying Citizens and Families of London, Occasioned Solely by the Dreadful Fire of That City, and Some Concurring Calamitous Events of Providence since.* London, 1675.

Rege Sincera. *Observations both Historical and Moral upon the Burning of London, September 1666.* London: Thomas Ratcliffe, 1667.

Rolls, S. *The Burning of London in the Year 1666.* London: R.I. for Thomas Parkhurst, Nathaniel Ranew and Jonathan Robinson, 1667.

Taswell, W. *Autobiography and Anecdotes by William Taswell, D.D*, edited by G.P. Elliott. London: Camden Society, 1853.

Waterhouse, E. *A Short Narrative of the Late Dreadful Fire in London.* London: W.G. for Richard Thrale and James Thrale, 1667.

Wycherley, W. 'Love in a Wood (1672)'. In *The Plays of William Wycherley*, edited by P. Holland, 1–113. Cambridge: Cambridge University Press, 1981.

Secondary sources

Acemoglu, D., Johnson, S., and Robinson, J. 'The Rise of Europe: Atlantic Trade, Institutional Change, and Economic Growth', *American Economic Review*, 95 (2005), 546–79.

Allen, R.C. 'The British Industrial Revolution in Global Perspective: How Commerce Created the Industrial Revolution and Modern Economic Growth', Nuffield College Research Paper, 2006. Accessed 12 January 2017, www.nuffield.ox.ac.uk/users/Allen/unpublished/econinvent-3.pdf.

Baer, W.C. 'The Institution of Residential Investment in Seventeenth-Century London', *Business History Review*, 76 (2002), 515–51.

Baer, W.C. 'Early Retailing: London's Shopping Exchanges, 1550–1700', *Business History*, 49 (2007), 29–51.

Baer, W.C. 'The House-Building Sector of London's Economy, 1550–1650', *Urban History*, 39 (2012), 409–30.

Baer, W.C. 'Using Housing Quality to Track Change in the Standard of Living and Poverty for Seventeenth-Century London', *Historical Methods: A Journal of Quantitative and Interdisciplinary History*, 47 (2014), 1–18.

Beier, A.L. 'Engine of Manufacture: The Trades of London'. In *London 1500–1700: The Making of the Metropolis*, edited by A.L. Beier and R.A.P. Finlay, 141–67. London and New York: Longman, 1986.

Beier, A.L. and Finlay, R.A.P. 'Introduction: The Significance of the Metropolis'. In *London 1500–1700: The Making of the Metropolis*, edited by A.L. Beier and R.A.P. Finlay, 1–33. London and New York: Longman, 1986.

Bell, W.G. *The Great Fire of London*. 1st ed. London: John Lane, 1920.

Ben-Amos, I.K. *Adolescence and Youth in Early Modern England*. New Haven and London: Yale University Press, 1994.

Berlin, M. '"Broken All in Pieces": Artisans and the Regulation of Workmanship in Early Modern London'. In *The Artisan and the European Town, 1500–1900*, edited by G. Crossick, 75–91. Aldershot: Scolar Press, 1997.

Bosker, M., Brakman, S., Garretsen, H., and Schramm, M. 'Looking for Multiple Equilibria When Geography Matters: German City Growth and the WWII Shock', *Journal of Urban Economics*, 61 (2007), 152–69.

Boulton, J.P. *Neighbourhood and Society: A London Suburb in the Seventeenth Century*. Cambridge: Cambridge University Press, 1987.

Boulton, J.P. 'Wage Labour in Seventeenth-Century London', *Economic History Review*, 49 (1996), 268–90.

Boulton, J.P. 'London 1540–1700'. In *The Cambridge Urban History of Britain, Volume II 1540–1840*, edited by P. Clark, 315–46. Cambridge: Cambridge University Press, 2000.

Brodsky, V.E. 'Widows in Late Elizabethan London: Remarriage, Economic Opportunity and Family Orientations'. In *The World We Have Gained: Histories of Population and Social Structure*, edited by L. Bonfield, R.M. Smith and K. Wrightson, 122–54. Oxford: Basil Blackwell, 1986.

Chartres, J.A. 'Trade and Shipping in the Port of London: Wiggins Key in the Later Seventeenth Century', *Journal of Transport History*, 1 (1980), 29–47.

Daunton, M.J. 'Industry in London: Reflections and Revisions', *London Journal*, 21 (1996), 1–8.

Davies, M. and Saunders, A. *The History of the Merchant Taylors' Company*. Leeds: Maney, 2004.

Davis, D.R. and Weinstein, D.E. 'A Search for Multiple Equilibria in Urban Industrial Structure', NBER Working Paper 10252 (2004).

Earle, P. 'Age and Accumulation in the London Business Community'. In *Business Life and Public Policy: Essays in Honour of D. C. Coleman*, edited by N. McKendrick and R.B. Outhwaite, 38–63. Cambridge: Cambridge University Press, 1986.

Earle, P. 'The Female Labour Market in London in the Late Seventeenth and Early Eighteenth Centuries', *Economic History Review*, 42 (1989), 328–53.

Earle, P. *A City Full of People: Men and Women of London, 1650–1750*. London: Methuen, 1994.

Earle, P. 'The Economy of London, 1660–1730'. In *Urban Achievement in Early Modern Europe: Golden Ages in Antwerp, Amsterdam and London*, edited by P.K. O'Brien, D. Keene, M. 't Hart and H. van der Wee, 81–96. Cambridge: Cambridge University Press, 2001.

Erickson, A.L. 'Married Women's Occupations in Eighteenth-Century London', *Continuity and Change*, 23 (2008), 267–307.

Field, J.F. 'Apprenticeship Migration to London from the North-East of England in the Seventeenth Century', *London Journal*, 35 (2010), 1–21.

Goose, N. 'How Accurately Do the Hearth Tax Returns Reflect Wealth? A Discussion of Some Urban Evidence', *Local Population Studies*, 67 (2001), 44–63.

Grassby, R.G. 'English Merchant Capitalism in the Late Seventeenth Century: The Composition of Business Fortunes', *Past and Present*, 46 (1970), 87–107.

Hammond, P. 'The Restoration Poetic and Dramatic Canon'. In *The Cambridge History of the Book in Britain, Volume IV 1557–1695*, edited by J. Barnard and D.F. McKenzie, 388–409. Cambridge: Cambridge University Press, 2002.

Hanson, J. 'Order and Structure in Urban Design: The Plans for Rebuilding London after the Great Fire of 1666', *Ekistics*, 56 (1989), 22–42.

Harding, V. 'London and Middlesex in the 1660s'. In *London and Middlesex 1666 Hearth Tax*, edited by M. Davies, C. Ferguson, V. Harding, E. Parkinson and A. Wareham, 25–57. London: British Record Society, 2014.

Hume, R.D. *The Development of English Drama in the Late Seventeenth Century*. Oxford: Clarendon Press, 1976.

Johns, A. 'Printing, Publishing and Reading in London, 1660–1720'. In *Urban Achievement in Early Modern Europe: Golden Ages in Antwerp, Amsterdam and London*, edited by P. O'Brien, D. Keene, M. t'Hart and H. van der Wee, 264–83. Cambridge: Cambridge University Press, 2001.

Keene, D. 'Growth, Modernisation and Control: The Transformation of London's Landscape, *c.* 1500-*c.* 1760'. In *Two Capitals: London and Dublin 1500–1840*, edited by P. Clark and R. Gillespie, 7–37. Oxford and London: Oxford University Press for the British Academy, 2001.

Kellett, J.R. 'The Breakdown of Gild and Corporation Control Over the Handi-craft and Retail Trade in London', *Economic History Review*, 10 (1957–8), 381–94.

Knights, M. 'A City Revolution: The Remodelling of the London Livery Companies in the 1680s', *Economic History Review*, 112 (1997), 1141–78.

Mandelbrote, G. 'From the Warehouse to the Counting-House: Booksellers and Bookshops in Late 17th-Century London'. In *A Genius for Letters: Booksellers and Bookselling from the 16th to the 20th Century*, edited by R. Myers and M. Harris, 49–84. Winchester and New Castle, DE: St Paul's Bibliographies and Oak Knoll Press, 1995.

Mandelbrote, G. 'Workplaces and Living Spaces: London Book Trade Inventories of the Late Seventeenth Century'. In *The London Book Trade: Topographies of Print in the Metropolis from the Sixteenth Century*, edited by R. Myers, M. Harris and G. Mandelbrote, 21–43. London and New Castle, DE: The British Library and Oak Knoll Press, 2003.

Michie, R.C. 'London and the Process of Economic Growth Since 1750', *London Journal*, 22 (1997), 63–90.

Muldrew, C. *The Economy of Obligation: The Culture of Credit and Social Relations in Early Modern England*. Basingstoke: Macmillan, 1998.

Newton, G. 'Clandestine Marriage in Early Modern London: When, Where and Why?', *Continuity and Change*, 29 (2014), 151–80.

Power, M.J. 'The Social Topography of Restoration London'. In *London 1500–1700: The Making of the Metropolis*, edited by A.L. Beier and R.A.P. Finlay, 199–223. London and New York: Longman, 1986.

Rappaport, J. and Sachs, J.D. 'The U.S. as a Coastal Nation', Research Working Paper, Federal Reserve Bank of Kansas City, 2002.

Raven, J. 'St Paul's Precinct and the Book Trade to 1800'. In *St Paul's: The Cathedral Church of London 604–2004*, edited by D. Keene, A. Burns and A. Saint, 430–8. New Haven and London: Yale University Press, 2004.

Raven, J. *The Business of Books: Booksellers and the English Book Trade 1450–1850*. New Haven: Yale University Press, 2007.

Sakata, T. 'The Growth of London and Its Regional Structure in the Early Modern Period', *Keio Economic Studies*, 38 (2001), 1–16.

Schwarz, L.D. *London in the Age of Industrialisation: Entrepreneurs, Labour Force and Living Conditions, 1700–1850*. Cambridge: Cambridge University Press, 1992.

Schwarz, L.D. 'London 1700–1840'. In *The Cambridge Urban History of Britain, Volume II 1540–1840*, edited by P. Clark, 641–72. Cambridge: Cambridge University Press, 2000.

Shammas, C. 'The Decline of Textile Prices in England and British America Prior to Industrialization', *Economic History Review*, 47 (1994), 483–507.

Shaw-Taylor, L. 'A Hidden Contribution to Industrialization? The Male Occupational Structure of London 1817–71', The Occupational Structure of Britain 1379–1911, Report 3. Accessed 12 January 2017, www.campop.geog.cam.ac.uk/research/projects/occupations/abstracts/paper3.pdf.

Slack, P. *The Impact of Plague in Tudor and Stuart England*. London: Routledge and Kegan Paul, 1985.

Smuts, R.M. 'The Court and Its Neighbourhood: Royal Policy and Urban Growth in the Early Stuart West End', *Journal of British Studies*, 30 (1991), 117–49.

Spence, C. *London in the 1690s: A Social Atlas*. London: Centre for Metropolitan History, 2000.

Stone, L. 'The Residential Development of the West End of London in the Seventeenth Century', In *After the Reformation: Essays in Honor of J. H. Hexter*, edited by B.C. Malament, 167–212. Philadelphia, PA: University of Pennsylvania Press, 1980.

Styles, J. 'Product Innovation in Early Modern London', *Past and Present*, 168 (2000), 124–69.

Ward, J.P. *Metropolitan Communities: Trade Guilds, Identity, and Change in Early Modern London*. Stanford, CA: Stanford University Press, 1997.

Whitteridge, G. 'The Fire of London and St Bartholomew's Hospital', *London Topographical Record*, 20 (1952), 47–8.

Yeo, M.G. *The Acquisition of Books by Chetham's Library, 1655–1700*. Leiden: Brill, 2011.

5 Cultural reactions to the Great Fire

The previous two chapters have focussed on London's material recovery from the Fire. By the late 1670s the ruined areas had been mostly rebuilt. London retained its prosperity, with its economy booming until the 1690s.[1] There was still a mental recovery to be made. The Fire was a traumatic event for Londoners and stoked fear in the rest of the country. Fire in general was viewed as an apocalyptic event, a precursor of internal division or foreign invasion.[2] Everything that was familiar and settled had been swept away.[3] Samuel Pepys expressed the psychological impact of the disaster, writing on 15 September 1666 that he was 'much terrified in the nights nowadays, with dreams of fire and falling down of houses'. Twelve days later he wrote his mind was 'still mightily perplexed with dreams and burning the rest of the town'.[4]

Conflagrations were an everyday part of early modern metropolitan life and often viewed providentially. Alexandra Walsham argues that it was believed fires were a means for God to chastise ungodly communities – a mode of instruction. In some cases, this instruction was heeded, and near annihilation of a community led to an ongoing commitment to moral regeneration.[5] A consolatory letter written from the civic officials of Derry to the City bemoaned the 'direfull & astonishing Judgments it hath pleased the Almighty to lay on you'.[6] Similarly, Sir Nathaniel Hobart wrote just after the Fire that

> the image of this terrible judgement has made such an impression in the soules of every one of us, that it will not be effaced while we live . . . God was not pleased, & we must submit to his will.[7]

There was not universal acceptance that the Fire was divinely ordained. A human culprit was needed. As Chapter 1, this volume, has shown, one of the first reactions of Londoners was to blame foreigners. Penny Roberts shows that blame for fires and conspiracy theories often became associated with fears of the 'other' – strangers and foreigners.[8] It is a 'common trait' of collective psychology to try to explain disasters in terms of the machinations of those who are regarded as a threat. For example, after the Lisbon

Earthquake of 1755 blame for the fires after the disaster (as well as loot-ing) was laid on Spanish deserters.[9] In 1666 the agents of destruction were generally thought to be Dutch or French, the two largest immigrant groups in early modern London.[10] Steven Pincus argues that the immediate predis-position of Anglican Royalists was to blame the Dutch.[11] The Royalist Lady Hobart wrote that it was a 'Duch fire, thar was one tacken in Westminster seting his outhous on fier & they have atempted to fier many plases & thar is a bundanc tacken with grenades & pouder'.[12] Over time general public opinion, if it was searching for a foreign culprit, tended to unanimously blame the French, the Papists, or both. This matched the long-term shift in popular sentiment from anti-Dutch to anti-French.[13] This mirrored the growing dissatisfaction with Charles II's regime. By the 1670s France was England's main European ally. Yet, the Protestant Dutch Republic (who England was again at war with from 1672 to 1674) was ignored when look-ing for a foreign enemy to blame.[14] Ultimately, France got the blame because of its association with Catholicism, absolutism and tyranny.

In Parliament a committee was organised to investigate the causes of the Fire. Its chairman was the Member of Parliament for Aldeburgh in Suffolk, Sir Robert Brooke. Reports flooded in. Witnesses testified to the presence of 7,000 Catholics in London and 100,000 in England. All were potential enemies: the Papist threat was omnipresent and elastic.[15] On 5 November Pepys dined at the house of John Crew, First Baron Crew, in Lincoln's Inn Fields. There his son, Sir Thomas Crew, Member of Parliament for Brackley in Northamptonshire, told Pepys that the committee 'conclude it as a thing certain, that it was done by plot . . . it was bragged by several papists that upon such a day or in such a time we should find the hot-test weather that ever was in England'.[16] The report was first presented to Parliament on 22 January 1667. It was never fully debated or discussed as Parliament was prorogued on 8 February. The Royalist John Milward, Member of Parliament for Derbyshire, was sceptical of the importance of the report, writing in his diary that it could not prove 'a general design of wicked agents, Papists or Frenchmen, to burn the city . . . I cannot conceive that the House can make anything of [it]'.[17] Not everyone shared this view. Late in 1667 fifty-five prominent London citizens petitioned City authori-ties requesting Parliament re-appoint the commission

> being fully persuaded that as the imediate hand and justice of God was therein, soe also very much of the Malice and practice of men . . . to the end that all persons may be encouraged to bring their informations concerning any foule practice therein.[18]

Shortly afterwards the City petitioned Commons requesting the commis-sion be re-appointed 'to discover the Wicked Instruments of that inexpress-ible Desolacon brought upon this City by the late dismall Fire' and hear evidence from 'Citizens and persons of good Quality and Esteeme Offering themselves to make out new and further Evidence then hath appeared of Fact and Design in that Deplorable Calamity'.[19] Despite these appeals, a new committee was not appointed. Supposed versions of Brooke's report soon appeared in print. In them, Robert Hubert, the Huguenot executed for starting the Fire, is claimed to be Catholic and working with a number of accomplices. It was suggested that large numbers of Catholic plotters, some from abroad, used various incendiary devices to spread the flames across London. It cast aspersions on York's loyalty as well as suggesting a wider Catholic conspiracy drawing on support from the French, perhaps leading to an eventual invasion of England.[20] Many subsequent anti-Catholic accounts of the Fire relied on Brooke's report to add verisimilitude to their claims.

When the report was published, many Royalists were convinced of its subversive nature. On 13 July 1667, Sir Thomas Langton, the Mayor of Bristol, and the local merchant Sir John Knight wrote to Arlington reporting that the radical bookseller Elizabeth Calvert of Little Britain had sent 'fifty bookes concerning the late fire in London' to Bristol, which had been seized, as they were deemed to be 'seditious and to be scattered abroad to seduce his Majestys subjects against his government'.[21] On 16 August 1667 Sir Daniel Fleming, a sheriff of Cumberland, reported to Joseph Williamson that the report had appeared in his locality recently, and he thought that it had been 'maliciously (& surely very falsely) published by some Presbiterian hand'. Three days after Fleming's letter, Sir Philip Musgrave, a Royalist officer and politician, wrote to Williamson from Carlisle notifying him that he had seen 'a printed booke containeing the informations given last winter to the House of Comons concerneing the burneing of London . . . also the informations concerning the insolenceys of Papists with some additions very seditious'. Musgrave reported that he had seized eighteen of the works from the shop of a 'fierce Presbiterian'.[22]

The reaction to the Fire revealed England's long-standing hostility to Catholics, which manifested itself most visibly at times of crisis.[23] Catholicism was doubly stigmatised as being both foreign and a familiar accompaniment of absolutism. It was identified with alien Irish barbarism, French despotism and Roman luxury, with its adherents being part of a vast international conspiracy.[24] Unlike other demonised groups, Catholics were not socially marginalised or powerless during the Restoration – they had a visible status at Charles II's court.[25] The easiest way to make sense of the Fire for many was to tell a story with a familiar, Papist, villain.[26] Due to the Gunpowder Plot of 1605 the association of fiery explosions with Catholics already existed. This is shown in a 1641 pamphlet, which recorded that Catholics planned to burn Dublin using 'many balls of wild-fire'.[27] The Great Fire made arson the most threatening of the fears about Papist conspiracies, and Jesuits in particular.[28] Rumours that Catholics had plotted to start the Fire quickly appeared. On 27 November Anthony Wood wrote that 'Papists at this time [were] very insolent in most parts of the nation; appear in publick; contrive the massacring of many; hundreds of strang knives being lately discovered . . . (in) a ruinous cellar at London'.[29] At the end of December Thomas Rugge reported that a poem, allegedly written by a 'friend of the church of Rome', was 'cast about the streets and put into windows at houses & shops'. It included the ominous lines, 'For Downe ye must ye hereticks/For all your hopes in sixty six/The hands against you is so steady/Your Babylon is fallen already'. It was also reported that this poem was scattered around Westminster Hall.[30] Jesuits in particular became associated with arson. In 1667 a tract called *Pyrotechnica Loyolana*, written by a 'Catholick-Christian', linked the order to numerous fires, actual and plotted, in England and across the world. Its frontispiece (see Figure 5.1) depicted members of the order planning fires across the world, as well as the pope fanning the flames in London. It stated that the Jesuits strove 'daily to bring forth new INVENTIONS, to bring men . . . to their *Religion* and *Society* by the use of Arms, Terror, FIRE'.[31] In 1670 a pamphlet was published that linked several small fires that had recently occurred in London to Catholic plotting.[32]

Throughout European history anti-Semitism was a common reaction to crises or disasters, including urban fires. In the aftermath of the 1728 Copenhagen Fire, the public clamour led to seven Jews (and a Swiss visitor) being interrogated under suspicion of starting the blaze – none were found culpable.[33] The few hundred Jews who had settled in London during the 1650s had been subject to hostility before the Fire. There had been several anti-Jewish petitions to Charles II, alleging that they were prone to conspiracy, disloyalty and avarice. The Court of Aldermen and the Lord Mayor also petitioned the king to expel London's Jewish community, claiming they were a threat to English merchants and that they would conspire with other immigrants. In 1664 Charles II pledged to protect Jews under his rule as long as they respected the laws of the realm.[34] The only contemporary source that blamed Jews was a 1676 letter. It claimed that France, using York as an agent, had paid Jews to spread fires 'not only in England, but in Germany, Poland and elsewhere' and went on to say that France 'had then several [Jews] in pay, not only in England, but all over Christendom; not only to give them Intelligence in which they are wondrous Active, but likewise to promote & act the worse of a mischiefs'.[35] In the aftermath of the Great Fire anti-Catholicism was a more common reaction than anti-Semitism.

Narratives of the Fire

The disasters of the mid 1660s led to a flood of polemical activity – 'all the literary forms, both popular and elite, were responsive to and helped shape and interpret the crises'.[36] The interpretation of events such as the Fire quickly became a contested site of interpretation, and thus politicised.[37] Narrative accounts of the Fire are divided into two binary, competing streams. The Royalist perspective tended to view the Fire as accidental. The event was a symbol of the Stuarts' commitment to London, as well as the consequence of the City's 'disloyalty' during the Civil Wars.[38] Opposing this

Figure 5.1 Frontispiece of *Pyrotechnica Loyolana* (1667)
(Reproduced with the kind permission of the Museum of London)

perspective was an anti-Catholic view, which tended to be Whiggish and dissenting. The Fire was used to question York's loyalty and Catholics in general, as well as criticise the Restoration administration. These two streams
drew their inspiration and many of their claims on upon two sources: the

account of the Fire in the *London Gazette* and the supposed report of the parliamentary committee investigating the causes of the Fire.

The account of the Fire in the *Gazette* embodied the 'official' perspective, treating it as an accident, and emphasising the role of Charles II and York in the fire-fighting effort. It stressed the role of God in starting the flames and of the king in helping to stem them and begin the reconstruction and recovery of London after the disaster.[39] One of the first books published on the Fire was 'Rege Sincera's' *Observations both Historical and Moral upon the Burning of London*, which drew its narrative of the Fire's progress entirely on that published in the *Gazette*, calling its account a 'true and naked Narrative of the Fact as it did happen'. The rest of the *Observations* identified the primary cause of the Fire as God, with all other factors acting as 'second causes'.[40] Edward Waterhouse's *Short Narrative Of the late Dreadful Fire in London* was another account that towed the establishment line. It took the form of a letter written to Sir Edward Turner, Speaker of the House of Commons and Member of Parliament for Hertford. Waterhouse reasoned that the Fire may have been caused by human agency from England's enemies, as it caused commotion and adversely affected the war effort. Waterhouse ultimately determined that the Fire was a divine judgment. His account praised Charles II and York and called for a halt in criticism so that England can recover: 'Nothing is a Curse of subversion to a Nation but Faction, Dissention, Jealousie'. He criticised London's nonconformists, claiming that '[l]evity and zealousness for Reformed Religion . . . has undone all'.[41]

Three nonconformist clerics published accounts of the Fire in 1667: Thomas Vincent, Samuel Rolls and Thomas Doolittle. They shared the providential view of the disaster, but not the admiration of Charles II. Vincent argued that divine displeasure had been increased by the 1662 Act of Uniformity and the 1665 Five Mile Act, as '*Gospel-Ordinances*, and *Gospel-Ministers* were the safe-guard of *London*, the glory and defence'. The eviction of dissenting ministers had presaged London's ruin. Vincent mentioned the dry weather, wind and combustible materials in the houses, as well as insinuating Catholic involvement. Sin was the primary cause of the Fire, which 'hath received its commission from God to burn down the City, and therefore all attempts to hinder it are in vain'. He goes on to give an account of the causes of the divine judgment, firstly arguing it was a national judgment, because London was the 'Metropolis of the Land, where all its Beauty, Riches, Strength and Glory' lay. He also mentions the godlessness of the gentry (a veiled criticism of Charles II's bawdy court) and the vast numbers of the 'ungodly crew' who reside there. Ultimately London's pride and sin brought about a divine judgment, and to forestall any other such events and prosper, London must turn from sin and be humble towards God.[42] Rolls' account includes a litany of sins, including Sabbath-breaking, debauchery and idolatry, that have previously brought the divine judgment of fire, and all of which London was guilty of. Rolls blamed Catholics for starting the Fire, 'the losse was Catholick (that is universall) in the consequences, as well as Roman Catholick in the Causes of it'. Like Vincent, Rolls argues they could not have done it unless God had ordained it because of the sins of the people.[43] Doolittle's account emphasised the sinfulness of man and the wrath of God. Sin is the bellows which fuels 'God's burning anger'. There is a catalogue of sins which especially kindled divine anger, with biblical examples of each. Doolittle reminded the reader that the Fire was a 'general' judgment, so all English people must forsake sin and pray for London, especially as many will have relatives in the metropolis.[44]

The Great Fire, the Popish Plot and the Exclusion Crisis

The mid 1670s saw a revival of popular political agitation against Charles II. On 15 March 1672 the Royal Declaration of Indulgence suspended the penal laws against Catholics and nonconformists. At the end of that month, England, as part of their alliance with France, declared war against the Dutch Republic, starting another expensive conflict. These two events were controversial and unpopular. In February 1673 Parliament compelled Charles II to withdraw the Declaration. It passed the Test Acts, which compelled public servants to deny transubstantiation and take Anglican Holy Communion (the next year they forced Charles II to make peace with the Dutch). Further controversy followed. By summer 1673 York's conversion to Catholicism was public knowledge. That September he married the Catholic Mary of Modena. As Charles II had no legitimate children, this created the possibility that York could produce a male Catholic heir who would usurp the claims of his Protestant daughters Mary and Anne. This led to the Exclusion Crisis, where the 'Country Party' (which became the Whigs) attempted to pass legislation to remove York from the line of succession to ensure a Protestant monarch. The Fire, and the association of Catholics with arson, became an essential polemical tool for those wishing to show the seriousness of the Popish threat to England. The huge material loss it had created tapped into fears about the loss of 'Liberty and Property', and made Whig attempts to save them from arbitrary and tyrannical government more resonant.[45] The memory of the Fire, as well as the constant threat it posed to urban areas, helped to foster popular belief in the Popish Plot.[46] Widespread anti-Catholic demonstrations started in London on 5 November 1673. At the annual election of London sheriffs at Guildhall in 1676 one candidate, the linen draper Francis Jenks (son-in-law of the Leveller leader William Walwyn) made a speech that summed up many of the concerns that Londoners felt. Jenks warned of the threat of Catholic arsonists. Jenks' speech also mentioned widespread concerns that Charles II's government had not been active enough since the Fire in protecting London's economy from French competition. Jenks closed by demanding that the City petition the king to summon a new parliament. As a result of his speech Jenks was imprisoned for three months.[47] A 1676 letter that purported to be written by the English translator and secretary of the Marquis of Louvois, France's secretary of state for war, claimed that York had helped spread the Fire, writing that he looked on the blaze 'Janus-like, with one Face seeming concerned for the lamentable Disaster, and with the other rejoicing to see that noble Pile reduced to Ashes, and its Citizens ruined; who had at all Times been the greatest Propugnators for Libertie, and Property'.[48] The poet Andrew Marvell's *Account of the Growth of Popery, and Arbitrary Government in England* (1677) asserted that the Pope had planned the Fire to weaken England.[49]

Paranoia about Catholic conspiracies reached its apogee during the Popish Plot. One of its key figures was Israel Tonge, who was made rector of St Mary Staining in June 1666. Just over three months later the church was destroyed in the Fire. It was not rebuilt. In 1670 Tonge petitioned Charles II for the rectory of Broadwater in Sussex, as 'amongst his sufferings by the dreadfull conflagracon . . . he . . . sustained the loss of his . . . parish Church together with his Parsonage and Glebe houses'. Tonge did not receive this preferment, but from 1672 he held the rectories of St Michael Wood Street and Aston, Herefordshire.[50] Tonge blamed Catholics (and Jesuits in particular) for his losses, and set about publishing reports of their sinister plotting. He was generally regarded as being unbalanced, and his theories did not gain much traction. In early 1677 Tonge met Titus Oates in London, and the two agreed to co-write anti-Catholic pamphlets. Oates was another clergyman with an unfavourable reputation. He had been dismissed as a naval chaplain for sodomy and recently been sacked from his post as the Protestant chaplain to the Earl of Norfolk's London household. Despite his agreement with Tonge, on 3 March Oates converted to Catholicism, and set off to study at Jesuit seminaries in France and Spain. In June 1678 Oates returned to London, claiming that his conversion had been false and that he had only carried it out to gain intelligence about Catholic plotting. Oates and Tonge reacquainted and wrote a manuscript detailing a Catholic plot to assassinate Charles II. The king was informed of the plot on 13 August but was sceptical about its existence. Even so, any threat to his life could not be ignored. On 6 September Oates and Tonge swore an affidavit of their claims before Sir Edmund Berry Godfrey, a timber merchant and justice of the peace. Godfrey had been knighted and rewarded with plate worth £200 for his role in stopping the Fire. At the end of the month Oates was summoned before the Privy Council to give an account of the plot, accusing dozens of people of being involved. The accused included Edward Colman, a Catholic courtier (and incidentally a friend of Godfrey's). Colman was arrested and a search of his papers found he had corresponded with Louis XIV's Jesuit confessor, raising suspicions further. It took the mysterious death of Godfrey for the plot to be seriously believed. On 17 October Godfrey's body was found in Primrose Hill, north of London. Oates used the memory of the Fire to whip up hysteria. He claimed that Popish agents had murdered Godfrey to show their malice towards him for preventing their plot to destroy London in 1666.[51] London was in uproar. John Evelyn recorded that 'The barbarous murder of Sir *Edmund Bery-Godfry*, found strangled about this time, as was manifest by the Papists . . . put the whole nation in a new fermentation against them'.[52] After Parliament reassembled on 21 October they heard testimony from Oates and Tongue. The House of Lords persuaded Charles II to order the expulsion of all Catholics from a twenty-mile radius around London. Oates was given apartments in Whitehall and an annual income of £1,200. His accusations had been entirely fabricated, but were taken seriously. This was partly because they were telling people what they wanted to hear, and confirming their long-standing fears and prejudices regarding Catholics.[53] The accusations led to the arrest and imprisonment of hundreds of Catholics and the execution of twenty-four people, including Colman, who was hung, drawn and quartered for treason on 3 December.

The Popish Plot raised concern in the City. In December 1677 it was ordered that the 1667 Act of Common Council to prevent fires be reprinted and sent to each alderman to be read at the wardmote.[54] The next year, it was legislated that 'in these times of Danger' there should be a curfew and that all cellar windows should have shutters 'for Prevencon of fire balls being thrown into the said windowes'.[55] Similar legislation was passed in sixteenth-century France after fears of plots to fire various urban centres.[56] This showed how claims made in Brooke's supposed report about the use of incendiary devices manifested themselves. It stated that fireballs were thrown or put 'at the end of a long pole, and lighting it with a peice of match, to put it in at a window'.[57] On 12 September 1679 Sir Thomas Player, the City Chamberlain and a prominent London Whig, led a large body of citizens to meet with the Lord Mayor (Sir James Edwards, a Tory) to express the gravity of the Popish menace. Player had been a supporter of the Court faction but he had turned against Charles II because of frustration at a perceived lack of support for London after the Fire. At Guildhall, utilising the memory of the Fire, Player stated, 'it cannot be forgot, That . . . this City was Destroyed . . . by the Cursed Designs of the *Papists*, it being now out of all Doubt, That they Burnt the City'.[58] Such claims were literally set in stone in June 1681 when an inscription was added to the Monument stating that Catholics were responsible for starting the Fire. When a large number of London apprentices addressed a petition to Lord Mayor Ward in September 1681, they emphasised the danger of Popish plots, and presented their petition on the anniversary of the Fire. They also brazenly appropriated the event by claiming Tories had helped to start the blaze.[59] By summer 1680 Whigs politically dominated London, controlling the Lord Mayoralty, sheriffs, the Common Council and livery companies. Even when Charles II began to recover his influence there by installing a Tory Lord Mayor, John Moore, in 1681, he was unable to totally bring London under his complete control.[60]

At the height of the Popish Plot panic in 1679, the Fire was frequently mentioned. Oates' account asserted that there had been an active Catholic plot to fire London since February 1665. During the fire the plotters had been helped by fifty to sixty Irishmen, using 700 fireballs. They had also employed men and women to plunder the ruined City.[61] William Bedloe, a fraudster and criminal who had supported Oates' claims, published a book setting forth the techniques used by Catholic plotters to start the Fire – for example, by using fireballs or firing their own houses. He denied the providential view of the Fire, writing that it had been propagated 'to make the Ignorant believe it was only the pure Effect of *Chance*'. Bedloe added the report of Brooke's committee, which was also included in two other texts published at that time.[62] The radical Whig Charles Blount's *Appeal from the country to the city* urged Londoners not to forget the ongoing danger of Popish plotters firing London, and their culpability in the blaze of 1666.[63] During the crisis, 'fires were confidently attributed to Papist incendiaries unless clear proof existed to the contrary'.[64] On 10 April 1679 there was a relatively minor fire in Fetter Lane, London. It was suggested it had been started by Elizabeth Oxley, a Catholic maid-servant. She was influenced by a Papist called Nicholas Stubbs, who had a supply of fireballs and the support of English, French and Irish Catholics.[65] Likewise in 1680, it was claimed that a Catholic member of York's guard bribed another maid, Margaret Clark, to start a fire in Southwark. The source also claimed that Catholics targeted neighbourhoods with old, closely packed buildings.[66]

In May 1679 the First Exclusion Bill was introduced in Parliament, attracting widespread support in the chamber and beyond. Charles II dissolved Parliament before the bill could be passed. A new Parliament assembled in October 1680. A Second Exclusion Bill passed Commons but was rejected by Lords. Parliament also passed a resolution stating that Papists had fired London in 1666 before it was dissolved in January 1681. This claim was repeated in the Oxford Parliament, which sat for one week in March 1681, where it was also alleged Tories had contributed to starting the Fire.[67] After 1681 Charles II regained control over the political situation. By this time the hysteria of the Popish Plot had died down. There was a backlash against Oates and he was arrested for sedition and imprisoned. His co-fabricants, Tonge and Bedloe, had died the previous year. The 1678 to 1681 period marked the highpoint of the polemical use of the memory of the Fire, but it would again be used to political ends in the eighteenth century.

The memory of the Great Fire in the early eighteenth century

Amidst of fears of a Jacobite invasion in the 1710s, the Fire was utilised again to remind the public of the Popish menace. Brooke's committee was frequently used. 'Opposing' this was a more providential view of the Fire. *London's Flames Set in a True Light* (1712) included the report of Brooke's committee, as well as a postscript of a supposed letter found at the Temple detailing a planned French invasion of England.[68] *The Burning of London by the Papists* appeared two years later. Although it did not include Brooke's report, its influence is clear. The Popish menace is still held to be a threat to the nation by dividing it against itself: 'They who before set our City on fire, are now as busie to set the Citizens themselves on fire one against another'. The Fire was just one branch of an overall plot, which included killing the king, subverting the government, carrying out a massacre and putting a Catholic on the throne.[69]

In 1720, two opposing tracts about the Fire were published: *An account of the Burning the City of London* and *The True Protestant Account of the Burning of London*. The former work included a verbatim copy of the report of the *Gazette*, and the latter includes the report of Brooke's committee. *The True Protestant Account* goes on to assert that all official accounts of the Fire were unreliable, as thousands of eyewitnesses saw Popish agents firing London as well as the fact that both Charles II and York were Catholics.[70] *An account of the Burning the City of London* combated this viewpoint by suggesting that the Fire was a providential event, or may have even been caused by nonconformist plotters. It included extracts from two contemporary historians; one, Dr White Kennet, Bishop of Peterborough, suggests that Republican plotters may be to blame for the Fire, whilst the other, an extract from a history of England written by Dr Lawrence Eachard, Archdeacon of Stow in Gloucestershire, took the view that the Fire was probably an accident caused by the conditions in London at the time, as well as the anger of God.[71] Eachard's opinion provoked a response from the Presbyterian historian and minister, Edmund Calamy (whose grandfather Edmund the Elder was a famed Presbyterian preacher and former curate of St Mary Aldermanbury who had been ejected for nonconformity). Calamy accused Eachard of having a 'great tenderness' towards Papists, even though 'they were evidently prov'd the authors and instruments' of the Fire.[72] Once 1666 ceased to be an event in living memory, it seems to have lost its relevance and effectiveness as a polemical trope. During the Jacobite Rising of 1745 there was little documentary mention of the Fire. A 1769 history of London by Gideon Harvey emphasised the providential nature of the Fire, and accepted that the true cause of the Fire was likely to be never known. The Stuarts, the French, the Dutch, Catholics, Jesuits and Republicans had all been blamed in the past, but ultimately Harvey determines that the Fire was probably an accident that had improved London – 'a more pardonable instance of doing evil that good may come of it, cannot perhaps be produced'.[73] By the later eighteenth century explanations for disasters began to shift away from religious, providential, interpretations to natural ones.[74]

The Fire in verse during the late 1660s

The immediate verse response to the Fire is an important study of how one of the chief modes of media in seventeenth-century England responded to a national crisis. The period after the Restoration saw poetry 'assume office'. By 1666, 'political and social circumstances had produced a situation in which poetry's immediate justification was its capacity to engage in topical issues'.[75] The representation of the Fire in contemporary verse therefore shows how this process of reflecting current events in verse took place. The Fire figured prominently in the most important political poems of the 1660s, the *Advice to a Painter* series, written by Marvell as a response to the corrupt and dissolute Restoration regime. The poems were in circulation between April and October 1666 and were published early in 1667.[76] In the *Third Advice* the catastrophes of Plague and Fire were used to lampoon the folly of the ongoing war with the Dutch. Marvell questioned the fact that fighting was allowed to continue while in the nation's capital one could 'See how men all like Ghosts, while *London* burns/Wander, and each o're his Ashes mourns'.[77]

Providential views were evident in verse representations of the Fire. *Londons Destroyer Detected* (1666) saw the Fire as providential and called for a return to godliness from London's people, so it may 'be a *place* of *praise* once more,/And *flourish*'.[78] *The Londoners Lamentation* (1666) stated that Londoners' 'sinful hearts' were guiltier than the French and Dutch agents suspected of starting the Fire.[79] John Dryden's *Annus Mirabilis* (1667) also treated fires 'as heavenly visitations', but 'brought on the nation by the guilt of Dissenters', amongst other groups.[80] He stated that God was in control of the Fire; 'Each element his dread command obeys'.[81] They are not so much judgments as 'trials of endurance' for the nation to show its loyalty. Dryden's work is essentially propaganda, an answer to the mid-1660s critique of Charles II's court and rule, and a chance for the nation to show its loyalty to the new regime.[82]

The Fire was not always viewed providentially. *The Burning of London* (1667) suggested that the causes of the Fire were ultimately unknowable, although the poem does target some likely culprits: the Dutch, the French, or the Pope.[83] The Royalist cleric Abraham Markland also pinned the blame on the French, although he suggested the Fire may have been 'helped' by a Dutch 'east-wind'.[84] Nonconformist poets tended to be more extreme in laying the blame on Catholics. The ejected minister Robert Wild left no bones about the causes of the Fire: 'Incendiary Priests, and subtile spies,/Who when our *Londons* fiery tryal came,/Like *Salamanders* feasted in the flame'.[85] Royalist poets side-stepped the issue of who caused the Fire by blaming the sins of the people. Royalists would have viewed the Fire as 'punishment' for the 'sins' of regicide and the Commonwealth, many of which occurred in London.[86] In particular, the execution of Charles I as a cause of the Fire was an important focus for Royalist-leaning poets. Eulogising Charles I had been an ongoing process since his execution. Although the numbers of Royalist eulogies may have declined since the early 1650s, they continued to re-appear, and with greater numbers after the Restoration. The typology of Charles I as 'royal martyr' was well known by 1666.[87] Therefore, there were numerous mentions of the 'martyrdom' of Charles I. *Englands Lamentation* called Charles I 'a Royal VICTIME on the stained Floor', whose death was partly due to the 'Factious Spirit' of London, which also had led to the Plague of 1665.[88] The elegist John Crouch's poem is more explicit in laying the blame on London's complicacy with Charles I's execution: 'Now *Loyal*

London has full Ransome paid/For that *Defection* the *Disloyal* made'.[89]
London thus assumed the guilt of the whole of England.

Other poets saw the Fire's purifying force as one which could improve the
fabric of London. *London Undone* (1666) portrayed the Fire as not so much
a tragedy, as an opportunity: 'When like the *Churches* you her Streets shall
see/Founded, and fronted *uniformallie/* . . . Then you'll conclude with me,
the Flames were kind,/She was not so much *ruin'd*, as *refin'd*'.[90] Jeremiah
Wells' 1667 poem *On the Rebuilding of London* predicted that London
would be improved after the Fire. This would echo the re-establishment of
the Stuart monarchy: 'So shall the City thank her cruel fate,/And bless those
flames that did their help afford,/Counting even Desolation no dear rate,/
Glad to be Ruin'd So to be Restord'.[91] Fire is therefore seen as a purifying
force, capable of wiping away sins of the past.

The verse reaction to the Fire in the later 1660s shows how strong the
providential view of the event was. The Fire became punishment for the sins
of England, and in particular London, during the years of Civil War and
Commonwealth. The Fire does not purge London of the sins of the people,
but of the sins of the past, creating a new symbol of a strong restored monarchy. Even so, poems about the Fire could also be used to criticise the
Restoration regime, and the memory of the event became a key part of the
satirical arsenal.

The Great Fire and religion

Fire was an important symbol of divine wrath. The Old Testament made it
clear that God was willing to use it to punish sinful people and nations and
move them to live more godly lives. In religious reasoning, 'disasters are
usually aimed at a group of people when their moral condition is at stake'.[92]
Fire would be there at the End of Days, when the material world would be
finally consumed. This section will examine how the Fire was described in
sermons to show how religious figures explained the Fire. It will also examine sermons given before 1666, as well as sermons given for other fires, in
order to determine what, if any, were the differences in how the Great Fire
was explained and how these explanations may have changed over time.
This section examines diaries by religious figures, as well as some other
religious writings, in order to gain a sense of how the Fire was understood
across the denominational spectrum.

The sermon was one of the chief modes of media in early modern
England. It was not just was heard from the pulpit. Printed sermons were
read, collected and used as a guide to personal piety. They were typically
sold in simple, unbound octavo pamphlets retailing at between two and four
pence.[93] Around 24,000 sermons were printed in England between 1660 and
1783.[94] For nonconformists in particular, the sermon was a key vehicle of
socialisation as well as an essential part of their spiritual life.[95] Public events
were frequently mentioned in sermons, especially disasters such as fires. The

early modern disaster sermon was an important part of the psychological recovery from trauma – the tragedy 'could only be overcome if it could be explained'.[96] The English Protestant clergy interpreted their world through a scriptural matrix, and it was scripture which formed the basis of their 'explanation' of disaster. Sermons for fast days in particular were frequently used by preachers as an occasion to rally against the sins of an undeserving people by listing the sins that had led to disaster.[97] In this section, fifty-four sermons dating from 1615 to 1770 were examined. The majority of the sermons in the sample were given on the fast day for the Fire. During the later seventeenth century the sermons regarding the Fire specifically were given, on the whole, by Anglican clergy. Sermons memorialising the Fire given by nonconformist ministers do survive, but all dated from the early eighteenth century.

Ninety per cent of the sermons examined viewed fires as the representation of the wrath of God against the sins of the people. This is consistent with John Spurr's assertion that 'Anglican preachers dwelt in morbid detail upon the "controversy" between a wrathful God and an incorrigible nation'.[98] Anglican preachers had similar views. In a sermon to the House of Lords on 10 October 1666 Seth Ward, then Bishop of Exeter, asserted that, 'The *breath* of the Lord *kindled* the fire, he *rode* upon *Cherub* . . . He made the *winds* his *Messengers*, and the *flames* of fire his *Ministers*'.[99] Similarly, in a sermon to the House of Commons directly after the Fire, Edward Stillingfleet noted that great fires represented 'the *kindling* of his [God's] *wrath* against us'.[100] Nathaniel Hardy, vicar of St Martin-in-the-Fields, in a sermon just after the Fire stated that 'this *Fire* which hath laid *waste* so many *beautiful Churches*, goodly *Fabricks* and *Houses* . . . [was] the *fire of God*, a fire of his *sending*'.[101] Nonconformists were no different. The dissenting minister Matthew Henry told his congregation in 1713 that 'God had made *London* as a fiery Oven in the Day of his Wrath, and the Flames went on like a mighty Army'.[102] Textual similarities between nonconformist and Anglican clergy are commonplace across all subjects, 'they found their inspirations in the same books, appealed to the same examples and even the same quotations'.[103] All preachers viewed their world providentially and saw God's hand active in everything. Thus, the vast majority concluded that any catastrophe in a sinful world would be regarded as symbolic of God's wrath against the transgressions of the people.

Fire was used to warn of the vanity of material goods. On the 1682 fast day for the Fire, the popular preacher Henry Hesketh argued that the event showed 'how fugitive and uncertain' the material world was.[104] Benjamin Ibbot, rector of St Vedast-alias-Foster and St Michael-le-Quern, argued in 1711 that people should not place their happiness in earthly things, as 'the World . . . which is the Support of these Things . . . is it self hastening to a Dissolution'.[105] Nonconformist sermons shared similar viewpoints. Philip Doddridge, minister of Northampton, in a 1738 sermon on the occasion of a fire in nearby Wellingborough, stated that the event showed 'the Vanity of worldly Possessions, and the superior Value of spiritual and eternal

Blessings'.[106] Preaching after a fire in London in 1748, the Independent minister Thomas Gibbons, urged his congregation to 'turn off our Eyes and Hearts from this empty delusive Scene, and fix them upon the incomparable Excellency, and unchangeable Perpetuity of the World above'.[107]

The Final Judgment was alluded to ten times in the sermons examined. Once again, neither established nor nonconformist clergy held a clear monopoly on mentioning it. Christopher Flower, rector of St Margaret Lothbury, preaching of the fast day for the Fire in 1669, stated that on the Last Day, Jesus' eyes would be like a '*Flame* of *Fire*, that is, agile, nimble, and able to penetrate any thing'.[108] Matthew Henry used the example of the Great Fire to show how much more dreadful Judgment Day would be, when Jesus would be revealed in 'the *flaming* Fire, the Fire that will *devour before him*; he will come with an *innumerable Company of Angels*, and each one of those Spirits is *a Flame of Fire*'.[109] Another London-based minister, Gibbons, called fire a 'premonition' of the last judgment, when Jesus would

> pour from his Throne a Flood of Fire, by whose inextinguishable, insufferable, and overwhelming Fury, not only Streets, Towns, Cities, and Countries, but the whole Globe shall be set on Fire, and become one general Heap and Wreck of burning Destruction.[110]

Fires were used to remind congregations of the coming of the ultimate judgment, and thus acted as an imperative towards personal reformation. Hellfire was mentioned in twelve sermons. Robert Elborough, vicar of St Lawrence Pountney, also made the difference between earthly and Hellfire clear when he reminded his listeners to repent in a sermon given just after the Great Fire: 'though our houses be destroyed by Fire on earth, our souls may not be destroyed by Fire in Hell'.[111]

The possible benefits of fire were dwelt upon. Such sermons urged their listeners to use fires as an occasion to purge their lives of sin and purify their lives. Hardy, preaching after the Great Fire, urged his listeners to use the event as a chance to purge their lives of sin: 'let the *heat* of that *flame* not only *thaw* our *frozen* hearts into *tears* of godly *sorrow*, but *melt* away the *dross* of our *corruption*'.[112] William Gearing, the rector of Christchurch, Surrey, preaching on the fast day for the Fire in 1688 stated that 'Fire cleaneth, purgeth, and getteth out the dross', and reminded his congregation that men can glorify God by losing their sins after a fire.[113] According to most sermons, the positive purgative effects of fire were not always felt. William Hopkins, curate of Mortlake in Surrey, said in his 1683 sermon on the fast day for the Fire, 'We have passed through the Fire, but are not purified'.[114] The physical properties of material fire are thus transmuted into the spiritual life of the congregation, as a reminder to desist from sin.

It was commonplace to give examples of previous fires. Around one in five of the sermons examined mentioned some past fire. The scriptural example of Sodom and Gomorrah was mentioned most frequently. The most frequently alluded to classical event was the Great Fire of Rome (64), allegedly started by Nero. This is because it could be used to show the mendacity and ruthlessness of the early modern ruler of Rome – the Pope. On a thanksgiving sermon for the twentieth anniversary of the Gunpowder Plot, the godly minister Theodore Hering compared Guy Fawkes to Nero, as they had both wished to fire a city and blame Christians – or in Fawkes' case, according to Hering, Puritans.[115] Contemporary fires were also mentioned. Thomas Cooke, rector of St Nicholas Worcester, in a sermon after a fire there in 1703 mentioned the fire which destroyed Port Royal in Jamaica that year.[116] The Great Fire eventually became a historical exemplar of how a city's transgressions were punished. William Parker in 1748 reminded his congregation that even through the Fire was nearly a century ago, and despite the fact that many of London's present inhabitants were not descended from the City's inhabitants in 1666, they should still learn from the example of 1666.[117]

Despite the popular belief in Popish arson plots, only one in five of the sermons examined specifically targeted Catholics as fire starters. All considered them secondary causes to the primary cause of popular sinfulness. No one ideological group tended to target Catholics more than any other; they are mentioned in statistically comparable numbers of sermons by Anglicans and nonconformists. A typical example is Hesketh's statement that even though there was a chance that Catholic plotters might be to blame for the Fire, God and sin should not be forgotten.[118] Other sermons were more explicit in blaming the Catholics, although they still dwelled on sin as the primary cause. Hopkins stated, 'neither the strong East-winds nor the famous *Popish* or *French* Fire-balls carried on the Fire so much as the Trains our Sins had laid in all quarters of the City'.[119] Ibbot, referencing the 'lost' report of Brooke's 1666 parliamentary committee, argued that the Popish faction were 'active and responsible' – but this does not make the Fire any less of a divine punishment.[120] It is probable that in many other sermons given in the years after the Fire, Catholic plotting was explicitly mentioned. On 16 December 1678, as the hysteria of the Popish Plot was beginning to emerge, Evelyn recorded hearing a sermon at St James Westminster from a royal chaplain, Dr John Butler, 'exhorting to stedfastnesse in the Faith, & Liberty, in which Christ had made us free in this Land especialy, reckning up the heavy Yoake of *Popish* bondage &c'.[121] Such sermons were never given in the 'official' context of the fast day, nor were they published in the years after the Fire. Ultimately, in the majority of sermons Catholics were not blamed wholly for any Fire because the vast majority of clergy believed fires, and other providential events, were divine punishments.

The Fire and nonconformist clergy

There are no surviving published sermons given on the subject of the Great Fire by nonconformist ministers until Matthew Henry's in 1713. It is likely that there was an 'alternative' nonconformist perception of the Fire in the years immediately after 1666. In some respects, the Fire was a vindication for nonconformist ministers, who had been banished from London in the early 1660s. To them, the Fire showed God's displeasure at this act. The Fire had deprived the established church of most of its 'physical assets' in the City. Nonconformist preachers such as Joseph Caryl, Thomas Brooks and John Owen flooded into the City to fill the vacuum.[122] Nathaniel Vincent, the younger brother of Thomas Vincent, 'came to the City soon after the Fire . . . and preach'd to large Multitudes. Sometimes he would have Thousands to hear him, as he was preaching in the Ruins'. He remained in London, and kept a meeting house in Southwark.[123] In spite of the fact that eight dissenting meeting houses were appropriated for the use of London's dis-placed Anglican parishioners, metropolitan nonconformity found ways to adapt, preaching in warehouses, company halls and quickly built structures. Ultimately London's nonconformist community was resilient in the face of the Fire, and even may have grown in size.[124] In 1675 the Court of Aldermen was informed that conventicles continued to be held in many public places and livery company halls. A year later it was recorded that the halls of eleven companies were used as conventicles.[125] The Fire was also a significant event for nonconformists in the New World. They believed that God had punished England for its transgressions by sending the Fire. Vincent's account of the Plague and Fire in London was reprinted in Cambridge, Massachusetts in 1668.[126] There was a significant nonconformist sermon reaction to the Fire in the late seventeenth century, but what form would it take?

Philip Henry, an ejected minister living in Wales in 1666, recorded his reactions in his diary. Sin was the ultimate cause – 'the nations sin, the sin of london, my own sin'. The event also showed how vain the material world was, 'how far it must needs bee from making a man happy, seeing in one moment it makes to itself wings and fly's away'. It was also a reminder of the End of Days, 'when all the world shall bee on fire and the elements shall melt with fervent heat, the earth also and all the works that are therein shall bee burnt up'. Henry also wrote that the Fire was a voice to the government saying 'let my people go' in response to legislation against nonconformists. He also wrote that it was a 'mercy' that dissenting ministers had been cast out of London before the Fire, as Lot had been cast out of Sodom.[127] Baxter had a similar view of the event, that 'It was a sight that might have given any Man a lively sense of the Vanity of this World, and all the Wealth and Glory of it, and of the future conflagration of all the World'.[128] Accounts of the Fire published by nonconformists such as Rolls, Vincent and Doolittle accepted that it was caused by divine anger and should serve as a reminder of the consequences of sin, the transitory nature of the material world and the eventual coming of the Final Judgment. Nonconformist sources on the Fire were also far more confident in ascribing the event to Catholic plotters. It is probable that many in the Quaker community believed that the Fire had been a consequence of Catholic arsonists; the Quaker George Whitehead recorded in his autobiography that the event was part of a Popish plot. He also records a foretelling of the Fire two days before it occurred, when a Quaker from Huntingdonshire came to London in great haste 'and foretold his Vision . . . That the City would be laid Waste by Fire'.[129] There were many similarities between the immediate responses of the established and nonconformist clergy to the Fire. Broadly, all agreed the event was caused by divine anger at the sins of the people. There were some key differences. Nonconformist sources tended to concentrate more on the moral decay of London. They also, predictably, emphasised the recent legislations against nonconformity as contributory to divine anger. Finally, they were far more certain in blaming Catholic plotters for the Fire than the established clergy were in the years after the Fire.

The exact descriptive language of fire in general was by no means consistent across any ideological group, event or time period. It was variously used as an occasion to dwell on Hellfire, the Last Judgment and the vanity of earthly things. There was one feature which the vast majority of sermons had in common – that it symbolised divine anger. This remained consistent before and after the Fire. Even criticism of Catholics and accusations of Papist plots remained secondary to these reflections on God's displeasure with the nation. In this respect there was significant continuity in the attitudes to fire revealed in early modern sermons. This did not extend to the other facets of the language of fire detailed above, none of which were mentioned nearly as frequently as the assertion that fire arose because of the fury of God.

Conclusions

The Great Fire was a heavily contested phenomenon, and was quickly 'politicised' across all forms of contemporary media. Royalists used the Fire to remind the reader of England's (and London's) sins during the Interregnum, and so viewed the event providentially. England's clergy frequently mentioned the Fire. It was almost always linked to the concept that it had been brought about by divine anger. This providential view of fire was not an innovation, but a familiar trope in early modern religious thought. The established clergy seem not to have linked Catholics to the Fire directly. However, nonconformists were quicker to associate Popish plotting with the Fire – although they still held that God was the ultimate author of the disaster. Competing with this view was the argument that England's earthly enemies had started the Fire. The notion that the Dutch had been responsible was quickly jettisoned in favour of blaming France and Catholics. This was utilised by Whigs in particular. During the Exclusion Crisis, the Fire was used to warn of the chaos that would befall England if it was to ever to have a Catholic monarch. These ideas resurfaced during the Jacobite threat of the early eighteenth century. The symbolic value of the Great Fire, therefore, had a longer-lasting impact than its damage on London's socio-economic fabric.

Notes

1 V. Harding, 'London and Middlesex in the 1660s', in *London and Middlesex 1666 Hearth Tax*, ed. M. Davies et al. (London: British Record Society, 2014), 37.

2 N. Smith, '"Making Fire": Conflagration and Religious Controversy in Seventeenth-Century London', in *Imagining Early Modern London: Perceptions and Portrayals of the City from Stow to Strype*, ed. J.F. Merritt (Cambridge: Cambridge University Press, 2001), 273–93.

3 C. Wall, *The Literary and Cultural Spaces of Restoration London* (Cambridge: Cambridge University Press, 1998), ix.

4 S. Pepys, *The Diary of Samuel Pepys*, ed. R. Latham and W. Matthews, 11 vols. (1st ed. London: G. Bell and Sons, 1970–83), vii, 296, 299.

5 A. Walsham, *Providence in Early Modern England* (Oxford: Oxford University Press, 1999), 122–3, 137–8.

6 LMA, Jour. 46, fol. 130r.

7 M.M. Verney, ed., *Memoirs of the Verney Family from the Restoration to the Revolution 1660 to 1696* (London: Longmans, Green, and Co, 1899), 142.

8 P. Roberts, 'Arson, Conspiracy and Rumour in Early Modern Europe', *Continuity and Change*, 12 (1997), 17–20; M.L. Allemeyer, 'Profane Hazard or Divine Judgement? Coping with Urban Fire in the 17th Century', *Historical Social Research*, 32 (2007), 163.

9 J. Miller, *Popery and Politics in England 1660–1668* (Cambridge: Cambridge University Press, 1973), 89; C.R. Boxer, *Some Contemporary Reactions to the Lisbon Earthquake of 1755* (Lisbon: Faculdade de Letras, Universidade de Lisboa, 1956), 9.

10 J. Selwood, *Diversity and Difference in Early Modern London* (Farnham: Ashgate, 2010), 3.

11 S.C.A. Pincus, *Protestantism and Patriotism: Ideologies and the Making of English Foreign Policy, 1650–1668* (Cambridge: Cambridge University Press, 1996), 347–51.

12 Verney, ed., *Memoirs of the Verney Family*, 137.

13 S.C.A. Pincus, 'From Butterboxes to Wooden Shoes: The Shift in English Popular Sentiment from Anti-Dutch to Anti-French in the 1670s', *Historical Journal*, 38 (1995), 333–61.

14 T. Harris, *Restoration: Charles II and His Kingdoms 1660–1685* (London: Allen Lane, 2005), 43–84.

15 F.E. Dolan, *Whores of Babylon: Catholicism, Gender, and Seventeenth-Century Print Culture* (Ithaca, NY and London: Cornell University Press, 2005), 20–2.

16 Pepys, *Diary*, vii, 356–7.

17 J. Milward, *The Diary of John Milward, Esq. Member of Parliament for Derbyshire, September, 1666 to May, 1668*, ed. C. Robbins (Cambridge: Cambridge University Press, 1938), 68–9.

18 LMA, Petition of Citizens to the Common Council relating to an enquiry after the causes of the late dreadful firing of the City of London, COL/SJ/03/004, 2, 1667.

19 LMA, Petition of the Common Council to the House of Commons touching the Fire, COL/SJ/03/004, 3, 1667.

20 *A True and Faithful Account of the Several Informations Exhibited to the Honourable Committee Appointed by the Parliament to Inquire into the Late Dreadful Burning of the City of London* (London, 1667), 5–24. See also: *Londons Flames Discovered by Informations Taken before the Committee Appointed to Enquire after the Burning of the City of London and after the Insolency of the Papists, &c* (London, 1667).

21 TNA, Letter from Sir Thomas Langton and Sir John Knight to Arlington, 13 July 1667, SP 29/209, 75.

22 TNA, Letter from Daniel Fleming to Williamson, 16 August 1667, SP 29/213, 118; Letter from Sir Philip Musgrave to Williamson, 19 August 1667, SP 29/214, 27.

23 T. Harris, *London Crowds in the Reign of Charles II: Propaganda and Politics from the Restoration until the Exclusion Crisis* (Cambridge: Cambridge University Press, 1987), 72.

24 R.D. Tumbleson, *Catholicism in the English Protestant Imagination: Nationalism, Religion and Literature, 1660–1745* (Cambridge: Cambridge University Press, 1998), 1–2, 13.

25 Dolan, *Whores of Babylon*, 8.

26 F.E. Dolan, 'Ashes and "the Archive": The London Fire of 1666, Partisanship, and Proof', *Journal of Medieval and Early Modern Studies*, 31 (2001), 382.

27 *A Wild-Fire Plot. Found Out in Ireland: Shewing How the Rebels Would Have Consumed the City of Dublin with Wild-Fire* (London: Thomas Bates, 1641), 1.

28 Miller, *Popery and Politics*, 89–90.

29 A. Wood, *The Life and Times of Anthony Wood, Antiquary, of Oxford, 1632–1695, Described by Himself*, Volume 2, ed. A. Clark (Oxford: Clarendon Press for the Oxford Historical Society, 1891), 93.

30 BL, T. Rugge, *Mercurius Politicus Redivius; or, a Collection of the Most Materiall Occurrences and Transactions in Publick Affaires, Since Anno Domini 1659, Volume II*. Additional MS 10117, 1659–72, fol. 182v; *True and Faithful Account*, 31.

31 *Pyrotechnica Loyolana, Ignatian Fire-Works: Or, the Fiery Jesuits Temper and Behaviour* (London: G.E.C.T, 1667), 57.

32 *Trap ad Crucem: Or, the Papists Watch-Word* (London, 1670).

33 H. Gamrath, 'The Great Fire of Copenhagen in 1728', in *Destruction and Reconstruction of Towns, Volume 1: Destruction by Earthquakes, Fire and Water*, ed. M. Körner (Bern: Paul Haupt, 1999), 299–300.

34 Selwood, *Diversity and Difference*, 1–2, 148–56.

35 BL, Letter of 1676 Relating to the Firing of London in 1666, Additional MS 15057, 1676, fol. 45r.

36 S.N. Zwicker, *Lines of Authority: Politics and English Literary Culture, 1649–1689* (Ithaca, NY and London: Cornell University Press, 1993), 94.

37 L.L. Knoppers, *Historicizing Milton: Spectacle, Power and Poetry in Restoration England* (Athens, GA: University of Georgia Press, 1994), 144.

38 Pincus, *Protestantism and Patriotism*, 394.

39 Wall, *Literary and Cultural Spaces*, 7–9.

40 Rege Sincera, *Observations both Historical and Moral upon the Burning of London, September 1666* (London: Thomas Ratcliffe, 1667), 1–7, 9–11.

41 E. Waterhouse, *A Short Narrative of the Late Dreadful Fire in London* (London: W.G. for Richard Thrale and James Thrale, 1667), 23–4, 65–6, 136.

42 T. Vincent, *God's Terrible Voice in the City* (London: G. Calvert, 1667), 20–3, 47, 51, 61–2, 70–1.

43 S. Rolls, *The Burning of London in the Year 1666* (London: R.I. for Thomas Parkhurst, Nathaniel Ranew and Jonathan Robinson, 1667), part 1, 25–88, part 2, 93, 102–3, 110–1, part 3, 11, 79.

44 T. Doolittle, *Rebukes for Sin by God's Burning Anger: By the Burning of London: By the Burning of the World: By the Burning of the Wicked in Hell-Fire* (London: Dorman Newman, 1667), 9, 89–95, 130–52, 190–216.

45 Harris, *London Crowds*, 111.

46 J.P. Kenyon, *The Popish Plot* (London: Heinemann, 1972), 13.

47 Harris, *Restoration*, 81–2; G.S. De Krey, *London and the Restoration, 1659–1683* (Cambridge: Cambridge University Press, 2005), 145.

48 BL, Add MS 15057, fol. 45r.

49 A. Marvell, *An Account of the Growth of Popery, and Arbitrary Government in England* (Amsterdam, 1677), 13.

50 TNA, Petition of Dr Israel Tongue to the King, 22 August 1670, SP 29/278, 30; A. Marshall, 'Tonge, Israel (1621–1680)', in *Oxford Dictionary of National Biography*, ed. H.C.G. Matthew and B. Harrison, 60 vols. (Oxford: Oxford University Press, 2004), liv, 966–9.

51 A. Marshall, *The Strange Death of Edmund Godfrey: Plots and Politics in Restoration London* (Stroud: Sutton, 1999), 32–3.

52 J. Evelyn, *The Diary of John Evelyn*, ed. E.S. De Beer, 6 vols. (Oxford: Clarendon Press, 1955), iv, 155.

53 Harris, *Restoration*, 136–7.

54 LMA, Rep. 83, fols. 45v–46r.

55 LMA, Rep. 84, fols. 4v–5r.

56 Roberts, 'Arson, Conspiracy and Rumour', 17.

57 *Londons Flames Discovered*, 3.

58 *An Account of the Proceedings at the Guildhall of the City of London, on Saturday, September 12. 1679* (London, 1679), 2; De Krey, *London and the Restoration*, 135; Player's father was also called Sir Thomas, and had also served as City Chamberlain from 1664 to 1672, preceding his son in the office.

59 *The Address of above Twenty Thousand of the Loyal Protestant Apprentices of London: Humbly Presented to the Right Honourable the Lord Mayor* (London: William Ingol the Elder, 1681); De Krey, *London and the Restoration*, 135.

60 Harris, *Restoration*, 193–6.

61 T. Oates, *A True Narrative of the Horrid Plot of the Popish Party against the Life of His Sacred Majesty, the Government, and the Protestant Religion* (London: T. Parkhurst and T. Cockerill, 1679), 22–5.

62 W. Bedloe, *A Narrative and Impartial Discovery of the Horrid Popish Plot: Carried on for the Burning and Destroying of London and Westminster, with Their Suburbs, &c* (London: R. Boulter, J. Hancock, R. Smith and B. Harris, 1679), 1, 4–12, 15–27; *London's Flames: Being an Exact and Impartial Account of Divers Informations Given in to the Committee of Parliament* (London, 1679); *London's Flames Reviv'd: Or, an Account of the Several Informations Exhibited to a Committee Appointed by Parliament, September the 25th 1666* (London: Nathaniel Ranew, 1680).

63 C. Blount, *An Appeal from the Country to the City, for the Preservation of His Majesties Person, Liberty, Property, and the Protestant Religion* (London, 1679), 1–7.

64 J.R. Jones, *The First Whigs: The Politics of the Exclusion Crisis, 1678–1683* (London: Oxford University Press, 1961), 24.

65 *The Papists Plot of Firing Discovered: In a Perfect Account of the Late Fire in Fetter Lane, London* (London, 1679), 3–7.

66 *Warning for Servants: And a Caution to Protestants: Or the Case of Margaret Clark, Lately Executed for Firing Her Masters Houses in Southwark* (London: Thomas Parkhurst, 1680).

67 Miller, *Popery and Politics*, 181–2.

68 *London's Flames Set in a True Light: Being a True and Faithful Account of the Several Informations Exhibited to the Honourable Committee Appointed by the Parliament to Inquire into the Late Dreadful Burning of the City of London* (London: J. How, 1712), 7–25, 34.

69 *The Burning of London by the Papists: Or, a Memorial to Protestants on the Second of September* (London: John Clark, 1714), 4–5, 9.

70 *The True Protestant Account of the Burning of London, or, an Antidote, against the Poyson and Malignity of a Late Lying Legend, Entituled an Account of the Burning of London, &c* (London: B. Baddam for S. Popping, 1720), 5–22.

71 *An Account of the Burning the City of London, as It Was Publish'd by the Special Authority of the King and Council in the Year, 1666: To Which Is Added, the Opinion of Dr Kennet the Present Bishop of Peterborough, as Publish'd by*

His Lordship's Order, and That of Dr Eachard, Relating Thereunto (London: J. Stone, 1720), 14–19, 22–9.

72 E. Calamy, *A Letter to Mr Archdeacon Echard, Upon Occasion of His History of England* (London: John Clark, 1718), 57.

73 G. Harvey, *The City Remembrancer: Being Historical Narratives of the Great Plague, at London 1665; Great Fire, 1666; and Great Storm, 1703, Volume 3: Of the Fire and the Storm* (London: W. Nicoll, 1769), 1–23, 52–67.

74 M. Mulcahy, 'Urban Catastrophes and Imperial Relief in the Eighteenth-Century British Atlantic World: Three Case Studies', in *Cities and Catastrophes: Coping with Emergency in European History*, ed. G. Massard-Guilbaud, H.L. Platt and D. Schott (Frankfurt: Peter Lang, 2002), 110–1.

75 R. Trickett, 'Samuel Butler and the Minor Restoration Poets', in *English Poetry and Prose 1540–1674*, ed. C. Ricks (London: Sphere, 1970), 311.

76 M. Dzelzainis, 'L'Estrange, Marvell and the *Directions to a Painter*: The Evidence of Bodleian Library, MS Gough London 14', in *Roger L'Estrange and the Making of Restoration Culture*, ed. A. Dunan-Page and B. Lynch (Farnham: Ashgate, 2008), 54–5.

77 A. Marvell, *The Second, and Third Advice to a Painter, for Drawing the History of Our Navall Actions, the Two Last Years, 1665: And 1666 in Answer to Mr. Waller* (1667), 31.

78 E.N., *Londons Destroyer Detected; and Destruction Lamented: Or, Some Serious Ruminations, and Profitable Reflections upon the Late Dreadful, Dismal, and Never-to-Be-Forgotten Conflagration* (London, 1666), 8.

79 R.A. Aubin, ed., *London in Flames, London in Glory: Poems on the Fire and Rebuilding of London 1666–1709* (New Brunswick, NJ: Rutgers University Press, 1943), 87–8.

80 G.D. Lord, *Classical Presences in Seventeenth-Century English Poetry* (New Haven and London: Yale University Press, 1987), 133.

81 J. Dryden, 'Annus Mirabilis', in *John Dryden: A Critical Edition of the Major Works*, ed. K. Walker (Oxford: Oxford University Press, 1987), 59.

82 C.V. Wedgwood, *Poetry and Politics Under the Stuarts* (Cambridge: Cambridge University Press, 1960), 138–43.

83 Aubin, ed., *London in Flames*, 56.

84 A. Markland, *Poems on His Majestie's Birth and Restauration, His Highness Prince Rupert's and His Grace the Duke of Albermarle's Naval Victories; the Late Great Pestilence and Fire of London* (London: James Cotterel, 1667), 18–20.

85 Aubin, ed., *London in Flames*, 154.

86 Smith, '"Making Fire"', 286.

87 A. Lacey, 'Elegies and Commemorative Verse in Honour of Charles the Martyr, 1649–60', in *The Regicides and the Execution of Charles I*, ed. J. Peacey (Basingstoke and New York: Palgrave, 2001), 225–46.

88 *Englands Lamentation for the Dismall Conflagration of Her Imperial Chamber the Citie of London: Sept. 2d. MDCLXVI* (York: F. Mawbarne, 1666), 6–7.

89 Aubin, ed., *London in Flames*, 52.

90 Aubin, ed., *London in Flames*, 55.

91 Aubin, ed., *London in Flames*, 128.

92 A. Akasoy, 'The Man-Made Disaster: Fire in Cities in the Medieval Middle East', *Historical Social Research*, 32 (2007), 77.

93 T. Claydon, 'The Sermon, the "Public Sphere" and the Political Culture of Late Seventeenth-Century England', in *The English Sermon Revised: Religion, Literature and History 1600–1750*, ed. L. Ferrell and P. McCullough (Manchester: Manchester University Press, 2000), 213–14.

94 J. Green, 'Teaching the Reformation: The Clergy as Preachers, Catechists, Authors and Teachers', in *The Protestant Clergy of Early Modern Europe*, ed. C.S. Dixon and L. Schorn-Schütte (Basingstoke: Palgrave Macmillan, 2003), 161.

95 C. Durston and J. Eales, 'Introduction: The Puritan Ethos, 1560–1700', in *The Culture of English Puritanism, 1560–1700*, ed. C. Durston and J. Eales (Basingstoke: Macmillan, 1996), 20.

96 Allemeyer, 'Profane Hazard or Divine Judgement?', 147.

97 P. Collinson, 'Elizabethan and Jacobean Puritanism as Forms of Popular Religious Culture', in *The Culture of English Puritanism, 1560–1700*, ed. C. Durston and J. Eales (Basingstoke: Macmillan, 2000), 46.

98 J. Spurr, 'Virtue, Religion and Government: The Anglican Uses of Providence', in *The Politics of Religion in Restoration England*, ed, T. Harris, P. Seward and M. Goldie (Oxford: Basil Blackwell, 1990), 30.

99 S. Ward, *A Sermon Preached before the Peers, in the Abby-Church at Westminster* (London: E.C. for James Collins, 1666), 24.

100 E. Stillingfleet, *A Sermon Preached before the Honourable House of Commons, at St. Margarets Westminster* (London: Robert White for Henry Mortlock, 1666), 2.

101 N. Hardy, *Lamentation, Mourning and Woe: Sighed Forth in a Sermon Preached in the Parish-Church of St Martin in the Fields, on the 9th Day of September: Being the Lords-Day after the Dismal Fire in the City of London* (London: Thomas Newcomb for William Grantham, 1666), 26.

102 M. Henry, *A Memorial of the Fire of the Lord, in a Sermon Preach'd Sept. 2d. 1713: Being the Day of the Commemoration of the Burning of London, in 1666: At Mr. Reynold's Meeting-Place Near the Monument* (London: John Lawrence, 1713), 20.

103 F. Deconinck-Brossard, 'Eighteenth-Century Sermons and the Age', in *Crown and Mitre: Religion and Society in Northern Europe since the Reformation*, ed. W.M. Jacob and N. Yates (Woodbridge: Boydell Press, 1993), 109.

104 H. Hesketh, *A Sermon Preached before the Right Honourable the Lord Mayor and Aldermen of the City of London at Bow Church, September the 2d. 1682* (London: Robert Sollers, 1682), 10.

105 B. Ibbot, *The Dissolution of This World by Fire: A Sermon Preach'd before the Right Honourable Sir Gilbert Heathcote, Knight, Lord-Mayor, the Aldermen, and Citizens of London, at the Cathedral-Church of St. Paul, on Monday, September 3. 1711* (London: John Wyat, 1711), 21.

106 P. Doddridge, *A Sermon Preached at Wellingborough, in Northamptonshire, November 9. MDCCXXXVIII* (London: R. Hett and J. Buckland, 1739), 31.

107 T. Gibbons, *The Divine Improvement of Desolating Judgments Represented: In a Sermon Preached at Haberdasher's-Hall, March 27: On Occasion of the Dreadful Fire in the City, on March 25, 1748* (London: J. Oswald, R. King, J. Buckland, J. Ward and E. Gardiner, 1748), 37.

108 C. Flower, *Mercy In the Midst of Judgment, with a Glympse of or a Glance on London's Glorious Resurrection, Like a Phoenix Out of Its Ashes* (London: Nathaniel Brooke, 1669), 13.

109 Henry, *Memorial of the Fire of the Lord*, 29.

110 Gibbons, *Divine Improvement*, 18.

111 R. Elborough, *London's Calamity by Fire Bewailed and Improved, in a Sermon Preached at St. James Dukes-Place* (London: M.S. for Dorman Newman, 1666), 13–14.

112 Hardy, *Lamentation, Mourning and Woe*, 31.

113 W. Gearing, *Londons Remembrance: Or, a Sermon Preached at the Church of St. Mary le Bow, on September the 3d 1688* (London: J. Richardson for T. Parkhurst, 1688), 20.

114 W. Hopkins, *A Sermon Preached before the Right Honourable the Lord Mayor, Aldermen and Citizens of the City of London, in the Parish Church of S. Mary Le Bow, September 3. 1683* (London: Walter Kettilby, 1683), 30.

115 T. Hering, *The Triumph of the Church Over Water and Fire: Or a Thankfull Gratulation for That Miraculous Deliverance of the Church and State of Great*

Britaine, from the Romish Tophet; or, That Barbarous and Savage Powder-Plot (London: I.D. for Nicholas Bourne, 1625), 34–5.

116 T. Cooke, *A Sermon Preacht in the Parochial Church of St. Nicholas in the City of Worcester, on Wednesday the 19th of January, Being the Day of the General Fast* (Oxford: John Butler, 1704), 19–20.

117 W. Parker, *The Natural Effect, and Religious Improvement of Extraordinary Divine Judgments, and of Solemn Fasts Instituted in Remembrance of Them: A Sermon Preached before the Right Honourable the Lord-Mayor, the Aldermen, and Citizens of London, at the Cathedral-Church of St. Paul, on Friday, Sept. 2. 1748* (Oxford: J. Fletcher, 1748), 24.

118 Hesketh, *Sermon Preached before the Right Honourable The Lord Mayor*, 18.

119 Hopkins, *Sermon Preached before the Right Honourable The Lord Mayor*, 24.

120 Ibbot, *Dissolution of This World*, 28–9.

121 Evelyn, *Diary*, iv, 157.

122 R. Baxter, *Reliquiae Baxterianae: Or, Mr. Richard Baxter's Narrative of the Most Memorable Passages of His Life and Times, Part 3*, ed. M. Sylvester (London: T. Parkhurst, J. Robinson, J. Lawrence and J. Dunton, 1696), 19.

123 E. Calamy, *A Continuation of the Account of the Ministers, Lecturers, Masters and Fellows of Colleges, and Schoolmasters, Who Were Ejected and Silenced after the Restoration in 1660, by or before the Act for Uniformity* (London: R. Ford, R. Hett and J. Chandler, 1727), 137.

124 R.H. Harrison, 'Temporary Churches after the Great Fire', *Transactions of the Ecclesiological Society*, 3 (1955–6), 251–8; De Krey, *London and the Restoration*, 91–2.

125 LMA, Rep.80, fol. 122r; Rep.81, fols. 148v-149r.

126 F.J. Bremer, *Congregational Communion: Clerical Friendship in the Anglo-American Puritan Community, 1610–1692* (Boston, MA: Northeastern University Press, 1994), 230–5.

127 P. Henry, *Diaries and Letters of Philip Henry, M.A.*, ed. M.H. Lee (London: Kegan Paul, Trench and Co, 1882), 192–3.

128 Baxter, *Reliquiae Baxterianae*, 17.

129 G. Whitehead, *The Christian Progress of That Ancient Servant and Minister of Jesus Christ, George Whitehead* (London: J. Sowle, 1725), 314–15.

Reference list

Primary sources

Manuscript

BL, Letter of 1676 Relating to the Firing of London in 1666, Additional MS 15057, 1676, fols. 44v-45r.

BL, Rugge, T. *Mercurius Politicus Redivius; or, a Collection of the Most Materiall Occurrences and Transactions in Publick Affaires, Since Anno Domini 1659, Volume II.* Additional MS 10117, 1659–72.

Letter from Sir Philip Musgrave to Williamson, 19 August 1667, SP 29/214, 27.

LMA, Journal of Common Council, Jour. 46, 1664–9.

LMA, Petition of Citizens to the Common Council Relating to an Enquiry after the Causes of the Late Dreadful Firing of the City of London, COL/SJ/03/004, 2, 1667.

LMA, Petition of the Common Council to the House of Commons Touching the Fire, COL/SJ/03/004, 3, 1667.

LMA, Repertory of the Court of Aldermen, Rep. 82–4, 1676–9.

TNA, Letter from Daniel Fleming to Williamson, 16 August 1667, SP 29/213, 118.

TNA, Letter from Sir Thomas Langton and Sir John Knight to Arlington, 13 July 1667, SP 29/209, 75.

TNA, Petition of Dr Israel Tongue to the King, 22 August 1670, SP 29/278, 30.

Printed

An Account of the Burning the City of London, As It Was Publish'd by the Special Authority of the King and Council in the Year, 1666: To Which Is Added, the Opinion of Dr Kennet the Present Bishop of Peterborough, as Publish'd by His Lordship's Order, and That of Dr Eachard, Relating Thereunto. London: J. Stone, 1720.

An Account of the Proceedings at the Guildhall of the City of London, On Saturday, September 12. 1679. London, 1679.

The Address of above Twenty Thousand of the Loyal Protestant Apprentices of London: Humbly Presented to the Right Honourable the Lord Mayor. London: William Ingol the Elder, 1681.

A True and Faithful Account of the Several Informations Exhibited to the Honourable Committee Appointed by the Parliament to Inquire into the Late Dreadful Burning of the City of London. London, 1667.

Aubin, R.A., ed. London in Flames, London in Glory: Poems on the Fire and Rebuilding of London 1666–1709. New Brunswick, NJ: Rutgers University Press, 1943.

A Wild-Fire Plot: Found Out in Ireland: Shewing How the Rebels Would Have Consumed the City of Dublin with Wild-Fire. London: Thomas Bates, 1641.

Baxter, R. Reliquiae Baxterianae: Or, Mr. Richard Baxter's Narrative of the Most Memorable Passages of His Life and Times, Part 3, edited by M. Sylvester. London: T. Parkhurst, J. Robinson, J. Lawrence and J. Dunton, 1696.

Bedloe, W. A Narrative and Impartial Discovery of the Horrid Popish Plot: Carried on for the Burning and Destroying of London and Westminster, with Their Suburbs, &c. London: R. Boulter, J. Hancock, R. Smith and B. Harris, 1679.

Blount, C. An Appeal from the Country to the City, for the Preservation of His Majesties Person, Liberty, Property, and the Protestant Religion. London, 1679.

The Burning of London by the Papists: Or, a Memorial to Protestants on the Second of September. London: John Clark, 1714.

Calamy, E. A Letter to Mr Archdeacon Echard, Upon Occasion of his History of England. London: John Clark, 1718.

Calamy, E. A Continuation of the Account of the Ministers, Lecturers, Masters and Fellows of Colleges, and Schoolmasters, Who Were Ejected and Silenced after the Restoration in 1660, by or before the Act for Uniformity. London: R. Ford, R. Hett and J. Chandler, 1727.

Cooke, T. A Sermon Preacht in the Parochial Church of St. Nicholas in the City of Worcester, on Wednesday the 19th of January, Being the Day of the General Fast. Oxford: John Butler, 1704.

Doddridge, P. A Sermon Preached at Wellingborough, in Northamptonshire, November 9: MDCCXXXVIII. London: R. Hett and J. Buckland, 1739.

Doolittle, T. Rebukes for Sin by God's Burning Anger: By the Burning of London: By the Burning of the World: By the Burning of the Wicked in Hell-Fire. London: Dorman Newman, 1667.

Dryden, J. 'Annus Mirabilis'. In John Dryden: A Critical Edition of the Major Works, edited by K. Walker. Oxford: Oxford University Press, 1987.

Elborough, R. London's Calamity by Fire Bewailed and Improved, in a Sermon Preached at St. James Dukes-Place. London: M.S. for Dorman Newman, 1666.

E.N. Londons Destroyer Detected; and Destruction Lamented: Or, Some Serious Ruminations, and Profitable Reflections upon the Late Dreadful, Dismal, and Never-to-Be-Forgotten Conflagration. London, 1666.

Englands Lamentation for the Dismall Conflagration of Her Imperial Chamber the Citie of London: Sept. 2d. MDCLXVI. York: F. Mawbarne, 1666.

Evelyn, J. *The Diary of John Evelyn*, edited by E.S. De Beer, 6 vols. Oxford: Clarendon Press, 1955.

Flower, C. *Mercy in the Midst of Judgment, with a Glympse of or a Glance on London's Glorious Resurrection, Like a Phoenix out of Its Ashes*. London: Nathaniel Brooke, 1669.

Gearing, W. *Londons Remembrance: Or, a Sermon Preached at the Church of St. Mary Le Bow, on September the 3d 1688*. London: J. Richardson for T. Parkhurst, 1688.

Gibbons, T. *The Divine Improvement of Desolating Judgments Represented: In a Sermon Preached at Haberdasher's-Hall, March 27: On Occasion of the Dreadful Fire in the City, on March 25, 1748*. London: J. Oswald, R. King, J. Buckland, J. Ward and E. Gardiner, 1748.

Hardy, N. *Lamentation, Mourning and Woe: Sighed Forth in a Sermon Preached in the Parish-Church of St Martin in the Fields, on the 9th Day of September: Being the Lords-Day after the Dismal Fire in the City of London*. London: Thomas Newcomb for William Grantham, 1666.

Harvey, G. *The City Remembrancer: Being Historical Narratives of the Great Plague, at London 1665; Great Fire, 1666; and Great Storm, 1703, Volume 3: Of the Fire and the Storm*. London: W. Nicoll, 1769.

Henry, M. *A Memorial of the Fire of the Lord, in a Sermon Preach'd Sept. 2d. 1713: Being the Day of the Commemoration of the Burning of London, in 1666: At Mr. Reynold's Meeting-Place Near the Monument*. London: John Lawrence, 1713.

Henry, P. *Diaries and Letters of Philip Henry, M.A.*, edited by M.H. Lee. London: Kegan Paul, Trench and Co, 1882.

Hering, T. *The Triumph of the Church Over Water and Fire: Or a Thankfull Gratulation for That Miraculous Deliverance of the Church and State of Great Britaine, from the Romish Tophet; or, That Barbarous and Savage Powder-Plot*. London: I.D. for Nicholas Bourne, 1625.

Hesketh, H. *A Sermon Preached before the Right Honourable the Lord Mayor and Aldermen of the City of London at Bow Church, September the 2d. 1682*. London: Robert Sollers, 1682.

Hopkins, W. *A Sermon Preached before the Right Honourable the Lord Mayor, Aldermen and Citizens of the City of London, in the Parish Church of S. Mary Le Bow, September 3. 1683*. London: Walter Kettilby, 1683.

Ibbot, B. *The Dissolution of This World by Fire: A Sermon Preach'd before the Right Honourable Sir Gilbert Heathcote, Knight, Lord-Mayor, the Aldermen, and Citizens of London, at the Cathedral-Church of St. Paul, on Monday, September 3. 1711*. London: John Wyat, 1711.

London's Flames: Being an Exact and Impartial Account of Divers Informations Given in to the Committee of Parliament. London, 1679.

Londons Flames Discovered by Informations Taken before the Committee Appointed to Enquire after the Burning of the City of London and after the Insolency of the Papists, &c. London, 1679.

London's Flames Reviv'd: Or, an Account of the Several Informations Exhibited to a Committee Appointed by Parliament, September the 25th 1666. London: Nathaniel Ranew, 1680.

London's Flames Set in a True Light: Being a True and Faithful Account of the Several Informations Exhibited to the Honourable Committee Appointed by the Parliament to Inquire into the Late Dreadful Burning of the City of London. London: J. How, 1712.

Markland, A. *Poems on His Majestie's Birth and Restauration, His Highness Prince Rupert's and His Grace the Duke of Albermarle's Naval Victories; the Late Great Pestilence and Fire of London*. London: James Cotterel, 1667.

Marvell, A. *The Second, and Third Advice to a Painter, for Drawing the History of our Navall Actions, the Two Last Years, 1665: And 1666 in Answer to Mr. Waller*, 1667.

Marvell, A. *An Account of the Growth of Popery, and Arbitrary Government in England*. Amsterdam, 1677.

Milward, J. *The Diary of John Milward, Esq. Member of Parliament for Derbyshire, September, 1666 to May, 1668*, edited by C. Robbins. Cambridge: Cambridge University Press, 1938.

Oates, T. *A True Narrative of the Horrid Plot of the Popish Party against the Life of His Sacred Majesty, the Government, and the Protestant Religion*. London: T. Parkhurst and T. Cockerill, 1679.

The Papists Plot of Firing Discovered: In a Perfect Account of the Late Fire in Fetter Lane, London. London, 1679.

Parker, W. *The Natural Effect, and Religious Improvement of Extraordinary Divine Judgments, and of Solemn Fasts Instituted in Remembrance of Them: A Sermon Preached before the Right Honourable the Lord-Mayor, the Aldermen, and Citizens of London, at the Cathedral-Church of St. Paul, on Friday, Sept. 2. 1748*. Oxford: J. Fletcher, 1748.

Pepys, S. *The Diary of Samuel Pepys*, edited by R. Latham and W. Matthews, 11 vols. 1st ed. London: G. Bell and Sons, 1970–83.

Pyrotechnica Loyolana, Ignatian Fire-Works: Or, the Fiery Jesuits Temper and Behaviour. London: G.E.C.T, 1667.

Rege Sincera. *Observations both Historical and Moral upon the Burning of London, September 1666*. London: Thomas Ratcliffe, 1667.

Rolls, S. *The Burning of London in the Year 1666*. London: R.I. for Thomas Parkhurst, Nathaniel Ranew and Jonathan Robinson, 1667.

Stillingfleet, E. *A Sermon Preached before the Honourable House of Commons, at St. Margarets Westminster*. London: Robert White for Henry Mortlock, 1666.

Trap ad Crucem; or, the Papists Watch-Word. London, 1670.

The True Protestant Account of the Burning of London, or, an Antidote, against the Poyson and Malignity of a Late Lying Legend, Entituled an Account of the Burning of London, &c. London: B. Baddam for S. Popping, 1720.

Verney, M.M., ed. *Memoirs of the Verney Family from the Restoration to the Revolution 1660 to 1696*. London: Longmans, Green, and Co, 1899.

Vincent, T. *God's Terrible Voice in the City*. London: G. Calvert, 1667.

Ward, S. *A Sermon Preached before the Peers, in the Abby-Church at Westminster*. London: E.C. for James Collins, 1666.

Warning for Servants: And a Caution to Protestants: Or the Case of Margaret Clark, Lately Executed for Firing Her Masters Houses in Southwark. London: Thomas Parkhurst, 1680.

Waterhouse, E. *A Short Narrative of the Late Dreadful Fire in London*. London: W.G. for Richard Thrale and James Thrale, 1667.

Whitehead, G. *The Christian Progress of That Ancient Servant and Minister of Jesus Christ, George Whitehead*. London: J. Sowle, 1725.

Wood, A. *The Life and Times of Anthony Wood, Antiquary, of Oxford, 1632–1695, Described by Himself*, Volume 2, edited by A. Clark. Oxford: Clarendon Press for the Oxford Historical Society, 1891.

Secondary sources

Akasoy, A. 'The Man-Made Disaster: Fire in Cities in the Medieval Middle East', *Historical Social Research*, 32 (2007), 75–87.

Allemeyer, M.L. 'Profane Hazard or Divine Judgement? Coping with Urban Fire in the 17th Century', *Historical Social Research*, 32 (2007), 145–68.

Archer, I.W. 'The Arts and Acts of Memorialization in Early Modern London'. In *Imagining Early Modern England: Perceptions and Portrayals of the City from Stow to Strype, 1598–1720*, edited by J.F. Merritt, 89–113. Cambridge: Cambridge University Press, 2001.

Boxer, C.R. *Some Contemporary Reactions to the Lisbon Earthquake of 1755*. Lisbon: Faculdade de Letras, Universidade de Lisboa, 1956.

Bremer, F.J. *Congregational Communion: Clerical Friendship in the Anglo-American Puritan Community, 1610–1692*. Boston, MA: Northeastern University Press, 1994.

Claydon, T. 'The Sermon, the "Public Sphere" and the Political Culture of Late Seventeenth-Century England'. In *The English Sermon Revised: Religion, Literature and History 1600–1750*, edited by L. Ferrell and P. McCullough, 208–34. Manchester: Manchester University Press, 2000.

Collinson, P. 'Elizabethan and Jacobean Puritanism as Forms of Popular Religious Culture'. In *The Culture of English Puritanism, 1560–1700*, edited by C. Durston and J. Eales, 32–57. Basingstoke: Macmillan, 2000.

Deconinck-Brossard, F. 'Eighteenth-Century Sermons and the Age'. In *Crown and Mitre: Religion and Society in Northern Europe since the Reformation*, edited by W.M. Jacob and N. Yates, 105–21. Woodbridge: Boydell Press, 1993.

De Krey, G.S. *London and the Restoration, 1659–1683*. Cambridge: Cambridge University Press, 2005.

Dolan, F.E. 'Ashes and "the Archive": The London Fire of 1666, Partisanship, and Proof', *Journal of Medieval and Early Modern Studies*, 31 (2001), 379–408.

Dolan, F.E. *Whores of Babylon: Catholicism, Gender, and Seventeenth-Century Print Culture*. Ithaca, NY and London: Cornell University Press, 2005.

Durston, C. and Eales, J. 'Introduction: The Puritan Ethos, 1560–1700'. In *The Culture of English Puritanism, 1560–1700*, edited by C. Durston and J. Eales, 1–31. Basingstoke: Macmillan, 1996.

Dzelzainis, M. 'L'Estrange, Marvell and the *Directions to a Painter*: The Evidence of Bodleian Library, MS Gough London 14'. In *Roger L'Estrange and the Making of Restoration Culture*, edited by A. Dunan-Page and B. Lynch, 53–66. Farnham: Ashgate, 2008.

Gamrath, H. 'The Great Fire of Copenhagen in 1728'. In *Destruction and Reconstruction of Towns, Volume 1: Destruction by Earthquakes, Fire and Water*, edited by M. Körner, 293–302. Bern: Paul Haupt, 1999.

Green, J. 'Teaching the Reformation: The Clergy as Preachers, Catechists, Authors and Teachers'. In *The Protestant Clergy of Early Modern Europe*, edited by C.S. Dixon and L. Schorn-Schütte, 156–75. Basingstoke: Palgrave Macmillan, 2003.

Harding, V. 'London and Middlesex in the 1660s'. In *London and Middlesex 1666 Hearth Tax*, edited by M. Davies, C. Ferguson, V. Harding, E. Parkinson and A. Wareham, 25–57. London: British Record Society, 2014.

Harris, T. *London Crowds in the Reign of Charles II: Propaganda and Politics from the Restoration until the Exclusion Crisis*. Cambridge: Cambridge University Press, 1987.

Harris, T. *Restoration: Charles II and His Kingdoms 1660–1685*. London: Allen Lane, 2005.

Harrison, R.H. 'Temporary Churches after the Great Fire', *Transactions of the Ecclesiological Society*, 3 (1955–6), 251–8.

Jones, J.R. *The First Whigs: The Politics of the Exclusion Crisis, 1678–1683*. London: Oxford University Press, 1961.

Kenyon, J.P. *The Popish Plot*. London: Heinemann, 1972.

Knoppers, L.L. *Historicizing Milton: Spectacle, Power and Poetry in Restoration England*. Athens, GA: University of Georgia Press, 1994.

Lacey, A. 'Elegies and Commemorative Verse in Honour of Charles the Martyr, 1649–60'. In *The Regicides and the Execution of Charles I*, edited by J. Peacey, 255–46. Basingstoke and New York: Palgrave, 2001.

Lord, G.D. *Classical Presences in Seventeenth-Century English Poetry*. New Haven and London: Yale University Press, 1987.

Marshall, A. *The Strange Death of Edmund Godfrey: Plots and Politics in Restoration London*. Stroud: Sutton, 1999.

Marshall, A. 'Tonge, Israel (1621–1680)'. In *Oxford Dictionary of National Biography*, edited by H.C.G. Matthew and B. Harrison, 60 vols., Volume 54, 966–9. Oxford: Oxford University Press, 2004.

Miller, J. *Popery and Politics in England 1660–1668*. Cambridge: Cambridge University Press, 1973.

Mulcahy, M. 'Urban Catastrophes and Imperial Relief in the Eighteenth-Century British Atlantic World: Three Case Studies'. In *Cities and Catastrophes: Coping with Emergency in European History*, edited by G. Massard-Guilbaud, H.L. Platt and D. Schott, 105–21. Frankfurt: Peter Lang, 2002.

Pincus, S.C.A. 'From Butterboxes to Wooden Shoes: The Shift in English Popular Sentiment from Anti-Dutch to Anti-French in the 1670s', *Historical Journal*, 38 (1995), 333–61.

Pincus, S.C.A. *Protestantism and Patriotism: Ideologies and the Making of English Foreign Policy, 1650–1668*. Cambridge: Cambridge University Press, 1996.

Roberts, P. 'Arson, Conspiracy and Rumour in Early Modern Europe', *Continuity and Change*, 12 (1997), 9–29.

Selwood, J. *Diversity and Difference in Early Modern London*. Farnham: Ashgate, 2010.

Smith, N. '"Making Fire": Conflagration and Religious Controversy in Seventeenth-Century London'. In *Imagining Early Modern London: Perceptions and Portrayals of the City from Stow to Strype*, edited by J.F. Merritt, 273–93. Cambridge: Cambridge University Press, 2001.

Spurr, J. 'Virtue, Religion and Government: The Anglican Uses of Providence'. In *The Politics of Religion in Restoration England*, edited by T. Harris, P. Seward and M. Goldie, 29–47. Oxford: Basil Blackwell, 1990.

Trickett, R. 'Samuel Butler and the Minor Restoration Poets'. In *English Poetry and Prose 1540–1674*, edited by C. Ricks, 311–27. London: Sphere, 1970.

Tumbleson, R.D. *Catholicism in the English Protestant Imagination: Nationalism, Religion and Literature, 1660–1745*. Cambridge: Cambridge University Press, 1998.

Wall, C. *The Literary and Cultural Spaces of Restoration London*. Cambridge: Cambridge University Press, 1998.

Walsham, A. *Providence in Early Modern England*. Oxford: Oxford University Press, 1999.

Wedgwood, C.V. *Poetry and Politics Under the Stuarts*. Cambridge: Cambridge University Press, 1960.

Zwicker, S.N. *Lines of Authority: Politics and English Literary Culture, 1649–1689*. Ithaca, NY and London: Cornell University Press, 1993.

Conclusion
The impact of the Great Fire

The Great Fire was a disaster for many of the Londoners whom it directly affected. However, it was not a disaster for the long-term development of the metropolis. This book has revealed the essentially stable and resilient nature of London's social and economic structure in the seventeenth century. The Fire was mostly constrained to the City within the Walls, an area of London that was declining in its importance in the overall structure of the metropolis – particularly, in terms of population. The longer-term impact of the Fire lay in its ideological and polemic value.

The most immediate problem caused by the Fire was the thousands of people it made homeless. Where and how would they resettle? Analysis of Hearth Tax assessments showed that many of the individuals burnt out did not return to their original location. The costs of rebuilding made London's suburbs a more attractive economic proposition for many. The Fire thus forced Londoners into the suburbs beyond the Walls. Such movement, in particular to the west and east, was part of an ongoing redistribution of London's population. Movement west was most associated with higher-status Londoners, particularly to the West End. Movement east was far more likely to be associated with a reduction in the social status of an address or household, and residence in a tenement, subdivided property or temporary lodging. Relocation north was the most significant direct consequence of the population resettlement forced by the Fire, as burnt-out individuals relocated to the open spaces like Moorfields there. Movement south of the river was relatively unimportant in comparison to other types of relocation. As a result of this population redistribution, the City must have grown more 'ordered', whilst the suburbs (in particular those north and east of the Walls) became more 'disordered'.[1]

Early modern metropolitan neighbourhood migration was usually short-distance.[2] Such movement was socially selective. Economic vulnerability before the Fire appears to have led to an increase in dislocation after it. Individuals who remained in the same location after the Fire were more likely to be from socially desirable areas of the City, and from higher social strata. The case study of the two neighbourhoods suggests that residential stability was far more likely to be associated with the prestigious area around St Paul's Cathedral than the lower-status area around the riverside. Even amongst poorer neighbourhoods there was still some degree of social continuity after the Fire. It was relatively commonplace for near-neighbours to relocate to similar areas after the Fire, even if they were a long distance from the pre-Fire address. Existing social links underlay movement after the Fire, whether it was a return to a pre-Fire location or resettlement in another part of London.

Change in London's economic topography after the Fire echoed trends in residential movement. The Merchant Taylors moved westward in large numbers in the decade after the Fire, regardless of whether they had been burnt out. In comparison, booksellers, whose business was largely reliant on passing consumer traffic, were more stable in their locations before and after the Fire. Londoners changed their occupations in response to the Fire. After 1666 there was a surge in Merchant Taylors engaging in the construction trade, particularly amongst younger members. It is likely that such shifts in occupation were repeated across the metropolis. London's economy was thus responsive to the consumer demands of its residents.

The symbolic value of the Fire had a longer-lasting impact than its damage on London's socio-economic fabric. The disaster was a heavily contested phenomenon, and was quickly politicised across all forms of contemporary media – including monuments in London's built environment. It was important propaganda tool for a number of reasons. 'Fire' was associated with disorder and the loss of property, and so had a powerful potential impact on the early modern psyche. Royalists used the event to remind the reader of England's (and London's) sins during the Interregnum. During the Exclusion Crisis the Fire was linked to Popish plotting and used to warn of the impending doom if Catholic influence on England was allowed to grow unchecked. The Fire's association with loss of property and liberty was utilised by Whiggish groups in particular. In comparison, Tory groups sought to maintain that the Fire was accidental – a providential event. The Monument, which was used by both Whigs and Royalists as a symbol of either the deliberate or accidental nature of the Fire, shows this duality. England's clergy frequently mentioned the Fire. It was almost always linked to the concept that it had been brought about by divine anger at the sins of the nation. This providential view of fire was not an innovation but a familiar trope in early modern religious thought.[3] This transcended both Anglican and nonconformist clergy, although the latter group was quicker to associate the Fire with Catholic plotting. In some respects, the Fire was a vindication for England's nonconformist ministers, who had been banished from London in the early 1660s. The Fire showed God's displeasure at this act. In the aftermath of the Fire, there was a rise in nonconformist activity in the metropolis, as its preachers filled the void caused by the disruption to London's established parochial system.

In spite of the often vicious nature of the polemic around the Fire, the popular reaction to the event was more measured. Although personal accounts of the Fire frequently blamed unnamed foreign conspirators for the disaster, there was no large-scale persecution of foreigners in London after the Fire. There was also no significant breakdown in public order in 1666. Rather, Londoners concentrated on fleeing or fighting the flames and preserving what possessions they could during the Fire. Fire was a frequent menace in urban early modern England.[4] Many Londoners reacted to the Fire phlegmatically – as one more metropolitan menace along with disease, unhygienic streets and inadequate housing.

London by no means had a monopoly on the concept and experience of a 'Great Fire'. Such events were not uncommon in the growth and development of major cities. 'Great Fires' and other disasters such as earthquakes or enemy invasion became stage posts in the history of a metropolis, just as they did for London. There were numerous general themes that occurred in major urban fires. A cause of the blaze was always sought. Major fires tended to be accidental, created by a random incident that escalated due to the existing pre-conditions of the urban environment and the immediate conditions of the moment, such as weather conditions. In the early modern context in particular, contemporary views of fires almost always eschewed an accidental view when seeking causes. Blame was ascribed to two main sources. Firstly, fires were mainly ascribed to the anger of a vengeful God – a providential event caused by the sins of a nation or people. Secondly, recrimination was often laid on a social group defined by their race or religion – frequently this took the form of a conspiracy. The rebuilding and resettlement of fired cities was often politicised – as after the Istanbul Fire of 1660 – and accompanied with government encouragement to return to the city and rebuild there – as after the Edo Fire of 1657.[5]

The Great Fire of London had the potential to severely disrupt the City's socio-economic structure, and by extension that of the country at large. However, because the Fire spread slowly and was mostly limited to within the Walls of the City, its negative effects were limited. Unlike other major early modern urban disasters the Fire did not have a high death toll. London did not experience a second mortality shock in 1666, following the 1665 Plague. The Fire did not spread west into western suburbs. Had it done so, it would have destroyed many of London's leisure attractions, as well as its political centre and the metropolitan homes of most of the nation's nobility. If the Fire had penetrated the walls of the Tower of London and ignited the stock of gunpowder there, the resulting flames could have razed most of the densely populated East End. This would have destroyed much of London's stock of cheap housing. As well as this, the Port of London – essential to the metropolitan economy – could have been destroyed. In fact, the Fire was mostly restrained to within the Walls, and although there was short-term disruption, London resumed its demographic and economic growth in the later seventeenth century. Despite the widespread destruction that the Fire caused, the area it destroyed showed remarkable long-term stability in many respects. Gregg Carr, using a comparison of the 1638 tithe assessments and the 1695 Marriage Tax, concluded that the structure of the reconstructed City within the Walls remained fairly similar over this period, with high rents and wealth in the centre, a surrounding poorer zone and concentrations of wealth in the western limits. In addition, the distribution of substantial households was similar in 1638 compared to 1695. The basic housing statistics of the City appeared to be stable during the seventeenth century.[6] However, its relative share of London's population was falling. By the beginning of the eighteenth century, the City within the Walls had a population of 70,000. In absolute terms the area's population was more or less unchanged since the Fire but in relative terms its share of London's population had declined from about one-third to one-seventh.[7] The Fire had the effect of speeding population growth outside of the Walls, a trend that was ongoing in 1666.

In the past London had dealt with serious fires and other disasters such as war and plague, and so it also recovered from the Great Fire of 1666. Ultimately, most Londoners recovered from the damage done by the Fire. Londoners' frequent mobility and relatively loose attachment to their homes, as well as the presence of the suburbs, meant that movement after the Fire became less traumatic, and metropolitan social and economic systems could be reconstructed. The Great Fire did not cause a significant lasting crisis in metropolitan society or economy. It became part of the fabric of civic history, representing the resilience of the City and the industry of its inhabitants. Its long-term impact lay ultimately in its symbolic value, which meant that the event retained its historic importance for centuries. London's resilience meant that the damage done by the flames of 1666 would ultimately be temporary, and reversed.

Notes

1 V. Harding, 'City, Capital, and Metropolis: The Changing Shape of Seventeenth-Century London', in *Imagining Early Modern England: Perceptions and Portrayals of the City from Stow to Strype, 1598–1720*, ed. J.F. Merritt (Cambridge: Cambridge University Press, 2001), 128.

2 J.P. Boulton, 'Neighbourhood Migration in Early Modern London', in *Migration and Society in Early Modern England*, ed. P. Clark and D. Souden (London: Hutchinson, 1987), 123–4; R.B. Shoemaker, 'Gendered Spaces: Patterns of Mobility and Perceptions of London's Geography, 1660–1750', in *Imagining Early Modern London: Perceptions and Portrayals of the City from Stow to Strype, 1598–1720*, ed. J.F. Merritt (Cambridge: Cambridge University Press, 2001), 155.

3 A. Walsham, *Providence in Early Modern England* (Oxford: Oxford University Press, 1999), 122–3, 137–8.

4 P. Borsay, 'Fire and the Early Modern Townscape', in *The English Urban Landscape*, ed. P. Waller (Oxford and New York: Oxford University Press, 2000), 110–1.

5 M.D. Baer, 'The Great Fire of 1660 and the Islamization of Christian and Jewish Space in Istanbul', *International Journal of Middle East Studies*, 36 (2004), 159–75; K. Ugawa, 'The Great Fire of Edo (Tokyo) in 1657', in *Destruction*

and Reconstruction of Towns, Volume 1: Destruction by Earthquakes, Fire and Water, ed. M. Körner (Bern: Paul Haupt, 1999), 213–38.

6 G. Carr, *Residence and Social Status: The Development of Seventeenth-Century London* (New York and London: Garland, 1990), 63, 90–1, 99, 106.

7 L.D. Schwarz, *London in the Age of Industrialisation: Entrepreneurs, Labour Force and Living Conditions, 1700–1850* (Cambridge: Cambridge University Press, 1992), 7.

Reference list

Baer, M.D. 'The Great Fire of 1660 and the Islamization of Christian and Jewish Space in Istanbul', *International Journal of Middle East Studies*, 36 (2004), 159–75.

Borsay, P. 'Fire and the Early Modern Townscape'. In *The English Urban Landscape*, edited by P. Waller, 110–1. Oxford and New York: Oxford University Press, 2000.

Boulton, J.P. 'Neighbourhood Migration in Early Modern London'. In *Migration and Society in Early Modern England*, edited by P. Clark and D. Souden, 107–49. London: Hutchinson, 1987.

Carr, G. *Residence and Social Status: The Development of Seventeenth-Century London*. New York and London: Garland, 1990.

Harding, V. 'City, Capital, and Metropolis: The Changing Shape of Seventeenth-Century London'. In *Imagining Early Modern England: Perceptions and Portrayals of the City from Stow to Strype, 1598–1720*, edited by J.F. Merritt, 117–43. Cambridge: Cambridge University Press, 2001.

Schwarz, L.D. *London in the Age of Industrialisation: Entrepreneurs, Labour Force and Living Conditions, 1700–1850*. Cambridge: Cambridge University Press, 1992.

Shoemaker, R.B. 'Gendered Spaces: Patterns of Mobility and Perceptions of London's Geography, 1660–1750'. In *Imagining Early Modern London: Perceptions and Portrayals of the City from Stow to Strype, 1598–1720*, edited by J.F. Merritt, 144–65. Cambridge: Cambridge University Press, 2001.

Ugawa, K. 'The Great Fire of Edo (Tokyo) in 1657'. In *Destruction and Reconstruction of Towns, Volume 1: Destruction by Earthquakes, Fire and Water*, edited by M. Körner, 213–38. Bern: Paul Haupt, 1999.

Walsham, A. *Providence in Early Modern England*. Oxford: Oxford University Press, 1999.

Index

account of the Burning the City of London, An (1720) 141

Account of the Growth of Popery, and Arbitrary Government in England (Marvell) 138

Act of Common Council for Preventing and Suppressing of Fires Within the City of London (1667) 139

Act of Uniformity (1662) 136

Advice to a Painter series (Marvell) 142

age, and post-Fire movement *see* economy of London, post-Great Fire

Albemarle, George Monck, First Duke of 16, 24

Alexander, Nicholas 88

Altham, Sir James 63

Andrews, John 115

Annus Mirabilis (Dryden) 142

anti-Catholicism 133–4; *see also* cultural reactions, to the Great Fire; Popish Plot and Exclusion Crisis

anti-French sentiment 131–3, 137

Appeal from the country to the city (Blount) 140

apprenticeships 103–4; *see also* economy of London, post-Great Fire

Arlington, Henry Bennet, Baron of 23, 39, 133

Ashley, Lord *see* Shaftesbury, Anthony Ashley Cooper, First Earl of

Ashmole, Elias 17

Ashurst, Henry 42

Aske, Frances 40

Baldwin, Henry 76

Barbon, Nicholas 36

Barnard, Frances 78

Batchelor, Grace 83

Baxter, Richard 18, 21, 39, 42, 147

Beck, Godfrey 62–3

Bedloe, William 140

Beier, A.L. 115

Belasyse, Baron John 15

Bell, Walter 62

Bennet, Henry *see* Arlington, Henry Bennet, Baron of

Berry, Daniel 85

Bill, John 111

Billers, Joseph 73

Blount, Charles 45, 140

Bludworth, Sir Thomas 9–14, 19, 23

Bolingbroke, Oliver St John, Second Earl of 75

Bolton, Clara 39

Bolton, Sir William 38, 87

booksellers 3, 17, 104–5, 107–12, 118–19, 161

Boston (Massachusetts) Fires (1679/1760) 42

Boulton, Jeremy 59, 76, 114, 117–18, 120

Bowdler, William 85

Box, Ralph 73

Boyle, Richard *see* Burlington, Richard Boyle, First Earl of

Boys, Thomas 61

Brett, Francis 41–2

Bridewell 16, 41

Bristol, George Digby, Second Earl of 82

Bristol 133

Brooke, Sir Robert 132–3, 139–41, 146

Brookes, Margaret 117

Brooks, Thomas 147

Browne, Abraham 77

Browne, Frances 77

Brudenell, Robert *see* Cardigan, Robert Brudenell, Second Earl of

Bunce, Sir James 101
Burlington, Richard Boyle, First Earl
    of 75
Burgesse, Deane 86
Burning of London, The (1667) 142
Burning of London by the Papists, The
    (1714) 140–1
Busby, Robert 61
Butler, James *see* Ormond, James Butler,
    First Duke of
Butler, John 146
Byfield, Gervaise 59–60

Calamy, Edmund 141
Calvert, Elizabeth 133
Calvert, George 76
Cambridge 14
Cardigan, Robert Brudenell, Second
    Earl of 75
Carlisle, Charles Howard, First Earl
    of 21
Carlyle, Ellen 85
Carr, Gregg 89, 162–3
Caryl, Joseph 147
Castlemaine, Barbara Palmer, Countess
    of 100
Charles I, King 17, 41, 142–3
Charles II, King: addresses to
    Parliament 30; attempts to control
    London, post-Fire 22, 24, 140;
    attends St Paul's Cathedral 43;
    Catholics at court of 133; depiction
    on Monument 45; dissatisfaction
    with 132, 136–7, 142; dissolution of
    Parliament 140; establishes national
    charitable collection 37–8; financial
    requests to, post-Fire 39–40, 100–1,
    108; orders expulsion of Catholics
    near London 139; oversight of Great
    Fire actions 13–14, 16, 18–19;
    oversight of rebuilding of London
    30–3; oversight of rebuilding
    of Royal Exchange 43; pledges
    to protect Jews 134; purported
    assassination plot 138; Restoration
    of 9
charts *see* illustrations, charts, and
    tables
Chetham's Library, Manchester 104–5
Chicago Fire (1871) 2, 35
Christ's Hospital 16–17, 37, 41
Church of England in London after the
    Fire 42–3

Civil Wars 9, 18, 39, 134, 143
Clarendon, Edward Hyde, First Earl
    of 9, 17
Clark, Margaret 140
Clark, Peter 73
Clever, Theophilus 41
coal duty 34–5, 41, 43–4
Colman, Edward 138–9
Compton, James *see* Northampton,
    James Compton, Third Earl of
Cooke, Thomas 146
Cooks' Company 101
Corbin, Gawain 78–9
Corporation Act (1661) 9
Country Party *see* Whigs
Crafts, Sarah 40
Craven, William Craven, First Earl
    of 14
Crew, Baron John 132
Crew, Sir Thomas 132
Croft, Robert 115
Crouch, John 142–3
Crumpton, Oliver 76
cultural reactions, to the Fire 131–59;
    anti-Semitism 134; assigning blame
    131–4; narratives on Fire during early
    eighteenth century 140–1; narratives
    on Fire in verse during late 1660s
    141–3; nonconformist clergy and
    146–8; polemical literary responses
    134–7; Popish Plot and Exclusion
    Crisis 45, 137–40, 146–7; providential
    views and 131, 136–7, 142, 143, 144,
    147, 161–2; summary conclusion 148
Cumberland, William 62

Davenport, John 42
Davis, Donald 119–20
Deakes, Ward 81–2
Denny, Foulke 76
Digby, George *see* Bristol, George
    Digby, Second Earl of
Doddridge, Philip 144–5
Doolittle, Thomas 36, 37, 136–7, 147
Dorset, Richard Sackville, Fifth Earl
    of 82
Dryden, John 18, 109, 142
Dudley, Alice 43
Dutch Republic 10, 30–1, 132, 137

Eachard, Lawrence 141
economy of London, post-Fire 99–130;
    booksellers 104–5, 107–9, 112,

118–19; effect of age on movement, pre/post Fire 116–17; female-run businesses, post-Fire 117–19; manufacturing 99, 113–14, 116; Merchant Taylors 103, 104, 106–7, 109–11, 113–19; occupational change, pre/post Fire 113–16; summary conclusion 119–21
Elborough, Robert 145
Eliot, John 42
Ellison, Francis 86
End of Days belief 143, 147
England: alliance with France 137; Clarendon Code 9; Parliament 8, 9–10, 30, 31, 44, 61, 62, 82, 101, 132, 137, 139, 140; population demographics 7; *see also* specific leaders, legislation and wars
Englands Lamentation (1666) 142
English Short Title Catalogue 105
Erection of Cottages Act (1588) 61
Evelyn, John: on anti-alien unrest 21; on charity post-Fire 37; designs for rebuilding London 31–2; on Dutch raid on Medway 30–1; on Great Fire 15, 17–18, 19; on hysteria of Popish Plot 146; on murder of Godfrey 138–9
Exclusion Crisis *see* Popish Plot and Exclusion Crisis

Farriner, Thomas 11
Fawkes, Guy 146
fear of others and conspiracy theories 131–2
Fincham, Thomas 40
Finlay, Roger 76
Finsbury Fields 9, 23
Fire Court 33–4, 40–2, 59–63, 77, 83, 85, 102, 108–9
fire-fighting practices 2, 12, 14–15, 19, 36–7
Fire of London Disputes Act (1667) 33
First Exclusion Bill (1679) 140
Five Mile Act (1665) 136
Fleming, Daniel 133
Flower, Christopher 145
foreigners, blaming of 15–16, 21, 131–2, 162
France: alliance with England 137; fire prevention legislation 139
freedom registers 116–17
Freeman, Henry 47
Freeman, Richard 36

Gaddesby, Thomas 22
Gearing, William 145
Geary, John 106–7
Gellibrand, Samuel 108, 112
Gibbons, Thomas 145
Gibbons, William 116
Gilborn, Percival 83
Godfrey, Edmund Berry 138–9
Gouge, Thomas 42
Granes, John 86
Great Fire of Chicago (1871) 2, 35
Great Fire of Copenhagen (1728) 2, 134
Great Fire of Edo (1657) 2, 20, 162
Great Fire of Istanbul (1660) 2, 20, 162
Great Fire of London (1666) 7–55; overview 11–19; aftermath 19–24; extinguishment of fire 19; memorialisation of Great Fire 45–8; outbreak of fire 11–14; social and political context 7–11; spread of fire 14–19; summary conclusion 160–3
Great Fire of Rome (64) 146
Guildhall 7, 16, 22, 35, 44
guild system 103–5, 116–17; *see also* Merchant Taylors
Gunpowder Plot (1605) 133, 146

Harding, Vanessa 2
Hardy, Nathaniel 144, 145
Hardy, Nicholas 39
Harris, Benjamin 45
Harvey, Gideon 141
Hawkins, William 60
Hearth Tax 63–7 *see also* residential patterns, post-Great Fire
Henchman, Humphrey 108–9
Henry, Matthew 144, 145, 146
Henry, Philip 12, 35, 147
Henry VIII, King 16
Hering, Theodore 146
Herringman, Henry 109
Hesketh, Henry 144, 146
Hilliard, Richard 84
Hinton, Charles 88
HMS *Loyal London* 10
Hobart, Sir Nathaniel 60, 131
Holmes, Robert 10
Hooke, Jane 42
Hooke, Robert 31, 33, 35, 43, 45
Hooke, William 42
Hopkins, William 145
Hothersall, Henry 83

household movement *see* residential
  patterns, post-Great Fire
Howard, Charles *see* Carlisle, Charles
  Howard, First Earl of
Hubert, Robert 21–2, 47, 133
Hurlock, George 112
Hyde, Edward *see* Clarendon, Edward
  Hyde, First Earl of

Ibbot, Benjamin 144, 146
illustrations, charts, and tables:
  booksellers, pre/post Fire 107;
  City plan post-Fire 19; hearths
  per household 67, 69, 70, 81;
  memorialisation of Fire 46; Merchant
  Taylors, movement 110; Merchant
  Taylors, occupational groups 113;
  Merchant Taylors, pre/post Fire 106;
  occupational change, pre/post Fire
  115; panoramic view of London 8;
  Pyrotechnica Loyolana frontispiece
  135; rebuilding designs 32; view of
  Great Fire from River Thames 13;
  see also maps
Inns of Court 8, 16, 19, 115
Isle of Wight 21
Islington 17, 18, 22, 111

Jacobite threats 140, 141, 148
James II, King: conversion to
  Catholicism 137; dissatisfaction
  with 137, 138; manages fire-fighting
  efforts 13, 14–15, 16, 19; possible
  depiction on Monument 45; seen as
  French agent 140–1
Japan, post-WWII recovery 119–20
Jenks, Francis 137
Jerman, Edward 33, 35, 44
Jesuits 133, 134, 138, 141
Jones, Inigo 17
Josselin, Ralph 35

Keene, Derek 2, 120–1
Kempe, Roger 60
Kendall, Elizabeth 39
Kennet, White 141
King, Gregory 70
King Charles' Hospital 41
King's Lynn 21
Kingston-upon-Hull 21
Kirton, Joshua 108
Knight, Sir John 133
Knight, Valentine 31

Lambeth 111
Lammas, Mary 74
Langton, Sir Thomas 133
Lauder, Sir John 103
Leicester, Robert Sidney, Second Earl
  of 75
Lenthall, Thomas 63
Le Roy, John 100
Linsey, Prudence 75
Lisbon Earthquake (1755) 131–2
Littlebury, Robert 104–5
Lloyd, Ann 40
Logsdon, Isaac 115
London: Court of Aldermen 17, 22–3,
  31, 36–8, 40, 61, 78, 101–3, 111,
  134, 147; Court of Common Council
  33, 38; deaths due to Plague 10–11;
  East End 8–9, 18, 82, 100, 162;
  population demographics 7, 10, 163;
  West End 8–9, 86, 100, 110, 111,
  160; *see also* economy of London,
  post-Great Fire; rebuilding London
London, parishes: All Hallows Barking
  76, 117; All Hallows Honey Lane 43;
  All Hallows Staining 86; All Hallows
  the Great 85; Christchurch Greyfriars
  17, 41; Holy Trinity Minories
  106; St Alban Wood Street 78;
  St Andrew Holborn 85; St Andrew
  by the Wardrobe 43; St Andrew
  Undershaft 42; St Anne and St Agnes
  72; St Bartholomew the Great
  68; St Bartholomew the Less 68;
  St Benet Gracechurch 83; St Benet
  Sherehog 83; St Botolph Billingsgate
  87; St Botolph without Aldersgate
  81, 84, 86, 105; St Botolph without
  Aldgate 68, 70, 83, 86, 106; St Bride
  Fleet Street 41, 61, 62, 68, 71, 76,
  82, 85; St Dunstan-in-the-East 43;
  St Dunstan in the West 40, 68, 81;
  St Dunstan Stepney 61, 75, 82,
  99; St Ethelburga Bishopsgate 76;
  St Faith under St Paul 17; St Giles-
  in-the-Fields 10, 20, 22, 61, 70, 71,
  75, 82; St Giles without Cripplegate
  68, 75, 76, 99; St Gregory by St Paul
  82, 87–8; St James Clerkenwell 68,
  71, 72, 107; St Katherine Cree 42;
  St Lawrence Pountney 42, 145;
  St Leonard Shoreditch 68; St Magnus
  the Martyr 12, 74, 80, 87–8, 112;
  St Margaret Lothbury 41, 145;

St Margaret New Fish Street 11, 45, 60; St Margaret Westminster 15, 80; St Martin-in-the-Fields 39, 68, 71, 75, 86, 114, 144; St Martin Pomary 73, 86; St Mary Aldermary 102; St Mary Aldermanbury 141; St Mary-at-Hill 63, 87; St Mary Colechurch 61, 73, 76; St Mary-le-Bow 43; St Mary Staining 74, 138; St Mary Woolchurch Haw 10; St Mary Woolnoth 62; St Michael Bassishaw 43; St Michael Cornhill 43; St Michael Crooked Lane 87; St Michael-le-Quern 144; St Michael Wood Street 138; St Nicholas Acons 60; St Nicholas Olave 62; St Pancras Soper Lane 43, 73; St Paul Covent Garden 68, 82, 88; St Sepulchre Holborn 37, 42, 43; St Vedast-alias-Foster 144

London, streets/places: Aldersgate Street 101, 107; Baynard Castle 15; Bedford Street 88; Billingsgate 120; Bishopsgate Street 22, 40, 108, 115, 116; Bothaw Lane 76; Broad Street 63, 103; Cannon Street 13, 14, 40, 74, 76, 101; Carter Lane 82; Chancery Lane 60, 85; Cheapside 7, 15–16, 34, 73, 83, 115, 117, 121; Clifford's Inn 33; Cornhill 15, 112; Cousin Lane 85; Covent Garden 17, 87, 105, 110; Cripplegate 19; Drury Lane 82; East Smithfield 106, 112; Fenchurch Street 73, 83, 101, 115; Fish Street Hill 11, 60, 79, 87; Fleet Street 8, 16, 20, 83, 85, 105, 107, 108, 110, 112; Gray's Inn Fields 15; Gresham College 22, 31, 33, 103, 108, 112; Great Queen Street 82; Henrietta Street 88; Holborn 36, 110, 115; Houndsditch 83, 110, 116; Ironmonger Lane 86; Jewen Street 76; Leadenhall Street 22; Leicester Fields 75; Lincoln's Inn Fields 15, 75, 82, 132; Little Britain 105, 107, 108, 112, 133; Lombard Street 15, 62, 73, 77; Long Lane 81; Lothbury 111; Ludgate Hill 62, 105, 112; Mark Lane 86; Minories 76, 110; Moorfields 1, 9, 16, 17, 22–3, 61, 103, 107; Newport Street 75; Old Fish Street 62; Old Jewry 116; Paternoster Row 73, 88; Pie Corner 47, 107; Portugal Row 75; Poultry 61; Pudding Lane 1, 11–12, 18, 21, 47, 86–8; Queenhithe 13, 120; Ratcliffe 9, 75; St John's Street 72; St Katherine's Street 86; St Martin's Lane 86; St Mary Ax 36; St Nicholas' Lane 60; St Paul's Churchyard 17, 76, 84, 86, 104–5, 107–9, 112, 119; Savoy 83; Seething Lane 117; Shoe Lane 20, 83; Silver Street 78; Smithfield 22, 103, 107, 110, 112; Snow Hill 40; Staining Lane 74; Strand 8, 36, 106, 112, 115, 121; Temple 8, 16, 17, 19, 105, 107, 108, 109, 110, 112, 140; Thames Street 11–13, 74, 87–8; Threadneedle Street 15; Tower of London 8, 16, 18, 22, 47, 83, 162; Tower Street 18; Walbrook 59, 60; Whitefriars 75; Wood Street 78

London, wards: Aldersgate Within 10; Aldersgate Without 9; Bishopsgate Within 64; Bishopsgate Without 9, 64; Broad Street 64; Candlewick 76; Castle Baynard 38; Cornhill 64; Cripplegate Without 9; Farringdon Without 40, 64; Langbourn 63, 101

London Bridge 2, 77, 87, 120

Londoners Lamentation (1666) 18

London Gazette, on Fire 14, 20, 22, 136, 141

Londons Destroyer Detected (1666) 142

London's Flames Set in a True Light (1712) 140

London Undone (1666) 143

Louvois, François Michel Le Tellier, Marquis of 137–8

Love in a Wood (1671) 102

Lowell, Paul 20

Maid of Stockholm (ship) 21

Manchester, Edward Montagu, Second Earl of 15

Mann, Samuel 40

Manufacturing in London 99, 113–14, 116

maps: London parishes xiii–xviii; London wards xix

Markland, Abraham 142

Marlborough 37

Martin, John 109

Marvell, Andrew 138, 142

Mary of Modena 137
Mather, Increase 42
Merchant Taylors' Company 38, 75–6, 103–7, 109–11; *see also* economy of London, post-Fire
Merchant Taylors' School 42
Mills, Peter 33, 35
Milward, John 132
Monck, George *see* Albemarle, George Monck, First Duke of
Montagu, Edward *see* Manchester, Edward Montagu, Second Earl of
Monument and memorialisation of Fire 45–8, 139, 161
Mortlock, Henry 109
Moxon, Joseph 105, 112
Musgrave, Sir Philip 133

Newton, Samuel 14
New England 42, 147
Norwich 21
Northampton, James Compton, Third Earl of 75

Oates, Titus 138–40
Observations both Historical and Moral upon the Burning of London ('Rege Sincera') 136
Ogden, Thomas 87
Ogilby, John 108
Oliver, John 35
On the Rebuilding of London (Wells) 143
Ormond, James Butler, First Duke of 23
Owen, John 102, 147
Oxley, Elizabeth 140
Oxford 21, 77

Page, Dixy 112
Palmer, Barbara *see* Castlemaine, Barbara Palmer, Countess of
Parker, William 146
Pawling, George 36
Peacock, Elizabeth 40
Pepys, Samuel: on attacks on foreigners 21; on cheating Lord Mayor 38; on economic recovery 121; on Fire 12, 13, 20, 131; on impact of Fire on booksellers 105, 108, 109; on losses on debts 100; on owners of White Horse Inn 77; on Papist Plot 132; on 1665 Plague 11; on rebuilding of London 103

Petty, Sir William 120
Pierce, Richard 101
Pigg, Ralph 80
Pigg, Robert 80
Pilley, Richard 87
Pincus, Steven 132
Plague (1665) 10–11, 64, 69–71, 88, 106, 120, 142, 147, 162–3
Player, Sir Thomas (d. 1672) 38
Player, Sir Thomas (d. 1686) 139
poems, on the Fire 141–3
Popish Plot and Exclusion Crisis 20, 44, 45, 137–41, 146–8, 161
Porter, Stephen 60
Port of London 9, 120, 162
Port Royal, Jamaica, Earthquake (1703) 146
Power, Michael 102, 113
Pratt, Roger 33
price-gouging 14, 85
Prince, Peter 88
Proctor, Elizabeth 100
providentialism *see* cultural reactions to the Fire
Pyrotechnica Loyolana (1667) 134–5

Quakers 147–8

Rapicani, Francisco de 13, 17, 21
rebuilding of London 30–55; charity in recovery effort 37–42; civic structures 44–5; memorialisation of Great Fire 45–8; parish churches 42–3; planning and financing of 31–7; St Paul's Cathedral 43–4
Rebuilding of London Act (1667) 34–6, 43, 45, 60, 102
Rebuilding of London Act (1670) 34–5, 43
'Rege Sincera' 24, 100, 136
residential patterns, post-Great Fire 59–88; case study of two neighbourhoods 86–8; change in social standing, post-Fire 80–5; effect of occupation on movement 85–6; hearths per household 67–71, 80–5, 88; number of households by ward, pre/post Fire 65–7; residential persistence and socio-economic status 73–5; social and geographic context 59–63; summary conclusion 88–9
Richardson, Randall 74
Ridley, Susanna 117

Rietvelt, Cornelius 15
Roberts, Penny 131
Robinson, Elizabeth 60
Robinson, Humphrey 112
Rochester, John Wilmot, Second Earl of
 45, 109
Rolls, Samuel 30, 35, 37, 60, 100, 106,
 136–7, 147
Royal Declaration of Indulgence (1672)
 137
Royal Exchange 15, 22, 35, 44, 100,
 103, 108
Royal Navy 10, 18
Rugge, Thomas 12, 16, 20, 23, 31, 134
Russell, Praise 82

Sackville, Richard *see* Dorset, Richard
 Sackville, Firth Earl of
St Bartholomew's Hospital 41, 103
St George's Fields 17, 78
St John, Oliver *see* Bolingbroke, Oliver
 St John, Second Earl of
St Paul's Cathedral: Fire destruction
 of 17–18, 20; previous fires of
 17; rebuilding of 34–5, 43–4, 47;
 surrounding residential patterns 73,
 86–8
Sare, Posthumous 78
A scheme of Popish cruelties
 (Harris) 45
Second Anglo-Dutch War 10, 30–1, 132
Second Great Fire of New York
 (1835) 14
Selby, Anthony 60
sermons, as mode of media 143–8
Shaftesbury, Anthony Ashley Cooper,
 First Earl of 15, 83
Sheldon, Sir Joseph 84
shipping industry in London 100, 120
Shirley, Frances 20
Shirley, James 20
*Short Narrative Of the late Dreadful
 Fire in London* (Waterhouse) 136
Sidney, Robert *see* Leicester, Robert
 Sidney, Second Earl of
Smith, Francis 112
Snow, Alice 75
Southwark 9, 12, 17, 23, 36, 37, 59,
 61, 68. 72, 74, 76, 78, 87, 111, 114,
 117–18, 140, 147
Spence, Craig 70
Spurr, John 144
Starkey, John 108

Stationers' Company 105
Stephens, Philemon 105
Stillingfleet, Edward 144
Stubbs, Nicholas 140
Sturt, Anthony 76–7

tables *see* illustrations, charts, and tables
Taswell, William 12, 16, 20
Test Acts (1673) 137
textile industry 16, 99, 104, 113–4,
 116–17
Thomas, Gilbert 22
Tombs, John 36
Tonge, Israel 138–9, 140
Treaty of Breda (1667) 31
Tremayne, John 12–13, 14, 15–16, 18
*True Protestant Account of the Burning
 of London, The* (1720) 141
Turner, Sir William 85–6, 87
Tutt, John 62

Utber, Richard 61

Vandenanker, Peter 101
Verney, Sir Ralph 14, 61
Vincent, Nathaniel 147
Vincent, Thomas 15, 31, 136, 147

Wadlow, John 100–1
Wakeford, Edward 88
Wall, Cynthia 33, 79
Walsham, Alexandra 131
Wapping 37
Ward, Sir Patience 38, 47
Ward, Seth 144
Wareham, Andrew 65, 69
Warwick 2
Waterhouse, Edward 11–12, 23–4, 42,
 100, 105, 136
Waterman, Sir George 38
Waynflet, William 23
Weinstein, David 119–20
Wells, Jeremiah 143
Westby, George 81
Westminster 8, 15, 16, 17, 21, 22–3,
 66, 69, 120
Whalley, Peter 116
Wheedon, Samuel 72
Whigs: anti-Catholic perspective
 135; blaming Tories for Fire 139;
 memorialisation of the Fire 45–7;
 support for Protestant monarch 137
Whitborn, Robert 11

Whitechapel 61
Whitehead, George 147–8
Wild, Robert 142
Williamson, Sir Joseph 23, 133
Wilmot, John *see* Rochester, John
  Wilmot, Second Earl of
women: female-run businesses, post-
  Fire 117–19; rebuilding assistance
  for widows 38–40; remarriage
  75–6; residential patterns of female
  householders, post-Fire 68, 72, 74,
  75, 77

Wood, Anthony 21, 77, 133–4
Wren, Sir Christopher: designs for
  rebuilding London 31–2; designs
  Monument 45–6; role in rebuilding
  effort 33, 43, 82; works on St Paul's
  Cathedral 17, 43
Wright, Abraham 114
Wycherley, William 102

York, Duchess of *see* Mary of Modena
York, James Stuart, Duke of *see* James II,
  King